FAMINE IN RUSSIA, 1891–1892

FAMINE IN RUSSIA 1891–1892

The Imperial Government Responds To A Crisis

RICHARD G. ROBBINS JR.

COLUMBIA UNIVERSITY PRESS
NEW YORK AND LONDON
1975

LIBRARY OF CONGRESS CATALOGING IN PUBLICATION DATA
ROBBINS, RICHARD G 1939–
FAMINE IN RUSSIA, 1891–1892.
INCLUDES BIBLIOGRAPHICAL REFERENCES.
1. RUSSIA—FAMINES. I. TITLE.
HC340.F3R6 361.5′5′0947 74-8528
ISBN 0-231-03836-4

PRINTED IN THE UNITED STATES OF AMERICA

* *To the memory of my mother* *

STUDIES OF THE RUSSIAN INSTITUTE, COLUMBIA UNIVERSITY

The Russian Institute of Columbia University sponsors the Studies of the Russian Institute in the belief that their publication contributes to scholarly research and public understanding. In this way the Institute, while not necessarily endorsing their conclusions, is pleased to make available the results of some of the research conducted under its auspices. A list of the Studies of the Russian Institute appears at the back of the book.

CONTENTS

PREFACE

Scholars holding widely differing views agree that the famine of 1891–92 was a turning point in Russian history. The crisis helped bring to an end the period of reaction which followed the assassination of Alexander II and marked the beginning of a new era of dissent. In the wake of the disaster, opposition to the Tsarist regime grew steadily and culminated in the revolution of 1905. But although the significance of the famine has long been recognized, not much is known concerning the hungry years, 1891 and 1892. Little has been written about the famine itself, and those passing references to the event which appear in almost all works dealing with late nineteenth-century Russia contain assertions which, somewhat uncharitably, may be labeled myths.

There are three important myths concerning the famine. The first tells us that the Imperial government tried to ignore the crisis and to suppress all news of the disaster. Second, we learn that when the regime was finally forced to act, its relief measures were inadequate and its officials incompetent. The third myth insists that, because of the government's inactivity and helplessness, the educated public of the country, that is, "society,"* moved in to fill the gap. Further, despite some opposition from state officials, public-spirited citizens carried out extensive relief work through the zemstvos and private volunteer groups. Their efforts did much to alleviate the sufferings of the peasants and exposed the bankruptcy of the state machine.

This book, based in large part on documents held in Soviet archives, dispels or modifies some of the accepted ideas about the famine, but it does

*Throughout this study I will use "society" to translate the Russian word *obshchestvo*.

not pretend to be a definitive study of the event. Many aspects of the problem—the economic causes of the disaster, the public's reaction, and the long-term political repercussions caused by the crisis—will be touched on only briefly. The present work concentrates on the formulation of government policy and the operation of state and zemstvo institutions. Its aim will be to show what the regime did to aid the needy in 1891–92 and, as far as is possible, to tell why specific actions were taken.

The focus of this work is narrow, but it has a broad purpose: an examination of government relief efforts can enhance our understanding of the way Russian institutions functioned in the late nineteenth century. This is an area of considerable weakness in historical literature. All too often the officials and institutions of the old regime are simply dismissed with a brief reference to "bungling bureaucrats" and the "creaking state machine." Little attention has been devoted to finding out what caused statesmen to err or to pinpointing the rusty joints in the government apparatus.

An account of relief operations in 1891–92 can help to bring these larger problems into focus. For the student of institutions, a crisis like the famine illuminates the actions of governments much as a signal flare sheds light upon a darkened landscape. Crises expose processes which are normally obscure; they uncover weaknesses which might otherwise pass unnoticed. The famine of 1891–92 is particularly valuable in showing the chain of command in Russian internal affairs. The disaster affected institutions at all levels of government, from the Committee of Ministers to the local peasant communes. These agencies were forced to react to the famine and interact with each other. By studying the way the various parts of the state apparatus responded, we can learn much about decision-making in the central government and we can see how well the institutions at the province and *uezd* level carried out the dictates of officials in the capital.

In addition to providing clearer insight into the functioning of the state institutions of Russia, a study of the famine of 1891–92 can make a contribution to the debate on the viability of the old regime itself. In recent years there has been renewed interest in the question whether Russian society in the late nineteenth and early twentieth centuries was pulling together or coming apart. By examining relief operations during the crisis we will certainly not find the answer to this great problem, but we can help accumulate the data needed for its solution. A study of the struggle against the famine will show to what degree the government and the public were able to cooperate in a common cause. It will help historians to assess better the strengths and weaknesses of the Russian state at the dawn of the revolutionary era.

ACKNOWLEDGMENTS

This monograph could not have been written without the assistance of many institutions and individuals. An NDEA Related Fulbright-Hays Fellowship and support from the Inter-University Committee on Travel Grants made it possible for me to do research in the Soviet Union during 1967–68. A New York State Regents Fellowship supported me while writing the dissertation upon which the present work is based. Awards from the Research Allocations Committee of the University of New Mexico enabled me to purchase a number of important materials which I had not previously used. Publication of the book was made possible by a grant from the Mellon Foundation.

At the research institutions where I was privileged to work, I encountered cooperation at every hand. The staffs of the Central State Archive of the October Revolution and the Manuscript Division of the Lenin Library in Moscow and those of the Central State Historical Archive and the Zemstvo Collection of the Saltykov-Shchedrin Library in Leningrad were unfailingly helpful. Equally generous of time and effort were the bibliographers and workers at the Helsinki University Library. In the United States, I was fortunate to obtain access to materials held in the Columbia University Archive of Russian and East European History and Culture. The curator of this unique collection, Lev Magerovsky, was extremely cooperative.

I owe a special debt to three scholars: Marc Raeff, Petr Andreevich Zaionchkovskii, and Leopold H. Haimson. Professor Raeff encouraged my original interest in the famine of 1891–92 and shared his extensive knowledge of Russian institutions. As my adviser at Columbia University, Professor Raeff read and commented on my dissertation and did much to improve it. Professor Zaionchkovskii, who directed my studies at Moscow State University, assisted me in gaining access to many important archival collections. He also generously permitted me to use the typescript of his study of the reign of Alexander III. Professor Haimson was most helpful during my first weeks in Moscow, taking time out from his own research to show a neophyte some of the tricks of working in the Lenin Library. Later, as a reader of my dissertation and the revised version of the manuscript, Professor Haimson put his finger on a number of weak spots. His perceptive criticism and his vast knowledge of late Imperial Russia enabled me to avoid some serious pitfalls.

I received help from many others. Professor George Vernadsky perused the work and made a number of valuable suggestions for its improvement. Zvi Gitelman kindly called to my attention and translated several important Yiddish language sources. My colleagues at the University of New Mexico, Jonathan Porter, Janet Roebuck, and Robert Slenes, aided me in matters relating to their areas of interest. This work especially benefited from the comments made by Nancy Frieden. She also shared many of the insights she had derived from her investigation of the Russian medical profession in the 1890s. Penelope Katson typed and retyped the entire manuscript with accuracy and good humor. The maps were drawn by Judith Bateman.

My greatest obligation is to my wife, Catherine. She read the manuscript in all its versions, subjecting the different drafts to her often harsh but always much appreciated criticism. If this book is at all readable, it owes much to her efforts. In addition, she endured the many inconveniences and troubles which are always associated with the writing and publication of a work of scholarship.

ALBUQUERQUE, NEW MEXICO
JUNE, 1974

FAMINE IN RUSSIA, 1891–1892

chapter one

THE FAMINE AND ITS CAUSES

On July 3, 1891 Count Illarion Ivanovich Vorontsov-Dashkov, Minister of the Imperial Household and an advisor to the Emperor Alexander III, wrote to His Majesty describing the unfavorable agricultural conditions in the Tambov countryside: "Here we are getting ready to go hungry. The peasants' winter crops have failed completely. . . . The situation is one of the utmost seriousness and demands immediate aid."[1] The Minister might have been commenting on the state of affairs in any one of sixteen provinces of European Russia, for the summer of 1891 saw the most serious crop failure since the 1830s. Now, the great, black earth granary of Russia would stand empty. By the end of December the Minister of Internal Affairs would estimate that 12.5 million people were in need of government relief.[2]

The immediate cause of the disaster was meteorologic. The winter of 1890–91 began early and was more severe than usual. In some places frost occurred in late October, but because of the cold the snowfall was light. The absence of snow and the premature frost were especially harmful because the dry autumn of 1890 had delayed the seeding of the fields, and the young plants had not had sufficient time to take root. Winter temperatures averaged about 20 to 25 degrees below zero on the Reaumur scale, and to the east, along the Volga, they fell as low as minus 30 to 40 degrees. Toward the new year there was some increase in snowfall, but heavy winds tended to drive the snow into the woods and ravines, leaving the fields with less than adequate cover. Spring arrived in the latter part of February and in the first weeks of March. The days were warm and bright; the snow melted rapidly, but the runoff of water into the cultivated areas was slight. In the middle of March the temperatures dropped sharply and there was renewed snowfall. From then until the first third of April there were low temperatures and high winds, conditions which had adverse effects on the winter crops, especially wheat. Starting in mid-April, the temperature began a steady rise, and the weather turned extremely dry. Little rain fell, except in Southwest Russia, and the drought in the black earth areas continued through the summer.[3] In some places in the blighted region, wells and ponds dried up, crops and pastures were scorched by the heat; dry, burning winds lifted the topsoil and sent clouds of dust racing over meadow and field. Several correspondents of the Department of Agriculture reported that "in the forests and groves the leaves withered and flew away in midsummer, giving, in the end, an autumnal appearance to heat-blasted nature."[4]

The combination of winter cold and summer drought brought disaster; the total grain harvest for European Russia was the smallest in a decade—26 percent below the norm. Worse still was the rye crop, the chief food of the peasantry, which fell to 30 percent of normal.[5] The situation in the central black soil provinces was particularly difficult: the rye harvest in Voronezh was 75 percent below normal, in Kazan it was down by 67 percent, and in Tambov by 65 percent. Other *gubernii* along the Volga and in south-central Russia experienced similar losses.[6] The net harvest of rye per rural inhabitant declined sharply: in Voronezh, 0.08 *pudy* were gathered as against an average of 14.98 *pudy* in the preceding two years; in Kazan, 2.22 as opposed to 10.94. The fields of Tambov province were somewhat more generous, but they gave only 5.14 *pudy* in contrast to the average of 17.32 for the period 1889–90.[7]

These figures do not, however, give a complete survey of the situation, for it should be noted that the harvest, even in the hard-hit regions, was not a total loss. In the very center of a stricken area, one could still find excellent crops.[8] Moreover, the impact of the crop failure on the population was influenced by the distribution of the harvest over the territory of a given province. Where the burden of the disaster fell evenly throughout the *guberniia*, the population was less likely to suffer than when a good or medium harvest was concentrated in one or two *uezdy*, leaving the rest of the province with nothing. Thus the situation in Voronezh, despite the almost total failure of the crops, was not as severe in terms of human need as in Samara or Simbirsk where the poor harvest was relatively less serious, because in Voronezh what crops there were, were distributed more or less evenly.[9]

The bleak picture of the harvest is somewhat lightened when several other factors are considered. Although the total collection of grains for European Russia was well below normal, the full impact of the disaster was largely restricted to the Volga and central agricultural areas. In the Southwest, the Ukraine, and in New Russia, harvests were only slightly below, and in some cases even above, the average for the period from 1883–87.[10] In the nonblack soil *gubernii*, the harvest was only a little less than average for the region.[11] Moreover, the harvest in the Caucasus was excellent. During the winter of 1891–92 this region would be a major source of food for the hungry areas of European Russia.[12]

So far we have spoken of crop failure, but not of famine; and we should be aware of the distinction between these two words. A nation can suffer one or even a series of bad harvests, and not experience famine.[13] On the other hand, famine may occur in a time of relatively good harvest when, for one reason or another, human decisions deprive areas of a country of needed food supplies.[14] The harvest of 1891 in Russia was extremely small, but there was enough food available to feed the population. Moreover, the harvest was not appreciably poorer than those of 1880 and 1885;[15] yet in those years the nation survived without resort to the extraordinary relief measures which were necessary in 1891. To understand why famine occurred in the winter of 1891–92, we must look at the situation of the peasantry and investigate some of the economic and financial policies of the tsarist regime.

Famine rarely strikes a prosperous nation. It happens only when a country's agricultural population has been reduced to a condition of chronic poverty and misery. By the 1890s the poverty and misery of the Russian peasantry was the one indisputable fact of the social life of the Empire. The deplorable state of the countryside was acknowledged by radicals and reactionaries alike. Descriptions of the peasants' plight could be found in the subversive tracts of revolutionaries and in the "most loyal reports" of the Tsar's own ministers.

There was, of course, considerable dispute as to the precise causes of rural poverty. But even about this question there was a growing consensus. By 1890 most Russians felt that much of the peasants' distress was rooted in the conditions created by the emancipation act of 1861. Modern historians, too, see the emancipation settlement as a major factor in the ruin of the Russian peasants in the last half of the nineteenth century, although the exact manner in which the freeing of the serfs impoverished them has been the subject of some debate. There is no space here to recount the arguments of nineteenth-century publicists and twentieth-century scholars. Let us say only that the Russian emancipation had three pernicious consequences. First, it set the size of peasant allotments so that, for the most part, the freedmen actually received less land than they had tilled in bondage. Second, the emancipation act stipulated that the peasants must pay for the land they were given. Thus the agricultural population was burdened from the outset with the heavy obligation to redeem their allotments from the state, often at a cost far above the actual value of the land. Finally, the emancipation locked the peasants into a system of collective land tenure by making the *mir*, not the individual cultivator, the real owner of the land with responsibility for meeting all obligations that accrued to it.

The effect of the emancipation arrangements on the peasant economy was highly detrimental. The reduced size of allotments meant that the peasants, hardly prosperous under serfdom, would now have to squeeze their living out of smaller resources. As a result, land hunger was a bitter constant in the Russian countryside, and that hunger became more intense with the steady growth of the rural population after 1861. Still, the amount of land held by the peasants was extensive, and with improved methods of farming they might have been able to break out of their poverty. But this escape was blocked in part by the financial aspects of the emancipation. The huge redemption payments sucked from the countryside money which could have been invested in new tools, livestock, and fertilizers.[16]

The possibility of the regeneration of peasant agriculture was further checked by the government's insistence on maintaining communal ownership of land. At the time of the emancipation, state officials had favored the *mir* as a fiscal and administrative device to guarantee the payment of redemption fees and taxes. They also saw the commune as a way to prevent the emergence of a landless rural proletariat. The commune fulfilled the hopes of the government in administrative and financial terms, but it did not benefit the peasant economy. Instead, the *obshchina* acted as a powerful brake on the rationalization of agriculture. It perpetuated the cumbersome and wasteful practice of parceling out land in small, widely separated strips, inhibited the diversification of crops, and made it almost

EUROPEAN RUSSIA, SHOWING AREAS OF POOR HARVEST IN 1891

impossible to modify the inefficient three-field system. The practice of repartition, customary in many communes, also curtailed the improvement of the land by peasant households. There was little incentive to invest in property which might be given to another family at some future date.[17]

The system created by the emancipation of 1861 made it hard for the peasants to escape rural poverty by moving to the cities. In theory it was possible for a *muzhik* to give up his allotment, but the process was complex and financially arduous. A peasant wishing to leave the *mir* had first to discharge all the debts and taxes he owed and then to make a considerable payment on the land he was abandoning.[18] Few peasants were capable of doing this; but even if they were, family pressure might keep a member of a household from moving away. His loss meant that the burden of taxes and work would have to be carried by fewer people. It also meant that the size of the household's fields might be reduced at the next repartition.

The legacy of the emancipation trapped the peasant in an almost unbreakable cycle of poverty. Each year he skirted the edge of disaster, his lot determined by the weather and the uncertain harvest. And yet he endured. Then, during the 1880s, the fates conspired to pile new troubles on the staggering farmers. A worldwide agricultural crisis caused a steady decline in grain prices, thus making the profit from the peasants' fields even smaller and increasing the weight of the obligations they carried.[19] At the same time the government adopted economic policies which applied even greater pressure on the villages. These measures were associated with the figure of I. A. Vyshnegradskii, who became Minister of Finance in 1887. Vyshnegradskii aimed to put the state economy on a firm footing. He was particularly concerned to stabilize the value of the ruble and to achieve its convertibility into gold. For this long-range goal to be attained, the budget had to be balanced and the national debt reduced. These reforms were costly, and Vyshnegradskii's policies placed the major portion of this burden on the peasants.

"*Nedoedim no vyvezem*—We may not eat enough, but we will export": this slogan summed up Vyshnegradskii's program. He felt that the quickest way to strengthen the national economy was to increase the sale of Russian grain abroad. Only by improving its balance of trade could the Empire accumulate the reserves of gold needed for financial stability and a sound currency. But in order to increase exports, the peasants had to be compelled to place more grain on the market even at the expense of their own consumption. Intense economic pressure would be needed to accomplish this goal.

Vyshnegradskii applied the required pressure vigorously. During his first half-year in office, the new Minister of Finance took steps which raised the price of many items of peasant consumption. Taxes on spirits were increased, and those on tobacco were raised by as much as 100 percent in some cases. State revenues from the land tax grew by 3 million rubles. The government imposed heavier duties on a number of imports, including iron and steel implements used by peasant agriculturalists. The apogee of this aspect of Vyshnegradskii's policy came in the very year of the famine when Russia adopted a new tariff, making her imposts among the highest in the world. The Minister of Finance also urged tax collectors to redouble their efforts in obtaining arrears due on the "soul tax" despite the fact that the tax itself had been abolished in 1886.[20]

Russian tax-gathering practices tightened the vise still further. Local treasury officials tended to collect the monies due the state just after the fall harvest. Autumn prices were low, however, and in order to meet their obligations farmers were forced to dispose of a larger proportion of their crop than they would had they been able to wait a few months. Huge quantities of grain were thus forced onto the market.[21] The amount of bread on peasant tables declined as more and more boxcars loaded with Russian rye, wheat, oats, and barley rumbled toward distant ports.

From the perspective of immediate state interests, Vyshnegradskii's tough policy was a brilliant success. Revenues from taxation grew steadily and the government's budget, which had shown a 3.5-million-ruble deficit in 1887, enjoyed a 65.9-million-ruble surplus by 1890. Another desired result was also obtained: grain exports rose sharply. The average yearly export of the four major grains increased from 269,129,000 *pudy* for the period 1881–85 to 367,908,000 for the years 1886–90. This massive sale of grain abroad enabled Russia to hold her place in the international market and to gain a favorable balance of trade. The growing strength of the Empire's finances heartened Vyshnegradskii. His chief goal—a gold standard for Russia—seemed within grasp.[22]

The mounting gold reserves of the Imperial treasury presented a sharp contrast to the growing wretchedness of the peasants. And the withering of the people while the state waxed fat did not escape the notice of contemporaries. In the wake of the famine of 1891, many critics would blame the disaster on Vyshnegradskii and his "system."[23] In our own day, too, scholars have accused the Tsar's government of sucking the country dry and have compared the causes of the crisis of 1891 with those of the tragic events of 1932–33.[24]

But it is probably too simple to assign the responsibility for the famine to the financial policies pursued by Vyshnegradskii. As we have seen, the long-term consequences of the emancipation were the main causes of rural poverty in Russia. Moreover, a precise link between the disaster of 1891–92 and the government's economic program in the years after 1887 has never been established. There is little doubt that Vyshnegradskii's policies would eventually have been detrimental to peasant interests. Yet these programs had been operative for only four years, and by 1891 their impact was just beginning to be felt. Even on the eve of the famine not all economic signs pointed to a sharp decline in peasant well-being.[25] Finally, it can be argued that, far from crushing the peasants, the reserves accumulated by the state during the late 1880s made possible extensive government relief in the hungry year.[26]

Although the exact impact of the government's economic policies is a matter for debate, there can be no doubt that by 1891 many Russian peasants, especially in the black earth regions, were in desperate straits and the regime was not attempting to develop programs for improving their lot. The rural economy had become so depressed that, for some, the line between normal existence and famine was very thin. In his study of the causes of famine in Russia, A. I. Skvortsov estimated that even in the best years peasant households which did not have over six *desiatinas* of land were unable to feed and clothe their members and pay taxes solely on the basis of the income from their property. Should some unexpected disaster occur—the death of a horse or a cow—the peasant living in these conditions found his back against a wall, and "if he did not completely starve, neither would he ever be full."[27] Among students of the peasant economy there was general agreement that the diet of the villagers was not sufficient to maintain good health. Moreover, the amount of grain available for consumption by the peasants in the early 1890s was less than it had been in the 1870s.[28] Even before the disastrous harvest of 1891, many of the signs associated with famine had begun to appear. According to

Dr. Petrov, a zemstvo physician in Tsivil'skii *uezd* of Kazan province, the use of surrogates for rye in the making of bread—a regular occurrence in times of bad harvest—had become a standard practice among the poorer peasants. In 1892, he wrote:

> The past year was different from the preceding, *only in that the number of users of "famine bread"* was significantly *higher*. . . . In my opinion [the following] circumstance deserves special consideration: *that part of the population cannot get by a single year without surrogate grains*, and [that] their use is in inverse proportion to the harvest of a given year.[29]

The tightening grip of misery caused the peasants to thrash desperately, seeking an escape. For most, increased production seemed the sole way out; but given the problems of peasant agriculture, this was extremely difficult. Only by bringing more land under the plow could bigger yields be obtained. The costs of renting and buying land were high, the chances for profit slim. Yet in the years preceding the famine, the peasants steadily acquired the use of more land. The way in which the Russian farmers worked their new fields was highly exploitative. They sought to wrest from the soil as much grain as possible, paying little attention to the condition of the land itself. In some areas, each harvest became a kind of lottery. According to the governor of Samara, peasants in the southern part of the province were influenced by the example of a few "big sowers" (*krupnye posevchiki*) who had become rich as the result of a single good harvest. The farmers of southern Samara concentrated all their efforts on the production of wheat, a major cash crop, virtually ignoring the needs of their own tables. They rented extra land and often went into debt hoping that a good yield would bail them out. Should their hopes be realized, they would risk the whole of their profits on a similar wager. A crop failure, however, left them ruined.[30]

Relatively few peasants engaged in this kind of desperate gamble. A much more common way in which the villagers sought to increase the size of their crop was to expand their tilled fields at the expense of fallow, pasture, and forest land. This trend, common throughout the black soil regions, was eloquently described by Ioann Sokolovskii, a priest in Lukoianovskii *uezd* of Nizhni-Novgorod province. Sokolovskii stated that although they possessed reasonable amounts of land, the peasants of his district "lived almost always on the edge of hunger." Their need caused them to reduce to the minimum the size of fields given over to making hay and they were seized by a mania for chopping down trees and clearing new land. "The forest allotments," the priest lamented, "were all cut down and [the land] plowed. The lowlands which had previously been meadow, were brought under cultivation." The farmers of the *uezd* even reduced the size of their herds so that areas once grazed by cattle could be used to grow grain.[31]

The peasants' efforts to increase their harvests had disastrous consequences. The expansion of tilled land at the expense of fallow rapidly exhausted the soil. By reducing the number of their animals, the peasants undermined agriculture at its foundations, eliminating a major source of farm power and depriving the earth of much needed fertilizers.[32] The destruction of the forests also had dire results. Cutting the trees robbed the land of natural wind breaks and created conditions which were highly conducive to drought.

By the end of the 1880s the stage was set for tragedy. The overburdened peasants and their exploited fields could take no more. The ability of the agriculturalists to meet their obligations had reached its limits and arrears on taxes and redemption payments grew steadily. The black soil provinces were especially pressed; in the period 1889–90 thirteen *gubernii* of that region were responsible for 54 percent of all cases of default.[33] Then the land itself began to fail. In 1888, 1889, and 1890 the Volga and central provinces experienced a series of bad harvests which destroyed what little remained of peasant well-being.[34] On the eve of the famine, official reports from the countryside indicated that farmers were selling their cows and work animals in order to feed their families. "Hunger typhus" had made its appearance. But the worst was still to come. For even as these correspondents wrote, the fields of winter grain were withering from lack of moisture. The terrible hungry year had begun.

When I arrived . . . in Novooksol'skii [*uezd*] and [passed] through Iablonovskaia *volost'*, I knew I had entered the famine region.

The first thing that tells you this is the appearance of the population. Everywhere, you encounter crowds of people. They look you in the eye; they literally seize upon every glance, every step you take. . . . But in addition, you notice that they all have a kind of dumbfounded expression; all are emaciated, defeated. This is understandable, because they have no idea of what will become of them. But worst of all are the children. The children leave the deepest impression. You can talk with the adults, discuss matters; but the children—that is the most terrible thing of all.[35]

The reports of men and women who traveled through the famine-stricken areas of Russia in the bitter winter of 1891–92 are varied. But as the historian examines the faded pages of journals, government documents, and memoirs, the distinctions begin to blur. The details of individual tragedies, no matter how poignant, tend to be forgotten. What remains is a dulling sense of despair, a gray picture of general misery. This is not to say that a visit to one stricken village would suffice to satisfy all curiosity about the conditions of the rural population during the famine year; yet the situation of the peasantry in all the black soil *gubernii* was fundamentally the same. In the years immediately preceding the crisis, the majority of the villagers had been poor, but their poverty was manageable. Maybe a horse or a cow had to be sold, some goosefoot[36] was added to the bread; yet, somehow, the winter was passed. Now, such palliative measures were to little avail. Most fields had produced nothing but goosefoot. Much of the grain that was harvested had been bought up by the *kulaks* and *skupshchiki*, sold for a big profit at the markets, and shipped by rail away from the province, toward the distant ports.[37]

A visitor to a famine village[38] in the winter of 1891–92 would, likely as not, have found the streets deserted—the population indoors, attending to the important business of warding off the cold. Fuel was scarce and money scarcer. The government decree permitting peasants to gather wood in state forests was the difference between limited warmth and frozen limbs. Still, some of the poorer denizens were beginning to use the thatched roofs of their huts as a source of heat and as food for their horses.

In the company of the village *starosta* and the local *zemskii nachal'nik* (land captain), the traveler might be invited to visit some of the houses. The *zemskii nachal'nik* is checking, no doubt for the third or fourth time, to see if the peasants have hidden away stores of grain in the stable or under the floorboards.[39] The stable, when examined, proves devoid of both grain and animals. Nor is this exceptional; in many villages, from one-half to two-thirds of the livestock has been sold. As for the contents of the *izba*, even men hardened to the realities of Russian country life are shocked by what they encounter. The appalling stench of burning dung,[40] human perspiration, and sickness is the first impression. When eyes adjust to the gloom of the hut, an old *baba* and an ancient *muzhik* come into view. Two children are curled on top of the stove. All are listless, with the dirty yellow skin, bloated features, and drooping eyes that are symptomatic of advanced hunger. The mother of the children lies on a bed in the corner of the room, stricken with typhus. Her husband and the oldest boy have left the village to seek work in a nearby town.

There is no real bread in the house; on the table there are the remains of what the peasants call *golodnyi khleb*. It is made from small amounts of rye with admixtures of surrogates, usually *lebedá* (goosefoot), a hardy plant which still grows when others fail. The government and the zemstvos have tried to encourage the peasants to use other, more healthful substitutes,[41] but tradition and easy availability result in the persistent consumption of goosefoot. Such bread has a yellowish color and a bitter taste. Continued use causes serious disorders of the digestive tract, depression, headaches, vomiting, and diarrhea. "Famine bread" has little nutritive value, passes through the system without being absorbed, and results in considerable protein deficiency.[42]

No cases of starvation in the village have been reported, but there is a sharp increase in mortality among infants and older people. Zemstvo grain loans are only about thirty pounds a month per "eater," but men of working age are frequently not listed on the relief rolls so as not to encourage sloth. But there is no work in the village, and many hands are idle. The usual source of seasonal employment—work in the fields of the nearby *pomeshchik* at harvest times—has been greatly curtailed this year by the crop failure. Jobs have been scarce, wages low.[43] Now some peasants seek work elsewhere; but the effects of the famine are making themselves felt even as far away as Moscow province, where there have been layoffs and factory closings.[44] Those who crowd into the cities often find conditions there as bad as at home. In the urban environment the peasants are ready prey for contagious diseases, especially typhus. On their return home they can infect entire villages.[45]

Our visit to other huts reveals little that is different. In some, the number of the sick is greater, in others, *slava Bogu*, the health of the family has been preserved. Only one case of concealed grain is discovered. The *kulak*, Foma K., had stashed away four *pudy* of rye in the barn and then convinced the village *skhod* to inscribe him on the relief lists. The *zemskii nachal'nik* crosses his name off the rolls with a blue pencil.

The dominant mood here is despair, resignation. For some, the burden is too great—there have been reports of mothers attempting to murder their children in order to spare them the pain of hunger.[46] But these are extreme cases. For the most part, the villagers are passive, even philosophical. The harvest—that is beyond the power of man. The Lord gives, the Lord takes. There is little outward resistance to authority, although in some regions there have been spontaneous mass movements of peasants with the intent to resettle in Siberia, and the number of migrants from the famine provinces has increased.[47] But loyalty to the Emperor is firm. Many peasants expect to be fed from the *tsarskii paek* (the Tsar's rations), and there is grumbling that the nobles have stolen the money that the Little Father has given them to distribute to the needy. Some rural officials have expressed fears of revolt. Yet for this winter, at least, the manor houses of the *pomeshchiki* are safe. The peasants are prepared to wait—wait for the zemstvo to deliver the grain, wait for the spring, wait for the new harvest.

chapter two

RUSSIA'S SYSTEM OF FAMINE RELIEF: ITS DEVELOPMENT AND ITS DEFECTS

As one of mankind's most ancient scourages, famine has presented a recurring challenge to organized society. And from earliest times, providing some form of help to the victims of such emergencies has been a recognized obligation of governments. The antiquity of the problem of famine does not mean, however, that an effective or universally acceptable system for aiding the needy has ever evolved. On the contrary, famine confronts modern leaders with many of the same unresolved difficulties which plagued their counterparts in previous eras.

The problem of immediate relief is straightforward enough: people are hungry, they must somehow be fed. But beyond this elementary task lies the job of working out a regular system which can guard the population against the consequences of future crop failures. Over the centuries, two basic approaches to famine have emerged. The oldest and simplest looks upon famine as primarily an administrative challenge provoked by an absolute, albeit localized shortage of food. The shortrun crisis is dealt with by distributing food to the needy either through sale, loan, or grant. A long-term solution is attempted by the establishment of storehouses in agricultural areas and in major cities. These granaries hold surplus food produced in years of good harvest. When crops fail, their contents can be used to help the destitute.

The food storage system, used in Egypt in biblical times, achieved its most comprehensive development in China during the Ming and Ch'ing dynasties. The rulers of the Middle Kingdom sought to create a universal network of storehouses which would enable the state and its officials to control food prices and to provide for the hungry in periods of crisis. Each county (*chou*) and district (*hsien*) was required to set up an "ever-normal granary" which was filled with foodstuffs purchased with government funds and managed by the local magistrate. The ever-normal granary was supplemented by charitable and community granaries, filled and controlled by the local population. The Chinese system proved enduring, but not very successful. Its proper functioning depended on too many variables: the vitality of the central government, the loyalty and honesty of local officials, the generosity of the gentry, and the cooperation of the peasants. The granaries worked well only in the best of times and even then in a relatively few locations. By the late nineteenth century China's traditional system of famine prevention was in a state of decay. The twentieth century witnessed its total collapse.[1]

A second, more modern approach to the prevention and relief of famine sees the problem largely in economic terms. The difficulties of the stricken population are viewed not as the result of an absolute grain shortage but as the consequence of temporary high food prices combined with local unemployment. The crisis caused by these conditions is treated by two devices. The first permits complete freedom of the grain trade so that foodstuffs will flow naturally into the areas of greatest demand and highest prices. The availability of food thus guaranteed, the government then seeks to provide work for the population so that with the wages earned the people can buy the necessary victuals. This approach to relief has a number of advantages over a system based on grain storage. It avoids the administrative headaches connected with maintaining the granaries. Since it allows direct grants of food only to those persons totally unable to work, the task of distributing aid to the needy is greatly simplified.

The economic approach to famine relief was used by the British to meet food supply difficulties in Ireland and India, but it enjoyed only mixed success. During the Irish crisis of the 1840s, reliance on the unhindered play of the market and public works programs proved disastrous. In India, however, the British gained more satisfactory results. The famine codes of the 1880s, which embodied the principles of free trade and public works, were able to mitigate the effects of crop failures. Between 1908 and 1943 India suffered no true famines. Yet the triumph of the British system was by no means complete. Its effectiveness was made possible only by a number of favorable factors: the efficiency of the British Indian administration, the regular import of foreign grain, the rapid and extensive spread of railroads on the subcontinent. The frailty of the system was demonstrated during 1943. In that year the strains of World War II disturbed the delicate economic and administrative balance. The result was the terrible Bengal famine which claimed over a million lives.[2] Since independence, the Indians have modified the relief arrangements inherited from the British, especially the emphasis on the unfettered operation of economic forces.[3]

If the Chinese and British systems can be seen as the opposite ends of the spectrum of relief procedures, the Russian approach to famine which developed during the eighteenth and nineteenth centuries lies somewhere between these two poles. By and large, the Russians, like the Chinese, viewed famine relief in administrative terms. But laissez-faire economic theories also had their impact on Russian thinking about food supply operations. Freedom of the grain trade became a central principle of the Russian antifamine system; public works were seen as an important supplement to the regular procedures for aiding the needy.

The details of the evolution of the Russian system of famine relief need not detain us long. But the *direction* of that evolution and some of the problems which determined the growth of relief arrangements are worth considering. Basically, the development of Russian antifamine measures witnessed a steady reduction of the central government's direct involvement in the management of relief. Gradually a system emerged which assigned to local people (state officials, the nobility, and, later, the zemstvos) the job of gathering, maintaining, and distributing relief supplies, while reserving to the center both the overall power to supervise affairs and ultimate financial control. Two problems forced the retreat of central authorities from the work of relief. The first was that the immense size and diversity of the Empire required a large degree of local autonomy and initiative. The second and more important difficulty was the weakness of the state apparatus which rendered intervention by St. Petersburg officials in food supply operations ineffective.

The Russian government's involvement in the matter of famine relief began in the last years of Peter I as the result of a series of bad harvests between 1721 and 1724.[4] Peter's antifamine legislation was, like so many of his other decrees, hastily improvised, unsystematic, and often draconian. Peter's most significant measures included the establishment of grain storage houses as strategic locations and the appointment of a special official to oversee them.[5] The Emperor ordered an inventory (*opis'*) of available food supplies in preparation for their possible confiscation or forced sale to the needy,[6] and he demanded that provincial officials supply the center with regular information on crops and prices in their localities.[7] At the height of the crisis, the Tsar-reformer reduced official salaries in order to raise relief funds, required the sale of household gold and silver to the treasury, slapped taxes on spirits, and banned grain exports, while authorizing the import of food from abroad.[8] In addition, Peter experimented with a whole series of measures designed to regulate the grain trade and to check the activities of speculators.[9]

Peter's legislation had little immediate, practical effect, but it clearly established the tradition of direct state action in the area of relief. During the rest of the eighteenth century, Peter's successors sought to rationalize his legacy. This process of regularization proceeded along four lines. First, grain storage, supplemented to some degree by public works and tax remission, became the backbone of the relief system. But as the network of granaries expanded, responsibility for maintaining and operating the storehouses increasingly passed into the hands of local officials and the nobility. Second, the state abandoned the use of extreme measures like the registration and requisition of grain or the reduction of official salaries in its struggle against famine. Third, the legislation of the eighteenth century saw a lessening of government intervention in the grain trade. This change of approach resulted in part from a recognition of the value of free trade and in part from an awareness that the state lacked the administrative machinery necessary to make its regulatory measures work. Finally, Russian rulers sought to develop an effective method of supervising the Empire's food supplies. Throughout the century central officials engaged in a continuous, but largely futile, attempt to secure a steady flow of reliable information about crops and prices in the provinces.[10]

Thus by the start of the nineteenth century the lineaments of Russia's antifamine system had been drawn. A network of granaries containing supplies gathered from the population was supposed to stand ready to provide the needy with quick assistance—usually in the form of loans—during times of distress. Management of these reserves was vested in local people under the watchful eye of the central government and its agents. In reality, however, the statutes which defined these relief arrangements had few practical results. Many of the granaries either did not exist or held precious little food. The peasants were, for the most part, too poor to make the necessary contribution to the storehouses. Even in prosperous villages, the granaries might be plundered by nobles, corrupt officials, or the peasants themselves. The failure of the local storage system meant that despite the intent of Russia's rulers, the central treasury almost always became the main source of relief in times of famine.

The continued dependence of the provinces on aid from the center was not only burdensome to the fisc, it also helped make the whole business of relief slow and cumbersome. When local officials appealed for aid, the authorities in the capital strove to determine the amount of assistance which would be required. This was difficult because St. Petersburg *chinovniki* were often unable to get a clear picture of the needs of the people in the stricken areas. Provincial bureaucrats frequently sent conflicting reports about the situation in the countryside. Consequently, before help from the center could be sent, lengthy, on-the-spot investigations were required. These procedures retarded the dispatch of relief unduly, and peasants were often forced to pass a hungry winter before aid began to reach them. Once the actual process of relief started, other difficulties ensued. There existed no uniform system for administering food supply assistance. Grants to the needy tended to be given out in the haphazard way which left many of the hungry unfed.[11]

The deficiencies of the eighteenth-century relief arrangements cried out for rectification, but it was not until late in the reign of Alexander I that the Imperial government undertook a major reform. The *ustav* of April 14, 1822 tried for the first time in Russian history to create a truly comprehensive famine relief system. The new law affirmed the obligation of state officials and the nobility to provide for the population in times of crop failure, but it permitted local people greater flexibility in the management of relief. Exclusive dependence on grain storage was abandoned. Each province was now given the option to establish either granaries or a monetary fund as the means of supplying the needy. At the same time, the statute outlined clearcut rules governing the collection of cash and grain reserves.

The most important innovation embodied in the legislation of 1822 concerned the administration of local relief. The law created a new set of institutions—the provincial food supply commissions, composed of elected representatives of the nobility and high-ranking members of the *guberniia* bureaucracy. The commissions were to keep watch on the state of agriculture in their provinces and were to supervise the monetary funds and granaries. They met annually at harvest time to determine whether or not the peasants would require aid during the coming year. Should assistance be needed, the commissioners were empowered to dispense monies from the capital reserves and to authorize loans from the granaries. If local needs exceeded provincial resources, the commissions could apply to the central government for further aid.

Although immediate responsibility for the management of relief was placed in the hands of the food supply commissions, the role of state officials was by no means negligible. Local bureaucrats assumed the task of gathering and systematizing the statistical information upon which the commissions based their decisions. Beyond this, the governors exercised enormous influence over the operation of the relief system. They chaired the provincial commissions and, more importantly, provided a link to the center which would be vital in times of serious crop failure.[12]

As Russia's first attempt to work out a general famine relief system, the law of 1822, not surprisingly, contained many serious flaws. Basically, it was too advanced for the time. Its framers failed to take into account sufficiently the poverty and backwardness of the Empire, the low level of provincial culture, and the weakness of rural administration. In many cases, local people did not properly understand the needs of their regions; and a number of *gubernii* established cash funds where granaries would have proved more useful. The grain and monetary reserves were collected at such a slow pace that the provinces never became self-sufficient, and aid from the center was constantly required. The food supply commissions were seldom equipped to grapple with the complex work of relief. The disbursal of assistance to the hungry often involved a number of conflicting agencies and so proved difficult and inefficient.[13]

The deficiencies of the law of 1822 soon became evident, but state officials proved unable to develop fundamentally different arrangements. In 1834 the government of Nicholas I undertook an extensive modification of the relief system without altering its basic principles. The new legislation reduced the freedom of the provinces to decide on the method of relief, requiring all *gubernii* to maintain both cash and grain reserves. The food supply commissions were now obliged to meet twice a year, and supervision of cash funds and grain stores was further regularized. Finally, stricter rules were established concerning the disbursal of relief loans which expanded the central government's control over local food supplies. The new law distinguished two categories of famine emergency: partial, when only a few households were in need, and general, when crop failure affected a whole province or a considerable portion of it. In the first case, local people were free to give out a portion of the reserves on their own initiative; actions designed to meet larger crises required authorization from officials in the capital.[14]

The food supply statute of 1834 did much to improve the relief system, at least in theory. But many basic problems continued unresolved. Local granaries remained only partially filled and carelessly managed. Provincial monetary funds were too small to be really useful in times of distress. The inadequacy of the resources at the *guberniia* level made necessary regular appeals to the center which slowed the flow of aid and caused a massive drain on the state treasury. The defects in the relief system led the government of Nicholas I to experiment with alternatives, particularly the use of public works as a means of helping the needy. Yet the fundamental rules governing food supply operations were unaltered until the reign of Alexander II.

The defects of the prereform relief system were reflections of a general problem which Frederick Starr has called the "under-government" of the Russian provinces.[15] There were not enough officials and institutions to provide the inhabitants of the far-flung *gubernii* with the kinds of basic services that other, more modernized states could supply. To their credit, the statesmen of the 1860s tried to come to grips with this weakness; to Russia's sorrow, their efforts were not entirely successful. The new laws which restructured provincial administration established neither effective bureaucratic management nor fully competent institutions of local self-government. As a consequence, inertia propelled old habits and methods of rule into a new era.

The famine relief statute of 1866 was just such an uneasy mixture of the old and the new. Like much of the legislation of the reform era, it bespoke the desire of the regime to preserve the essence of the traditional system while equipping the state with improved methods of administration and control. Accordingly, the reformed law kept the basic relief arrangements established by earlier legislation, but it abolished the provincial commissions and turned over the management of food supply operations to the zemstvos, the newly created organs of local self-government. At the same time, the supervisory powers of the governors, the Ministry of Internal Affairs (MVD), and the Committee of Ministers were maintained and even enhanced.

The new food supply statute, which remained basically unchanged until the end of the century, established a three-tiered system of relief supplies. As in the past, peasant communes were to set up local grain storage houses. The law stipulated that the granaries were to hold 1.5 *chetverty* (about nine bushels) of grain for each male "soul." In order to see that the reserves were maintained at the desired level, a portion of the required grain was collected annually.[16] Special peasant officials were assigned to stand guard over the grain stores.[17] The *uezd* zemstvos were to gather information on the status of granaries twice each year, and at regular intervals would conduct detailed inspections of the reserves.[18] In addition to their supplies of stored food, peasant communes were entitled, but not required, to possess monetary funds. This communal food supply capital was usually turned over to the zemstvos for safe keeping.

The local supplies of grain and money were backed up by two separate capital funds, one held at the *guberniia* level in the hands of the provincial zemstvo, the other maintained by the central government under the control of the Economic Department of the Ministry of Internal Affairs.[19] These monies were to be kept distinct from the other revenues of the zemstvo and the state. They could, however, be deposited in banks or used to purchase interest-bearing government securities.[20] The food supply funds could be used only for the purpose of famine relief, and were to be constantly on hand in case of emergency.[21]

The reformed food supply system was designed to enable the authorities to provide immediate relief in the form of loans to needy individuals and, if necessary, to whole peasant communes.[22] Elaborate safeguards were established, however, to see that the loans were of moderate size and not made without cause. Before granting a loan from its own granary or cash reserve, a commune was required to draw up a special declaration (*prigovor*) which stated to whom the loan would be made and how much would be given. The *volost'* administration was then to attest to the accuracy of the declaration and pass it on to the *uezd* zemstvo *uprava*.[23] The *uezd upravy* were empowered to authorize the loan and make adjustments as to its size, but they could not permit the disbursal of more than half of the available communal reserves. Should larger grants be needed, permission had to be obtained from the provincial *uprava*.[24] In the event that local resources were not sufficient to meet the crisis, the *uezd upravy* could appeal to the *guberniia uprava* for monies from the provincial fund. When the reserves of the province proved insufficient, the zemstvo could ask for a loan from the central fund. A request for such aid would be presented to the governor who would forward it with his comments to the Minister of Internal Affairs.[25] Even the power of the Minister to grant money was limited. On his own authority, he could make loans of no more than 50,000 rubles to a single province. In order to obtain permission to make larger grants, the Minister had to present a special request to the Emperor through the Committee of Ministers.[26]

Loans to the needy could be made in two ways, either in the form of a direct grant of money or the distribution of seed and food grain. Loans from local granaries and monetary funds were supposed to be repaid at the next harvest or, if this proved impossible, within two years.[27] The provincial zemstvos were empowered to fix the terms of loans from their capital, but the schedule of repayments should be agreed upon at the time the grant was made.[28] Loans from the central fund were first turned over to the zemstvos, not to individuals, and the zemstvos were obliged to collect the money from the borrowers and to repay the government within three years. Failure to do so resulted in a penalty in the form of a 3 percent per annum interest on the principal.[29]

Like its predecessors, the food supply statute of 1866 required local institutions to obtain detailed information on the state of the harvest and on the prices of grains in their regions. The zemstvos were assigned a major share of this burden, but the law stated that the governors were to order the rural police to make independent observations which could be used to check zemstvo statistics.[30] The information on crops and prices was to be systematized by the *guberniia upravy* at regular intervals. Zemstvo calculations were to show, among other things, how food costs varied from region to region within a particular province.[31] When these computations had been completed, the governors were to pass them on to the Ministry of Internal Affairs.[32]

The food supply law stipulated that the grain trade remain free even in times of crisis. Provincial authorities were forbidden to take any actions which would either hold foodstuffs within a given area or prevent their entrance into a region.[33] The framers of the statute realized that in the past government attempts to control the grain market had been ineffective, and they counted on the free play of economic forces to aid in provisioning needy areas. Grain, it was reasoned, would flow to those regions where prices were highest. Any restriction on the movement of produce would only slow or prevent the work of relief.

The famine relief system which emerged from the era of the great reforms was by far the most comprehensive ever designed by the Imperial government. To be sure, many of its features—grain and cash reserves, food supply loans—had been drawn from older legislation, particularly the *ustavy* of 1822 and 1834, but there were new departures as well. Of major significance was the creation of an Empire-wide capital fund which aimed, for the first time, to put the business of relief on a national as well as a local and provincial basis. Beyond this, the new law established a much clearer chain of command and communication and a more precise division of obligations among various agencies than had existed under previous statutes. The reformed food supply system seemed to have achieved the illusive goal of Russian administrators: to divest the state of immediate responsibility for relief, while enabling the central authorities to supervise affairs and to intervene if necessary.

Unfortunately, however, the new relief system was not significantly more effective than earlier programs. The local granaries, the first line of defense against famine, could not be filled any better under the new procedures than they had been under the old. The peasants continued to be too poor, too burdened by taxes and other obligations, to put aside the needed reserves. As in the prereform era, corrupt local officials and desperate peasants often plundered what little food was stored.[34] The zemstvos soon proved unable to establish firm control over the granaries. Frustrated, many *zemtsy* either ignored the problem entirely or pushed for the conversion of grain supplies into more manageable monetary funds.[35] Finally, repeated bad harvests during the 1870s and 1880s caused the villagers to borrow constantly from their granaries. By 1891 a large part of the grain stores in the provinces affected by the crop failure was already on loan to the peasants.[36] The provincial and Imperial capital funds were also difficult to maintain. Because the village economy was so weak, the peasants often required aid but were frequently unable to pay back their loans.[37] Thus cash reserves remained small and would be of little use in meeting a large-scale food supply crisis. In the event of a serious crop failure, the state would have to spend sums far in excess of the amounts put aside for famine relief.

Peasant poverty was a major, but by no means the only, reason that the new food supply system failed to operate as intended. Other debilitating factors were the weakness of the zemstvos and the inadequacy of the state's administrative machinery in the countryside. Given the absence of a viable network of village granaries, effective famine relief would depend largely on the ability of local institutions and officials to gather accurate information about the needs of the people and to distribute swiftly the aid supplied through zemstvo and government auspices. The accomplishment of these tasks would prove extremely difficult, however, because neither the zemstvos nor the state had any direct link with the peasants. The zemstvos extended only to the *uezd* level. Consequently, their ties with the villages were tenuous and, from the peasants' point of view, artificial.[38] State agents also were often unable to intervene in local affairs: their number was too few, their contact with the people too infrequent. The occasional visits of tax collectors and the police did not constitute a real penetration by the government into village life. Despite the reforms of the 1860s, the rural population continued to live as it had for centuries: segregated from the rest of Russian society, ruled by its own institutions, customs, and laws.[39]

The lack of contact between the peasants and the zemstvo and state apparatus hindered the development of solid relief programs in times of famine. Having no local agencies of their own, zemstvo and government personnel were forced to rely on data supplied by peasant officials as to the size of the harvest and the number of those requiring aid. The figures obtained from the villages, however, were often inaccurate. Sometimes peasants would exaggerate their needs in order to obtain as much bread as possible. On other occasions the more prosperous farmers might force a commune to pare its relief lists to the bone. The *kulaks* frequently took this step because they realized that as a consequence of the system of collective responsibility (*krugovaia poruka*) they, and not the poor, would have to pay back the loan.[40]

The distribution of relief supplies entailed further difficulties. Peasant officials assumed this task with little supervision. As a result, grain and seed loans often did not reach the households for which they were intended. There were times when *kulaks* succeeded in diverting relief for their own purposes. A far more likely development would be the peasants' decision to divide the relief equally among the members of the commune without regard to actual need. The absence of any public institutions capable of guaranteeing the rational administration of relief meant that much of the aid given out simply disappeared, producing, at best, only a part of its intended impact.

The incompleteness of the local administrative network was the Achilles' heel of the Russian food supply system. But at other, higher levels of the state and zemstvo apparatus there were also weaknesses which hampered relief work. A particularly glaring and pernicious defect was the almost total lack of coordination between the main agencies involved in the struggle against famine. No national zemstvo organization existed and, consequently, in the event of a crop failure affecting a number of *gubernii*, cooperation and communication among the several provincial zemstvos would be difficult to arrange. In addition, the link between the zemstvos and the state machine was imperfect. When the zemstvos were created in the 1860s they had been viewed as private corporations designed to handle local economic matters. And although they assumed certain important governmental functions—education, rural medicine, and the administration of the food supply system—the zemstvos were not supposed to share in state power.[41] The separation of state affairs from local economic concerns was artificial and often broke down in practice. Yet in periods of crisis, this peculiar setup opened the way for misunderstanding and conflict between zemstvo personnel and government officials at both the provincial and national levels.

Among the chief branches of the central administration, too, proper coordination was difficult to obtain. The various ministries whose activities affected famine relief were frequently at loggerheads. Nor was there any institution, like a cabinet, to harmonize government operations. The Committee of Ministers which appeared able to perform this function was, by and large, unequal to the task. The Committee had almost no policy-making powers; its purpose was largely informational. The institution had been designed to provide a channel of communication between the ministers and the Emperor. It could neither make major decisions on its own nor enforce cooperation between the main departments of the state.[42]

The poor cohesion among the elements concerned with famine relief would clearly have undesirable effects on food supply campaigns. This was especially true in major crises embracing a significant number of provinces. Such circumstances called for the maximum coordination of the work of local and central agencies. The government would have to locate needed supplies and provide the zemstvos in the stricken regions with reliable information on available grain stores and food prices in other parts of the Empire. A transportation policy capable of facilitating the movement of provisions into the afflicted *gubernii* was also vital. These goals could only be achieved by the closest cooperation between the zemstvos, the provincial administrations, and the Ministries of Finance, Transportation, and Internal Affairs. But the fragmented state of governmental and zemstvo machinery made the easy realization of the necessary cooperation unlikely.

Had the administrative weaknesses outlined above affected only the management of famine relief, their continued existence would not have been anything surprising. The fact is, however, that these defects had detrimental consequences for a wide range of other governmental operations. Moreover, they prevented the Tsarist regime from exercising anything like direct control over the bulk of its subjects. These deficiencies had, of course, long been recognized, yet Russian statesmen had been unable to implement reforms which might substantially improve the situation. Explaining this failure is not difficult, but to do so we must briefly look beyond the question of famine relief. For the inadequacy of the state administration in Russia reflected broader problems: the general poverty of the Empire and a number of basic political conflicts which were inherent in the autocratic system.

The economic causes of administrative weakness are fairly straightforward. Good government, especially an effective network of local institutions, is expensive. The Russian treasury was usually poor, and the demands of the central ministries, particularly the Ministry of War, were always much more pressing. Thus in the area of local affairs the Imperial regime traditionally tried to get by on the cheap; it refused to create viable state institutions in rural areas. Instead the state assigned to various agencies of self-administration a large number of governmental duties without giving these institutions the power or the authority to do a truly effective job.

In the last analysis, however, political rather than economic considerations did most to perpetuate the administrative weakness of the state. At the center, for example, the continued ineffectiveness of the

Committee of Ministers resulted from the concern on the part of Russian autocrats that a western style cabinet might limit their powers. Likewise, the refusal to permit a national zemstvo organization and the failure to integrate these institutions into the state were the products of the long-standing distrust which the bureaucracy felt toward all forms of local self-administration. More specifically, many *chinovniki* feared that a unified zemstvo structure and the participation of elected representatives in the work of government might be a first step toward the establishment of a Russian republic.[43]

Political concerns were also responsible for many of the defects in local administration. The feeling that institutions of self-government constituted a potential threat to the well-being of the state blocked the extension of the zemstvos to the *volost'* or village level in much the same way as it prevented the creation of a national zemstvo organ.[44] Beyond this, there was another political problem which slowed the rationalization of provincial administration: the traditional conflict between the bureaucracy and the nobility. Many state officials, particularly those of a more liberal stamp, believed that the *dvorianstvo* had outlived its usefulness. The class privileges of the nobility and its powers at the local level were a brake on the development of effective provincial government. On the other hand, the *dvorianstvo* desperately struggled to hold on to its position and bitterly opposed the extension of bureaucratic agencies into the countryside. The rival claims of the nobility and the bureaucracy produced a kind of Mexican standoff with regard to local government. The regime delayed the much-needed reform of rural administration while it sought measures which might increase state power at the local level without compromising the status of the second estate.

The way in which political conflicts hindered the achievement of rational administration in the countryside is illustrated by the fate of the reform proposals discussed in the Kakhanov commission. This body, which labored between 1881 and 1885, had been created because the weaknesses of provincial government became painfully obvious during the crisis of autocracy in the last years of Alexander II.[45] The commission's staff included a significant number of reform-minded officials who, in the initial phase of its existence, dominated the proceedings. Within the commission, a subcommittee (*soveshchanie*), headed by Kakhanov himself, produced a project which outlined sweeping alterations in the area of local administration. Among the changes suggested was the creation of new, all-class governmental units at the village and *volost'* levels. In addition, the subcommittee urged the establishment of firmer institutional links between the zemstvos and the state which would give the elected representatives a more direct voice in the management of *uezd* and provincial affairs. The project also proposed to expand zemstvo powers in certain important areas such as the assessment of taxes and the gathering of statistics. Finally, the subcommittee's scheme would have achieved greater coordination between zemstvos by permitting inter*uezd* and even inter*guberniia* zemstvo conferences.[46]

The plan advocated by Kakhanov's subcommittee would have done much to improve the provincial administration and, in the process, might have made possible the more effective working of famine relief procedures. Had the subcommittee plan been adopted, many of the fissures in local government could have been eliminated. The village and *volost'* administrative units would have enabled state and zemstvo personnel to oversee properly the compilation of relief lists and the disbursal of aid to the needy. The improved integration of the zemstvos into the state machine at the *uezd* and province levels would have considerably lessened the potential for conflict there. In addition, the possibility of inter*guberniia* zemstvo conferences could have fostered a much more coordinated assault on food supply problems in times of national emergency.

But the potential inherent in the Kakhanov subcommittee's project was never realized. The full commission watered down many of the more sweeping proposals. The plan for an administrative unit at the *volost'* level was blocked by the opposition of representatives of the conservative *dvorianstvo* headed by A. D. Pazukhin. More importantly, even the much tempered suggestions of the full commission proved unacceptable to the government of Alexander III which by the mid-1880s was fully embarked upon a reactionary course. At the behest of D. A. Tolstoi, then Minister of Internal Affairs, the commission was dissolved in April 1885 without any of its proposals being implemented.[47]

Alexander III and his ministers might disband the Kakhanov commission and reject its disturbing program for change. Yet the institutional problems of the state could not be ignored. Consequently, the Imperial government continued to work for better provincial administration through a series of limited improvements in existing arrangements. The result was the counterreform legislation of the late 1880s and early 1890s. These laws introduced two major changes in rural life. The first, embodied in the statute of July 12, 1889, created a new official, the *zemskii nachal'nik* (land captain), who was to operate below the *uezd* level. The *zemskii nachal'nik*, chosen from among the local nobles, was to exercise "paternal" supervision over the peasants of his district (*uchastok*), and was given wide discretionary powers to intervene in communal affairs. A second counterreform altered the makeup of the zemstvos by setting up a special electoral curia for the *dvorianstvo*. The zemstvo statute also bound these institutions more closely to the state, bureaucratizing to some extent the provincial *upravy*, and establishing tighter administrative supervision of zemstvo work.[48]

The retrograde direction of the counterreform legislation is evident from even the most cursory examination. It was unquestionably designed to shore up the social and political power of the decaying *dvorianstvo* and to reduce the influence of peasant and *raznochinets* elements. The counterreforms sought to insure that the nobles remained in control of the zemstvo organizations and to restore some of the authority over the peasants which the *dvorianstvo* had lost as a consequence of the emancipation. The reactionary character of these laws is further underlined when we compare them with the proposals of the Kakhanov commission. Moreover, such a comparison shows clearly that the framers of these statutes willingly sacrificed administrative rationality to political considerations. They strengthened the "loyal" nobility not only at the expense of less trustworthy classes, but also to the detriment of governmental efficiency.[49]

Our awareness of the reactionary aims of the counterreforms should not, however, blind us to the fact that in some limited areas these statutes represented a step forward. This was especially true with regard to rural medical programs which were considerably strengthened by the new zemstvo law.[50] The possibility of effective famine relief was also improved by the counterreforms. Although relief procedures were not altered in any significant way, the creation of the land captains meant that there would now be officials stationed closer to the peasants who would be better able to oversee and direct food supply operations at the local level.[51] Even the consequences of bureaucratizing the zemstvos were not entirely negative for famine relief. Closer ties between zemstvo and government personnel had long been needed. Applied in the proper spirit, the zemstvo law of 1890 might help to achieve this aim.[52]

While the counterreforms promised some improvement in the

management of famine relief, they were far too little and much too late. The basic institutional problems of the state remained unaffected. Thus when hunger seized the Volga and black earth provinces in 1891, Russia's government and her people had to struggle against famine using inadequate weapons. The food supply campaign of 1891–92 would quickly and clearly reveal not only the weakness of relief arrangement but also the defects in the state apparatus which slowed and blocked the proper flow of aid. With thousands, even millions of lives threatened, the Imperial regime and the Russian public would be forced to improvise, to forge new tools which would enable them to come to grips with the crisis. The success of these efforts would depend on the resourcefulness of state officials, *zemsty*, and private citizens. Beyond this, the situation would demand close cooperation between government and "society." A spirit of national unity was vital if the hungry were to be fed and the tragic prospect of mass starvation averted.

chapter three

THE CRISIS BEGINS: THE FIRST STEPS OF THE GOVERNMENT

If the historian of the famine of 1891 were to be guided solely by the writings of journalists, diarists, and memoirists of the period, he would have the impression that the disaster came upon the Russian government like a thief in the night, catching the Tsar and his ministers completely unprepared.[1] This view is only partially true. To be sure, at the beginning of the year 1891 the government of the Russian Empire had no idea of how serious the food supply situation would grow to be in the months ahead, but it was aware that trouble was brewing in the Volga and central black earth provinces. The harvest of 1890 had been poor in these areas. The central government had given aid to some of the provincial zemstvos, but for the most part local resources had proved sufficient to meet local needs.[2]

While unfavorable agricultural conditions produced no alarm in St. Petersburg, they did provoke action. Significantly, the first to move was I. A. Vyshnegradskii, the Minister of Finance. As the cautious husband of the Empire's economy, Vyshnegradskii sought to prevent the development of a situation which might divert national resources from the achievement of his primary goals. The Minister of Finance realized that a major crop failure requiring massive relief would destroy his hopes for a favorable balance of trade and a stable currency. Consequently, he worked to head off such a crisis. Vyshnegradskii could not alter the weather, but he could take steps to alleviate part of the distress which drought had caused. Control of railroad shipping rates gave him a useful tool. By reducing the tariff on the transport of grain destined for the afflicted regions, he could increase the availability of food and regularize local prices. This method of indirect assistance had another signal advantage: it would cost the treasury little.

Shortly after the new year, Vyshnegradskii began to put his scheme into effect. He turned to S. Iu. Witte, head of the Ministry's Railroad

Department, with a request for information on grain prices throughout the Empire so as to have a factual basis for decisions concerning shipping rates. On January 23, 1891 Witte approached the Director of the Department of Direct Taxes, Dmitri Fomich Kobeko, asking him to provide data received from tax inspectors about the state of the grain market as of January 1, the extent of food needs in various provinces, and any other information which might illuminate the situation.[3] Kobeko dispatched the information on grain prices the following day,[4] and it was passed on for the consideration of a railroad tariff committee composed of Ministry personnel and representatives of the interested railways. At the same time, Vyshnegradskii sought the cooperation of the Minister of Internal Affairs, Ivan Nikolaevich Durnovo. In a memorandum dated January 23, Vyshnegradskii noted that the poor harvest of 1890 might necessitate a temporary revision of the railroad rates in the affected areas. He asked Durnovo to give the MVD's assessment of the situation, supplying data on the needs of the population and the requests of the provincial institutions for government aid.[5]

On January 27th, Durnovo presented Vyshnegradskii with a lengthy report on conditions in the provinces hit by crop failure in 1890. The document included an outline of the correspondence received from officials in the stricken *gubernii* and a detailed list of the needs of these areas. Durnovo was enthusiastic about the possibility of reduced railroad rates. Surveying the situation in the provinces, he wrote: "I can state with positive assurance that [present] food supply difficulties would have been reduced by half if the movement of grain shipments into the areas of poor harvest had increased in accordance with actual need, . . . in such circumstances the prices of grain would not have risen as rapidly as they . . . have now."[6] Durnovo felt that a number of provinces could benefit from special rates: Kazan, Nizhni-Novgorod, Orenburg, Penza, Samara, Saratov, Simbirsk, and Ufa.[7] The Minister of Internal Affairs described in detail the plight of some of the provinces. Of Nizhni-Novgorod he wrote:

> The extremely poor harvest of spring [grains] and especially grass . . . has had a very unfortunate influence on the well-being of the rural population of the province. True, food supplies, as a result of a satisfactory rye crop, are almost everywhere in good order (*obezpecheno*); but the failure of the grass and spring hay has led to a marked reduction in the amount of peasant livestock [which is] being sold . . . for a song. Besides this, in many areas an insufficiency of seed oats is expected.[8]

The situation in Kazan was similar to that in Nizhni-Novgorod, but, if anything, more serious. The harvest of spring and winter grains had turned out poorly in the southeastern part of the province, and lack of food for cattle caused massive sales of peasant livestock. In some localities "hunger typhus" had appeared. In Spasskii *uezd* the peasants had become so impoverished that they had to dispose of their cattle in order to pay their taxes.[9]

Furnished with information submitted by Durnovo and Kobeko, the tariff committee of the Railroad Department met to consider the question of new rates on February 7, 1891. It decided to reduce by 50 percent the tariff on the shipment of grain into areas hit by the crop failure the previous year. These rates were to apply to deliveries of grain made to Kazan, Nizhni-Novgorod, Orenburg, Samara, Saratov, Simbirsk, Stavropol', Ufa, and Viatka provinces, Kuban oblast', and select *uezdy* in Ekaterinoslav, Kharkov, and Crimea provinces. The special rates were to remain in effect until September 1, 1891.[10]

While the Minister of Finance and the Director of the Railroad Department worked out the new tariff rates, the Committee of Ministers as a whole tried to obtain a clearer picture of the situation with regard to food supplies and the funds available to meet a crisis. On January 26 the Director of Affairs (*upravliaiushchii delami*) for the Committee, Anatolii Nikolaevich Kulomzin, requested Durnovo to present information on the status of the central food supply capital fund. The Minister was asked to list all loans made to individual provinces since the establishment of the central fund. He was also to indicate what conditions had been made concerning the repayment of these loans, and how much in fact had been returned.[11]

Durnovo prepared his report in a leisurely fashion, indicating that he, at least, was not overly aroused by the situation. The document was not drawn up in final form until April 25, and the Committee of Ministers did not discuss it until the session of May 21.[12] After their examination of the data, the ministers felt that they needed more information in order to have "complete clarity as to the amount of food supply need which has arisen in various areas in the course . . . of time, and the means [available] for satisfying [this need]."[13] The Committee therefore requested Durnovo to provide material on local food supply capital and grain stores. Specifically, the Committee wished to know how much money and grain was on hand

and on loan, what amounts had been returned, and how much was in arrears.[14]

Durnovo did not present this second report to the Committee of Ministers until much later, but it is clear that information of the sort requested by the Committee eventually became available at the center.[15] In the meantime, informed persons, both within and outside the government, were growing more and more concerned about the food supply situation. The correspondents of the Department of Agriculture reported that the outlook for the harvest of winter grains was not good.[16] In April, newspapers noted poor harvests in Europe and a resulting increase in the export of Russian grains.[17] By the end of May, *Russkie vedomosti* was estimating that people in the areas affected by bad harvests might not be able to provide for their own needs. The newspaper expressed the hope that the zemstvos and local administration would take whatever steps were necessary to see that supplies of food and seed were provided and that the peasants would be given relief in the form of tax remissions and the suspension of other obligations.[18] But somewhat later *Russkie vedomosti* stated that further, more far-reaching governmental measures would have to wait until a clear picture of the harvest had been obtained from the provincial authorities and the zemstvos.[19]

If in late May and early June the scope of the growing crisis was not yet completely apparent to the bureaucracy and educated public in St. Petersburg, it was becoming more than obvious to people in the provinces and to those who had occasion to pass through the stricken areas. In May 1891, Aleksei Sergeevich Ermolov, then Director of the Department of Indirect Taxation of the Ministry of Finance, toured some of the Volga and black earth *gubernii* in connection with Department business. As he traveled by the ravaged fields, it seemed to him that not only had all the crops succumbed, but also that even the ancient trees would not long survive the destructive onslaughts of the weather. His discouragement increased when, riding through Voronezh, Samara, and Saratov, he read articles in the newspapers calling for the export of grain in view of the excellent prices on the continent.[20]

Upon his return to the capital, Ermolov tried to inform Vyshnegradskii of the dangers ahead. His report to the Minister concluded with the following warning: "'The terrible spectre of famine is advancing on

Russia. It is necessary now, while it is not too late, to take the most decisive measures to prevent the impending disaster.' "[21] Vyshnedgradskii was most disturbed by Ermolov's statement, for it must have seemed that the circumstances described were an immediate threat to all his efforts to stabilize the finances of the Empire. According to Ermolov, the Minister seized the report, thrust it into his desk, and locked it. " 'Your notes will never come out of this drawer,' " Vyshnegradskii told Ermolov firmly. " 'No one should know of this—otherwise you will spoil my rate of exchange [of the ruble].' "[22]

The actions taken by the Ministry of Finance at the beginning of 1891 show that Vyshnegradskii was not indifferent to the fate of the population of the stricken regions. But his abrupt rejection of Ermolov's report reveals that, as of May, the Minister's charity had relatively narrow limits. The interests of the treasury were paramount; and Vyshnegradskii was eager to avoid any major outlay of state funds for relief purposes. He sought to restrict government aid to indirect means like reduced railroad tariffs. The Minister of Finance tried to silence any voice which called for direct intervention on the part of the central government.

The weight of evidence that disaster had fallen upon the fields of Russia was growing rapidly, however. It would soon become too great to be denied, even by the powerful Minister of Finance. A stream of reports of trouble and requests for aid now began pouring across the desks of the *chinovniki* of the MVD's Economic Department. Typical of these early reports was that of Baron Vladimir Platonovich Rokasovskii, the Governor of Tambov. On June 7, 1891, he wrote to Alexander Grigorevich Vishniakov, Director of the Economic Department, outlining the critical situation in the *guberniia*. The Governor stated that there was little hope for the rye crop, and it was conceivable that the fields would not even produce enough for seed. The *uezd* zemstvos were already meeting to take stock of the harvest, and an extraordinary assembly of the provincial zemstvo was planned for July 3 in order to request loans from the central capital fund. Rokasovskii did not request aid at this point, and he stated that some of the estimates of need already prepared by the *uezd* zemstvos were extreme. Nonetheless, he felt that the province would probably require from 1.5 to 2 million rubles in the near future. In view of the steadily rising price of grain, even this sum might not suffice. The Governor noted that the crop failure was hurting other provinces, and he asked the Economic Department to advise him how much aid could be expected from the Imperial capital fund so that he might better guide the zemstvos in framing their requests.[23]

Vishniakov replied to Rokasovskii a few days later. His confidential letter gave little ground for optimism about the possibility of extensive loans from the central fund. Vishniakov estimated that the central government had only 7.5 million rubles on hand to meet the food supply needs of the country, and he stated that provincial authorities would have to be cautious when asking for aid. In the past decade, he noted, the largest loans had never exceeded 1 million rubles, and even a grant of this size had been made only when the situation was extremely serious. As for Tambov itself, Vishniakov argued that it was not among the provinces most adversely affected by the crop failure. Moreover, it had considerable grain and capital reserves. Vishniakov suggested that the zemstvos be encouraged to undertake measures which would aid the peasants without causing them to rely on loans. One such technique might be the sale of grain by the zemstvos at prices below the going rate in the province. Special attention should also be paid to the question of public works. Loans, Vishniakov insisted, should be made only when absolutely necessary, and should be restricted whenever possible to that part of the population which was unable to work.[24]

Vishniakov's letter to Rokasovskii indicated that in the first weeks of June the Ministry of Internal Affairs and the Ministry of Finance saw eye to eye on the question of relief. Like Vyshnegradskii, Durnovo and his colleagues were cautious. As yet unsure of the extent of the trouble in the countryside, they were fearful lest the sums on hand prove inadequate to meet the situation. Durnovo was not of a mind to appeal for significant expenditures of state funds. He was aware of the precarious condition of the Empire's finances, and he knew of Vyshnegradskii's efforts to accumulate sufficient reserves to make possible the conversion to the gold standard. Also realizing that Vyshnegradskii's financial goals enjoyed the support of the Tsar, Durnovo in all likelihood felt that his main duty was to hold relief outlays to a minimum and to encourage the population to provide for itself whenever possible.

Given Durnovo's outlook at the time, it is not surprising that his first response was to push for the expansion of the kind of indirect aid to the stricken area which the Ministry of Finance had developed in January. Thus on June 19 Durnovo proposed to Vyshnegradskii that railroad tariffs on grain shipments into the blighted provinces might be reduced even further than they had been at the beginning of the year. Durnovo felt this measure was necessary because "the economic difficulties of this year . . . [were] going to be much more significant than [those] of the previous year; already there . . . [had] begun a rapid rise in the price of foodstuffs."[25] The Ministry of Finance had obviously been considering the possibility of such measures for some time. Even before Durnovo's request, it had been attempting to gather information on the harvest and the existing grain stores in the affected regions.[26] Now it responded quickly. On June 25 Vyshnegradskii wrote Durnovo and outlined the new tariff rates. Shipments of grain purchased by zemstvos for use in the stricken provinces would be carried by the railroads at the cost of 1/100 kopek per *pud-verst*. All other shipments of grain into these provinces would be made at 50 percent of the regular cost.[27] A few days later the Minister of Finance explained the significance of the new railroad shipping rates to the Emperor. Vyshnegradskii stated that this measure was designed to help regularize grain prices and limit speculation. He also expected that the new railroad tariff would encourage merchants to cut back on exports and reship grain from the ports back to the internal market. Vyshnegradskii felt that the role played by the new rates would be especially important, since without them the poor harvest in Western Europe and the low exchange rate of the ruble would encourage exports to a degree not consistent with the interests of the population of the Empire. The Tsar approved the Minister's proposal and expressed the hope that the measure would be of genuine benefit to the people.[28]

In the latter half of June the first requests for substantial relief from the central capital fund came to the attention of the MVD. On June 15, the Governor of Tula province, N. A. Zinov'ev, petitioned the Ministry for 500,000 rubles, and at about the same time Governor A. A. Goriainov of Penza asked for 1 million rubles. Somewhat later, on June 24, N. M. Baranov of Nizhni-Novgorod wired a request for 1 million rubles.[29] The demands of Governors Zinov'ev and Baranov were based only on the sketchy preliminary figures drawn up by the zemstvo *upravy* and local officials. The governors admitted that the state of the harvest and the needs of the population in their provinces were not yet clear, and that a more detailed picture of the situation would have to wait until the provincial zemstvo assemblies convened in extraordinary sessions during the first weeks of July. But both Zinov'ev and Baranov felt that some relief should be given out even before the zemstvos met and submitted their formal requests.

While Governor Baranov limited his presentation of the situation to a telegraphic message, Zinov'ev accompanied his request with a lengthy report. The Governor of Tula stated that although the question of food for the population was not critical at the moment, the likelihood of a serious crop failure was clear. At this point, seed for the fall planting was most necessary. In many areas of the province the spring harvest had been so poor that even seed grain was lacking. The exact amount of seed that would be required was still not certain, but since local supplies of grain and cash were very small, a loan from the Imperial food supply fund was mandatory. Zinov'ev pledged that under his supervision the zemstvo *uprava* would exercise the utmost care in the granting of any loans.[30] The Governor stressed the fact that when the zemstvos had clarified the extent of need, it would be wise to respond to their requests as quickly as possible. Sowing of the winter fields was soon to begin,[31] and the continuing drought threatened the outcome of the fall harvest.[32] Zinov'ev concluded with the ominous statement that, according to one of the local landowners whose estate records went back to 1805, present climatic conditions closely resembled those which had prevailed in the famine year of 1840.[33]

In contrast to Baranov and Zinov'ev, Governor Goriainov of Penza presented the Ministry with the results of the deliberations of the provincial zemstvo assembly. The zemstvo estimated that the province would need 2,645,000 rubles between June and September 1 in order to stave off disaster. Of this sum, 816,000 rubles would be used to obtain food and 1,829,000 rubles would be allocated for seed purchases. The zemstvo also requested permission to begin buying grain without waiting for peasant communes to request such action. It asked that the favorable railroad rates introduced in February be continued and that peasants be allowed to postpone payment of taxes, arrears, and redemption dues.[34]

Governor Goriainov, however, disagreed with the zemstvo's estimates. Although he affirmed the existence of real poverty among the population as the result of continued bad harvest, he felt that at present it was impossible to determine the true extent of need. On the basis of information gathered through his own agents, the Governor judged the zemstvo requests to be exaggerated. Goriainov felt that 1 million rubles would suffice for the moment: 730,000 for seed, 270,000 for food. He supported zemstvo demands with regard to railroad tariffs, but he argued that tax relief should be given with caution, in accordance with the economic situation of given communes.[35]

The reaction of the Ministry of Internal Affairs to the above requests is instructive, since it not only points up the views of Durnovo and his colleagues but also reveals the pattern the MVD would follow in dealing with similar petitions. The Ministry accepted without much question the statements of Governors Zinov'ev and Baranov concerning the needs of their provinces despite the fact that they did not present volumes of statistics to justify their demands. On the other hand, the MVD showed an unwillingness to believe the estimates of the Penza zemstvo and readily sided with the views of the Governor.[36] The reluctance to grant the 2,645,000 rubles requested by the Penza zemstvo was caused in part by the knowledge that the Ministry's funds were limited.[37] But it is clear from these and later documents that the MVD was receptive to the idea that zemstvo requests were bound to be excessive.[38]

The MVD's caution concerning loans to the zemstvos may have been influenced by political considerations. The government of Alexander III was ill disposed toward the institutions of local self-administration and had demonstrated this clearly by its counterreform legislation. But whatever doubts St. Petersburg bureaucrats may have harbored regarding the loyalty of the zemstvos, they did not seem to fear that the zemstvos would mismanage relief. To be sure, Durnovo attempted to lay down some general guidelines for zemstvo relief (chiefly that loans to peasants be given out in the form of grain, not cash), yet he insisted on allowing the zemstvos the maximum freedom of action. When he submitted the Penza governor's request for 1 million rubles to the Committee of Ministers, Durnovo stated that the provincial zemstvo should not be restricted in its use of the assigned sums. It ought to be permitted to fight rising food prices by selling grain at cost or even below, and it should not be prevented "from taking any other measures with regard to food supply which it . . . [saw] fit, in accordance with local conditions."[39] Durnovo stoutly resisted attempts by overly ambitious governors to limit the activities of the zemstvos or to exclude them from relief work.[40]

Although phrased in the undramatic language of the bureaucracy, Durnovo's decision to give the zemstvos a relatively free hand in the management of relief was one of the most important acts of the entire food supply campaign. This ruling did much to prevent the politization of relief work and laid the basis for effective cooperation between government and zemstvo personnel. Given the thrust of state policy in the late 1880s, however, the actions of the Minister of Internal Affairs appear puzzling. Alexander III's regime had acquired a well deserved reputation for *proizvol*—the arbitrary abuse of authority. The crisis engendered by the famine seemed to create a golden opportunity for even more bureaucratic high-handedness.

Yet upon reflection, Durnovo's motives are not difficult to understand. At the start of the food supply operations, the government viewed the famine primarily as an administrative problem and not as a political challenge. The regime was prepared to work closely with the zemstvos because it did not see relief as a very sensitive issue. The basic question before the government was a strictly practical one: how much aid was needed; how should it be given out? The problem of the political ramifications of the crisis was secondary. The government's willingness to cooperate with the zemstvos also reflects the regime's awareness of its own institutional weaknesses. The state lacked both the apparatus and the personnel necessary for it to manage relief by itself. If the job of feeding the hungry was to be accomplished, the zemstvos would have to assume a major role in the food supply campaign. Durnovo and the leading state officials recognized that a rift between the zemstvos and the government over the control of relief operations would be dysfunctional. The best policy was to proceed along the lines established by the *ustav narodnogo prodovol'stviia*.

Because the sums requested by Penza, Tula, and Nizhni-Novgorod exceeded 50,000 rubles, the law required that the MVD submit these petitions to the Committee of Ministers.[41] Accordingly, Durnovo presented the requests of the provincial authorities and his own recommendations to a meeting of the Committee on June 25. He proposed that Tula receive the 500,000 rubles requested by the Governor and that, likewise, the 1 million rubles demanded by Baranov be assigned to Nizhni-

Novgorod. Durnovo also supported the Governor of Penza's view that 1 million rubles would suffice to meet the immediate needs of that province. The Committee accepted the proposals of the Minister of the Interior virtually without debate, and the requests were forwarded to the Emperor for final approval.[42]

Since the June 25th session would be the last meeting of the ministers until the end of the Committee's summer recess in October, Durnovo suggested that arrangements be made to provide for the possibility of additional relief in the near future. The Minister of Internal Affairs expressed his conviction that the coming months would see increasing demands for loans from the central capital fund. These, he felt, would demand immediate attention. Durnovo therefore proposed to the Committee that, during the vacation period, he be authorized to grant loans as he saw fit, even if they exceeded the 50,000-ruble limit prescribed by law.[43] The Committee approved the idea of granting Durnovo special powers. In its view, the situation in the country was "extremely serious." The exact extent of need was not yet clear, but it would be considerable.[44] Still, the Committee did not feel that it was necessary to remain in session over the summer or to establish a special temporary institution to deal with the problem. Nor did it attempt to work out a general plan for relief. The Committee regarded the special powers given the MVD as sufficient. Thus, placing the management of affairs in the hands of Durnovo, the ministers proceeded to their *dachas* and foreign spas.

chapter four

SETTING THE PATTERN FOR RELIEF: THE WORK OF THE MINISTRIES OF INTERNAL AFFAIRS AND FINANCE

The resolutions of the Committee of Ministers on June 25 marked the beginning of a new stage in the struggle with the famine. The government had recognized that a serious crisis existed and had authorized extraordinary measures to deal with it. But many problems concerning the developing relief campaign remained unresolved. Nor had the officials at the center worked out a detailed plan of action. Given this unclear state of affairs, the decision of the Committee of Ministers to recess, allowing its members to depart for their vacations, seems frivolous. In fact it was not. At that moment there was little more for the Committee to do. Before it could begin to act effectively it had to receive much more complete data on the size and scope of the disaster and the extent of need in the countryside. The Committee also had to know what kinds of programs might be undertaken to counter the effects of the crop failure.

The Committee of Ministers could not gather this kind of information itself, since it lacked local agencies directly subject to its authority.[1] The Committee was dependent on the various Ministers for its supply of data, particularly the Ministries of Internal Affairs and Finance. In recessing, the Committee of Ministers was not washing its hands of the famine. Rather, it was giving the MVD and the Ministry of Finance the go-ahead to accumulate the needed information and to work out some basic programs. The members of the Committee hoped that when they resumed sitting in October they would be in a better position to assess the situation and to take further action.

In the absence of the Committee of Ministers, the Ministry of Internal Affairs and its head, Ivan Nikolaevich Durnovo, assumed the major responsibility for developing the central government's approach to the crisis. During the summer the judgments made by the officials of the

MVD would set the pattern for the entire relief campaign and would, to a large extent, determine its success or failure.

Without question the most crucial decision made in this period was to abandon the emphasis on indirect methods of relief and to begin massive, direct grants of money to the afflicted provinces. By the time the Committee of Ministers reassembled, Durnovo and the MVD had awarded over 29 million rubles to finance the purchase of seed and food grain in the *gubernii* affected by the crop failure.[2] This sum far exceeded the meager resources of the Imperial capital fund, and the MVD was forced to borrow directly from the treasury. Moreover, the events of the summer convinced Durnovo that it would be impossible to hold the line at 29 million rubles. Writing to the Emperor in late September or early October, the Minister stated: "Only by means of further . . . significant expenditures of state monies will it be possible to spare the population of the stricken region the distressing consequences of the disaster which has befallen them."[3]

The decision to embark on a major relief campaign involving a sizable disbursement of state resources was a victory for those who had been urging the government to take more vigorous steps in the face of the developing crisis. It ended Vyshnegradskii's program of husbanding the monetary reserves of the state; the interests of the treasury were sacrificed to the common weal. Even the Ministry of Finance was ultimately forced to embrace this new course. During the summer, Vyshnegradskii reluctantly abandoned his policy of encouraging exports. The sale of Russian grain abroad was restricted in order to ease the task of feeding the hungry at home.

Available records do not show in detail how the decision to expand the relief campaign was reached. Unquestionably the Committee of Minister's recognition that a serious crisis was developing provided the essential background to the new policy. But the conversion to large-scale, state-financed relief was not sudden. Pressure from Vyshnegradskii and treasury officials to hold the line on requests for aid must have been considerable; and the evidence we have indicates that Durnovo was hesitant to challenge the powerful Minister of Finance. Whenever possible, Durnovo avoided a direct confrontation with Vyshnegradskii. Instead of asking for a single large appropriation from the treasury to pay for relief, the Minister of Internal Affairs made at least four separate appeals for relatively small sums.[4] Similarly, Durnovo disbursed the food supply loans to the stricken provinces by means of a series of modest grants made over the course of the summer. This piecemeal approach to relief helped to reassure the officials in the Ministry of Finance that awards were being made only after the most careful study. It also mollified the treasury by holding out the hope that each grant might be the last.

Pressure from Vyshnegradskii was not the only reason that Durnovo was slow to commit himself to a massive relief effort. Another factor—the difficulty of obtaining a clear and accurate picture of what was going on in the countryside—would have considerable impact on ministerial decision-making. The MVD's problem was not a shortage of information; on the contrary, it suffered from surfeit. The Ministry's primary dilemma was making sense out of the intelligence it received. The data coming in from the provinces was often contradictory and in many cases the MVD lacked the means to make a proper evaluation of individual reports.

Throughout the summer, the zemstvos and the provincial governors provided Durnovo and his colleagues with the bulk of the information about conditions in the stricken region and the needs of the population. Unfortunately, these two sources seldom agreed. The initial requests of the zemstvos tended to be huge, projecting the requirements of the peasants for seed and food over the coming six to nine months. The governors, in their reports and comments on zemstvo figures, painted a different picture. While admitting that the crop failure presaged serious food supply problems, the governors urged caution. In general they told the Ministry to meet the immediate needs of the population for seed to sow the winter fields, but they advised Durnovo to be wary about requests for food loans.

The conflicting character of the data received from the provinces confronted Durnovo with the crucial question: Whom to trust? This problem was made even more troublesome by the fact that the Economic Department, the section of the Ministry charged with supervising matters relating to food supply, proved to be a frail reed. Not much is known about the structure and personnel of the Economic Department, but the little information we have is hardly flattering. The work of the Department was neither glamorous nor exciting, and service there offered little prospect for advancement. As a result, the Economic Department was unable to attract energetic and able people. Over time it acquired the reputation as a resting place for dead souls, and was looked upon with disdain by the other workers in the MVD.[5]

The poor quality of its personnel made it impossible for the Economic Department to play an effective advisory role during the famine. It responded to the crisis in the spirit of musty routine. Surveying the documents held in the files of the Economic Department, the historian is struck by the fact that so few of the reports, telegrams, and appeals for aid display any marginal notation. Although the Department was supposed to evaluate all requests from the provinces and to oversee the development of relief programs, the bureaucrats there seem to have been unable or unwilling to exercise judgment. They simply passed most of the communications from the *gubernii* on to Durnovo without comment. The Minister was thus forced to resolve the conflict between the views of the zemstvos and those of the governors with little guidance from the "specialists" in the Economic Department.

Given the lack of reliable advice from the Ministry's staff, Durnovo tended to regard the testimony of the governors more highly than that of the zemstvos. The reasons for this preference are obvious. Because the governors' assessment of the needs of their provinces were much smaller than zemstvo estimates, they could be satisfied without destroying Durnovo's credit with the Ministry of Finance. But in addition to the problem of their size, there were other explanations for the MVD's distrust of the zemstvos' requests. Zemstvo sources themselves admitted that the data upon which their estimates were based had been gathered with great speed at a time when the final outcome of the harvest was not clear. The MVD also favored the views of the governors because it was possible to bring the information they presented up to date quite rapidly. The *uezd* and provincial zemstvos met infrequently, even during the famine crisis. The MVD found it difficult to get clarification from the zemstvos concerning their requests. Nor could the Ministry easily address the zemstvos on specific issues. The governors, however, were always on call, providing a ready line of communication with the provinces. Should new data cast doubt on a governor's view concerning a particular matter, it was possible to query him directly to clarify the situation and hopefully correct any errors.

Despite his preference for the views of the governors on the question of relief, Durnovo was not prepared to accept the information they supplied without question. In mid-July, therefore, the MVD resorted to the time-honored device of sending out a *revizor* to survey the stricken region.

The Director of the Economic Department, A. G. Vishniakov, was assigned the task. Although the Minister's instructions to Vishniakov seem to have been lost,[6] it is clear that Durnovo hoped to achieve several ends by means of this "revision." First, and most important, he reasoned that an outsider might provide a detached and reliable picture of conditions in the Volga and black earth regions. Beyond this, the Minister of Internal Affairs intended to use Vishniakov's tour as an occasion to inform both *zemtsy* and governors that the government's ability to satisfy provincial needs was limited and to insist that local people exercise restraint in formulating their requests for aid.[7] Finally, Durnovo may have hoped that by sending Vishniakov to gather first-hand information on the problems arising from the crop failure he might stir the somnolent Economic Department to action and so provide the MVD with a more useful analysis of the situation.

Vishniakov's tour of the famine region did not realize Durnovo's expectations, however. The Director of the Economic Department approached his mission in a spirit which was to have undesirable consequences for the relief campaign. Instead of concentrating on an investigation of local conditions and needs, Vishniakov made his main task the reduction of provincial requests for aid. Pursuant to this goal, Vishniakov often adopted extremely high-handed methods. After a whirlwind tour of a stricken province, the Director of the Economic Department would announce to *zemtsy* and provincial officials that the situation in the *guberniia* was not really as bad as they had reported, and he would demand a sharp cut in the estimates of need. On occasion, Vishniakov bullied the zemstvos into submission by calling local tax collectors to discredit zemstvo figures.[8] Governors who defended zemstvo demands, even in part, were quick to feel Vishniakov's wrath.[9]

The kind of information Vishniakov supplied the MVD during his "revision" is illustrated by a telegram he sent to Durnovo concerning the state of affairs in Nizhni-Novgorod. Vishniakov admitted that the province had suffered severe crop failures for several years, but he felt that present zemstvo requests for aid were overdrawn. Vishniakov insisted that the estimates concerning the size of the loans needed were based on "extremely problematic (*gadatel'nye*) and obviously exaggerated data."[10] The inadequacy of zemstvo figures was proved, he continued, by the fact that the special provincial food supply conference,[11] which met in his presence, reduced the size of zemstvo demands by half—from 8 million to 4 million rubles.[12] Vishniakov cautioned Durnovo against burdening the population with a loan of even this size, and he reckoned that zemstvo requests could be cut further. The 2 million rubles which had already been granted to the province were sufficient to meet immediate needs.[13] In Vishniakov's opinion it would be "more prudent and convenient" to delay further grants of money to Nizhni-Novgorod until the question could be discussed by the Committee of Ministers.[14]

Vishniakov's final report to Durnovo has not been preserved, but it is possible to surmize its contents on the basis of references to it in other documents. The general tone of the report was probably similar to that found in Vishniakov's telegram of July 17—a distrust of zemstvo estimates coupled with the insistence that the situation was not as black as it had been painted by provincial authorities. Vishniakov may well have denied the existence of "famine,"[15] but there is no question that he affirmed the presence of real need in many areas of the *gubernii* he visited.[16] The main thrust of Vishniakov's argument, however, was the need for extreme caution in the disbursal of relief monies, and this mood clearly infected the Ministry. The impact of Vishniakov's findings is illustrated by the tentative conclusions Durnovo himself drew from the report. According to the Minister's own statement,

> [Vishniakov's] investigations . . . led me to the conclusion that although the data collected by the zemstvo institutions . . . [were] not sufficiently precise and cannot be left without necessary corrections . . . [it would be] impossible to refuse to satisfy a certain part of the food supply needs [of the afflicted provinces] without obvious damage to the proper course of relief.[17]

Durnovo's acceptance of the view that only "a certain part" of the provincial requests for aid should be satisfied unquestionably slowed the process of giving loans to the stricken *gubernii*. But it did not prevent relief from reaching sizable proportions by the end of the summer. Despite his desire to spare the treasury undue expenditures and his conviction that local demands for assistance were excessive, Durnovo found it impossible to ignore the steady stream of petitions which flowed into the offices of the MVD. Ministerial resistance began to crumble as more detailed information on the poor harvest became available at the center. In addition, during the period from July to October the reports of many of the governors began to come into closer agreement with the views of the zemstvos. Thus the dispatch of funds from the center proceeded steadily, although the amount of money disbursed did not equal the total of the requests made by the zemstvos.

The changing character of official communications was not the only factor which pushed the MVD in the direction of steadily enlarging relief grants. On occasion, the intervention of an important outsider could influence the decisions of the Ministry concerning the outlay of funds. This happened in the case of Tambov province. In early July, when the zemstvo assembly presented its views on the needs of the local population, it requested 2.9 million rubles: 1,770,000 to be used for food loans, 1,130,000 for seed. Governor Rokasovskii agreed with the zemstvo estimates regarding seed, but felt the demands for food relief were excessive and premature. In his own evaluation of the province's needs, Rokasovskii argued that no more than 1.5 million rubles were required at this stage of the food supply operations. The Ministry accepted the Governor's reasoning and granted the sum he requested on July 16, 1891.[18] On the 22nd, however, the MVD received a telegram from the Minister of the Imperial Household, Count Vorontsov-Dashkov, who was visiting his estate in Tambov. The Count stated that the loans being granted to the province were not sufficient to meet its requirements for seed grain. On the basis of his personal observations, Vorontsov-Dashkov estimated that without further grants, 15,000 *desiatinas* of peasant land would lie fallow in Shatskii and Morshanskii *uezdy*.[19] It was not clear from Vorontsov-Dashkov's telegram whether or not he knew of the loan assigned by the MVD on the 16th, but Durnovo was taking no chances lest he offend the powerful Minister. He immediately requested the Ministry of Finance to grant another 500,000 rubles to the Tambov zemstvo.[20] Durnovo wired Voronstov-Dashkov to inform him of all the loans that had been made to the province.[21] The Ministry of Internal Affairs also telegraphed Governor Rokasovskii, ordering him to see to it that all peasant allotment lands were fully sown.[22]

The advantage of hindsight makes it easy to criticize the policy pursued by the MVD with regard to relief loans during the summer of 1891. For it is clear that Durnovo and his colleagues failed to assess correctly the scope of the disaster which had afflicted the Volga and black earth provinces. The 29 million rubles disbursed between July and October was an enormous sum, but it did not begin to meet the needs of the stricken *gubernii*. Moreover, the Ministry's insistence on giving out relief grants piecemeal hampered zemstvo grain purchases and prevented the build-up of reserves of food at the local level. Grain prices rose sharply during the summer months. The inability of the zemstvos to buy large stocks of grain at the beginning of the relief campaign meant that the value of the loans they received from the MVD declined steadily. In the end the Ministry would be forced to make much more money available to the zemstvos. It can be argued that had the government been more generous during the summer of 1891, not only could relief have been more effective but also some of the expense the state was to incur later could have been reduced.

Such criticism is easy, but it is not entirely accurate or fair. The MVD's initial caution with regard to relief grants was at least partially justified by the fact that the final outcome of the harvest could not be known until mid-August. Moreover, during the early summer false hopes concerning the crops had been raised by increased rainfall in some of the stricken regions.[23] Even if the Ministry of Internal Affairs had placed the entire 29 million rubles in zemstvo hands at the start of the relief campaign, however, the problem of building up reserves of food might not have been significantly eased. As we will have occasion to note in another context,[24] the zemstvos were not well equipped to undertake the large-scale purchase of grain. Their efforts in this sphere often proved clumsy and self-defeating. Zemstvos frequently competed with one another for available grain stores, forcing prices up and thus wasting a good portion of their alloted sums. A large grant from the Ministry early in the summer would not have avoided this problem. Indeed, it might have hastened the appearance of panic conditions on the grain market and so have made matters even worse.

The slow disbursal of relief monies was not the main weakness of the MVD's antifamine program. Most needed in the early phase of the food supply campaign was some kind of overall direction from the center. But events were to prove that the Ministry of Internal Affairs was unable to provide this guidance. As in the case of monetary grants, Durnovo and his colleagues resorted to a piecemeal approach. Instead of putting forth a unified plan of attack, the MVD restricted its intervention to the dispatch of circulars designed to established some ground rules for relief.

Perhaps the most important suggestion from the Ministry came in

July. As the governors of the various provinces presented the zemstvos' requests for loans, the MVD issued orders putting forth some general regulations for the actual disbursement of relief funds by the zemstvos. These ministerial instructions contained five basic points: (1) seed loans to peasants should be made for allotment lands only, and peasants who had rented additional fields would have to provide for those themselves; (2) seed loans should not exceed eight *pudy* per *desiatina*; (3) food loans were not to be given to persons of working age, so as not to cause the population to avoid available work; (4) the highest food loans should not be greater than thirty *funty* per month per "soul;" and (5) at all times the greatest possible economy should be observed, and grain should always be bought where prices were lowest.[25]

The initial guidelines established by the MVD were later attacked, with considerable justification, as ungenerous and too restrictive.[26] There can be little doubt that the Ministry's insistence on the strictest economy encouraged zemstvos to make undue cuts in their relief rolls, in some cases even excluding young children between two and five years of age.[27] The ban on aid to persons of working age was also unnecessarily parsimonious given the unavailability of jobs during the crisis. To its credit, however, the MVD quickly recognized this error and modified the rules to permit loans to all persons whose economic situation warranted them.[28]

The size to the loans themselves (30 *funty* per "eater" per month) also appears niggardly, but here some words may be offered in the MVD's defense. First of all, Durnovo and his colleagues did not consider the "full feeding" of the needy as goal of the government's assistance program. Food loans were only supposed to be a supplemental ration. Moreover, the 30-*funt* monthly allotment corresponds closely to the acceptable modern standard for relief grants.[29] Finally, as the crisis developed, the MVD became increasingly flexible, permitting the expansion of loans to an amount well above the stipulated norm.[30]

The Ministry continued to insist on the complete freedom of the zemstvos in their use of the sums assigned to them. But to insure greater cooperation between the zemstvos and provincial administrations, the MVD proposed that special "conferences" on food supply be established. These conferences were to meet under the chairmanship of the governor. They were to be composed of persons directly concerned with the food supply question and who were in a position to offer information on the state of the province and the course of relief. Such conferences usually included the vice-governors, the provincial marshals of the nobility, the chairman of the *guberniia* zemstvo *upravy* and other representatives of the zemstvos, the mayor of the provincial capital, the directors of the local *kazennye palaty*, and *udel'nye kontory*, the permanent member of the provincial council on peasant affairs. When the situation required it, representatives of the *uezd* zemstvos, *uezd* marshals, land captains, and any other persons whose presence might aid the deliberations of the conference were to be invited.

Precisely when the Ministry decided to order the establishment of these conferences is not certain. Toward the end of June, Governor Baranov proposed to the MVD that a special committee on food supply be set up in Nizhni-Novgorod province. This idea was approved by Durnovo shortly thereafter.[31] The Ministry may have been impressed by Baranov's suggestion; at any rate, in July, the MVD sent out instructions to the other governors to set up their own special conferences.[32] Despite the Ministry's orders, however, these conferences did not come into existence in all provinces at the same time.[33] For whatever reasons, some governors were slow to act, and in August, Durnovo sent out a supplemental circular reminding the governors that they should organize the food supply conferences.[34]

By means of its circulars, the MVD sought to guide the zemstvos and provincial officials in the task of relief and, wherever possible, to point out potential dangers. On several occasions in the course of the summer, Durnovo ordered the governors to see to it that those peasants who were able to do so store up sufficient supplies of spring grain. This would guarantee that the fields would be sown in the spring of 1892, and would make it possible for government loans to be kept to a minimum.[35] In September the MVD expressed concern that zemstvo grain purchases were not being properly managed. The Ministry noted that competition between zemstvos from different provinces had resulted in a significant rise in grain prices. It suggested that the governors help to work out local plans for grain purchases so as to avoid such conflicts.[36] In two other circulars, the MVD called the attention of the governors to zemstvo abuse of the special railroad tariffs[37] and noted that some zemstvo agents were charging more for the grain they purchased than it actually cost. In the latter case, however, there was no implication of dishonesty. The circular stated that these agents were simply trying to cover the costs of commissions to grain merchants and other expenses incurred in purchase. The Ministry urged that zemstvo agents be given extra money so that they would not have to pad their accounts.[38]

In August, as the outlook on the harvest became clearer, the MVD turned its attention to the problem of tax collections. On August 1 the *zemskii otdel* issued a circular urging the governors to exercise caution in gathering taxes and arrears "so as not to weaken the individual peasant economies and deprive them of the possibility of recovery in the future."[39] When necessary, collections of taxes and arrears could be suspended, but this should be done with great care, on the basis of accurate information gathered by the *zemskie nachal'niki* and the tax collectors. Since many of the stricken provinces contained areas with relatively good harvests, there would be households and whole communes able to fulfill their obligations. When it was possible for the population to pay, it should be made to do so, lest the state lose revenue and the peasants be burdened with an enormous debt.[40] The Ministry suggested that deferment of payments be applied only to a part of the peasant obligations—redemption payments—and that regular land taxes be gathered as usual.[41]

The MVD also sought to encourage and guide the development of private charity. In a circular dated September 1, the Ministry noted with pleasure the growth of nongovernmental relief and attempted to establish some rules governing its operation. As if to counter the suspicions of "society," the MVD denied that the guidelines it was setting forth were designed to delay or hamper the work of private individuals. The public was assured that these rules were simply intended to insure the "proper direction of charitable activity."[42]

The actual instructions, however, indicated that Durnovo wished to see that the authorities retained a large measure of control over charitable operations. Under the rules laid down, collections for the needy could be made only with the permission of the governor and under his supervision. Similarly, private citizens could not establish their own relief committees without the governor's approval. The governor was also to have a say in determining the composition of these committees and the scope of their activities. Donations made for the benefit of specific regions or persons could be sent to local charitable bodies or to the governors for distribution. Contributions of a general nature were not to be dispensed until the MVD had been informed and had reached a decision regarding their use.[43]

The rules laid down may seem to have been unduly restrictive, but closer examination shows that they were not entirely unreasonable. The main purpose of governmental control was to see to it that the monies gathered were actually assigned to charitable purposes, and also to insure that these contributions went to meet the needs of persons who were not able to receive loans from the zemstvos. The network of private charity in the provinces was thin even in the best of times. Now, in some areas, it had already broken down under the strain of the disaster.[44] At this critical moment, there could be no duplication of effort. Thus some coordination was vital to the success of private efforts to aid the needy.

Still, it is very likely that the MVD's rules concerning private charity were also designed to prevent the proliferation of local committees and other organizations which might, among other things, provide avenues by means of which seditious persons could enter the countryside and spread their views among the peasantry. At any rate, many representatives of "society" were apprehensive concerning the government's motives. Mutual distrust between the authorities and the public came to be an important influence on the development of private relief during the famine. Even after the Special Committee on Famine Relief was set up in November under the chairmanship of the Tsesarevich (Heir Presumptive), many persons engaged in relief work preferred to avoid contact with "official" bodies, although as they later admitted, they might have rendered their own efforts more effective by doing so.[45]

The above survey of ministerial instructions shows clearly that the MVD's activities in connection with the food supply campaign during the summer of 1891 were not negligible. Still, the guidelines established by Durnovo and his colleagues fell far short of the overall management the situation required. Of course, Russia's food supply law (*ustav narodnogo prodovol'stviia*) provided for considerable local autonomy in the matter of famine relief. But the enormous scope of the disaster of 1891 called for some kind of action by the MVD to coordinate the efforts of the various zemstvos and provincial administrations. The modest and limited character of the Ministry's actions seem strange given the well-known propensity of the Russian government to try to manage affairs from the capital. Why, then, did the MVD hold back?

Part of the answer to this question lies in the character of Durnovo.

On paper the Minister appears to have been exceptionally well qualified to lead the struggle against the famine. He had been a provincial governor, and so was familiar with the workings of local administration. He enjoyed extensive experience in the MVD including several years as Assistant Minister. Moreover, before his appointment to head the Ministry of Internal Affairs, Durnovo had served as Director of His Majesty's own Chancellery of the Institutions of the Empress Maria. This post undoubtedly gave Durnovo insights into the problems of managing charitable work.

Yet for all this excellent background, Durnovo lacked force in his conduct of office. He was timid—a feature of his personality which appears to have been the consequence of a feeling of inferiority. Durnovo did not have the respect of his colleagues in government. Almost all of them describe Durnovo as having the qualities of a typical *pomeshchik*, personally affable and hospitable, but "uncultured, unintelligent and extremely limited."[46] Whether Durnovo deserved this low opinion is difficult to say with certainty. (Durnovo was hardly a statesman of the first order; on the other hand, his policies during the famine did not expose him as an incompetent bungler.) In any case, Durnovo himself seems to have accepted the judgment of his peers. His feeling that he was somehow not fit to hold the post as head of the MVD[47] does much to explain Durnovo's caution and his routine approach to the famine crisis.

Serious deficiencies in the apparatus of the MVD reinforced Durnovo's timidity. The inadequacy of the Economic Department hampered the acquisition of a detailed picture of the famine and so retarded ministerial action. But other factors, too, prevented Durnovo from attempting centralized direction of relief work. The most important of these was the inability of the MVD to impose its will on its main local agents—the governors.

The lack of effective central control over the governors was a longstanding problem in the Imperial administration which reflected the peculiar nature of gubernatorial authority. The governors were both the personal representatives of the Emperor and the agents of the MVD. But because they derived their powers from the Tsar and could not be removed from office without his sanction, the governors enjoyed a strong sense of independence from the Ministry of Internal Affairs. Separated from the capital by vast distances, and unchecked by any local institutions, the governors often ruled as virtual sovereigns in their *gubernii* and resisted attempts by the MVD to guide and supervise their activity.[48]

The independence of the provincial governors was tolerable (although not desirable) in ordinary times. But during a crisis like the famine, the absence of genuine ministerial control over the *nachal'niki* made central coordination of relief efforts in the several afflicted *gubernii* extremely difficult. For although the Minister of Internal Affairs might propose policies, it was up to the governors to implement them. When gubernatorial actions ran counter to ministerial directives or even to the law itself, there was little the MVD could do. A governor might defy an order from the Ministry and sustain his opposition for months. Such acts of defiance occurred a number of times during the famine year. One of the most interesting and illustrative instances took place in Viatka in connection with the question of banning grain exports from the province.

The conflict between the MVD and Governor A. F. Anis'in of Viatka arose out of a misunderstanding concerning the proper method of dealing with grain speculators in the province. During the summer of 1891, "*skupshchiki*" seeking to buy foodstuffs from the peasants had appeared in Viatka. This alarmed zemstvo and *guberniia* officials who feared that such activity might deprive the local population of its grain reserves. Viatka authorities sought the guidance of the Ministry of Internal Affairs, and on July 30 the MVD responded with a statement encouraging the adoption of measures to curtail speculation and to limit peasant grain sales.[49] Provincial bureaucrats and *zemtsy* took this to mean that all methods designed to achieve these ends were acceptable, and went to the point of prohibiting the export of grain from Viatka.[50] Even shipments to the stricken *gubernii* of Kazan, Ufa, and Perm were banned. Viatka police stopped and searched travelers at border checkpoints in the hope of discovering contraband grain.[51] Plainclothesmen skulked about bazaars in several *uezdy* of Kazan to see to it that Viatka peasants did not smuggle out fodder for sale in a "foreign" province.[52]

The actions of the Viatka authorities were in direct violation of Russia's food supply law, which insisted on the complete freedom of the grain trade on the internal market. These measures also threatened the success of the antifamine campaign in neighboring provinces where zemstvos were counting on being able to acquire grain in Viatka. The free movement of supplies in the northern Volga area was especially important because Viatka and the other nearby provinces were without railroad links to the rest of the country. No main lines passed through Kazan or Perm, and the railroad in Ufa was so far to the south as to have almost no influence on the grain trade in the northern *uezdy*. This weakness in the local transportation network made it necessary to purchase food stores for the winter and seed for the spring planting early, before the Volga froze and navigation ceased. Viatka's restrictions threatened to disrupt the balance of trade in the region, for in normal times Viatka often exported grain to its neighbors.[53]

It is not surprising, therefore, that Durnovo was alarmed by Governor Anis'in's ban on grain exports and refused to approve the measure.[54] The Minister became further concerned when he began to receive complaints from the Governor of Kazan, Petr Alekseevich Poltaratskii. On September 4, Poltaratskii informed the Ministry that Viatka's trade restrictions were creating obstacles to relief work in Kazan, and asked that Durnovo intervene in the situation.[55] The Minister responded on the 7th by demanding that the Viatka administration explain and justify its actions.[56] Durnovo's query produced only a curt reply from Anis'in: "Not possible to permit Kazan zemstvo to obtain rye, oats, barley in Viatka province. Needs of areas of poor harvest in Viatka hardly met."[57] The Ministry continued to press, however, insisting that Viatka officials render assistance to Kazan authorities since "Kazan province . . . [was] in a more difficult position than Viatka."[58] Somewhat later, Durnovo repeated his objections. On September 19 he informed Governor Anis'in that the MVD could not support Viatka's ban on grain exports. The province should strictly limit itself to measures against speculators and artificial price rises.[59]

The Minister's strict orders met with continued opposition from the authorities in Viatka and, as a result, officials of the MVD were bombarded by bitter complaints from Governor Poltaratskii.[60] In late September Durnovo tried to persuade Anis'in to cooperate, but could only gain permission for agents of the Kazan zemstvo to take limited amounts of grain from Viatka.[61] During October the Minister again sought to bring Anis'in into line. In a letter to the Governor, Durnovo stated firmly that "my permission to take measures against the artificial inflation . . . of prices by speculators did not give a basis for the unconditional prohibition of exports of grain beyond the border of the province."[62]

Once more the Minister's directive produced no results. During November the zemstvos in Kazan complained that Viatka authorities were still interfering with grain shipments.[63] Not until December 14, 1891 could the MVD state that it had received assurances from Governor Anis'in that he had "given orders for the abolition of all restrictive measures concerning the grain trade in Viatka province."[64] By this time, however, winter snows had made transportation extremely difficult and other *gubernii* were far less interested in Viatka's grain than they had been earlier. Governor Anis'in had won his struggle with the Ministry.

The Viatka affair was the most serious instance of gubernatorial defiance of ministerial authority to occur during the famine crisis. But it was not an isolated case. In other provinces, too, governors would act to thwart or distort orders from the center. Such events clearly show that Durnovo's power to shape events in the countryside was severely limited, and they explain why the independence of local agencies was to be an outstanding feature of the relief campaign. On the whole, local autonomy would have a beneficial effect on the struggle with the famine. Too much central control would undoubtedly have stifled the initiative of provincial officials and zemstvo workers. Still, the inability of the Ministry of Internal Affairs to coordinate the efforts of the institutions in different *gubernii* and to prevent the kind of conflict which developed between Viatka and Kazan had undesirable consequences. After large-scale grain purchases were underway, the absence of central direction led to unnecessary and harmful competition between zemstvo agents. Moreover, Durnovo's awareness of the MVD's institutional shortcomings inhibited him from working out more vigorous relief programs even when the situation warranted and his colleagues on the Committee of Ministers pressed him to do so.[65]

Although the Ministry of Internal Affairs dominated the central government's relief efforts, few if any of its measures aroused much excitement among the public. Ironically, the actions of the Ministry of Finance caused far more commotion and discussion than did those of the MVD. Certainly the most dramatic move by the Ministry of Finance was the ban on the shipment of Russian grain abroad, decreed with regard to rye at the end of July and later expanded to include other grains as well.[66]

The decision to impose these trade restrictions came as a result of the steady growth of Russian exports during the early part of the year. According to data published in *Vestnik finansov*, exports of food grains for the period January 1 to June 1, 1891 were larger than those for the same period in the two preceding years. A comparison of exports for 1890 and 1891 showed that exports of wheat had risen by almost 6 million *pudy*, rye by 1.5 million *pudy*, and oats by over 4.5 million *pudy*.[67] The reason for this growth in exports was two-fold. First, the harvest of 1891 had been poor all over Western Europe, and thus the demand for Russian grains was unusually high. Second, news of Russia's food supply problems had helped to cause a decline in the value of the ruble on the international money markets. The drop in the rate of exchange of the ruble made Russian money cheaper, and this enabled foreign merchants to pay higher prices for rye without increasing their expenditure of gold or credit *valiuta*.[68]

The outflow of grain at a time when the country was experiencing an extremely bad harvest and a sharp rise in domestic food prices must have alarmed many officials in the central government. This was especially true in the early phase of relief operations when the precise size of harvest and the needs of the people were not yet clear and requests for aid were beginning to pour into the MVD. In late June, Vyshnegradskii, undoubtedly in conjunction with Durnovo, considered the possibility of a ban of grain exports.[69] But the idea was rejected in favor of less stringent methods. At this stage, both the Ministries of Finance and Internal Affairs hoped to deal with the crisis by indirect means which would not do damage to the interests of the treasury. Thus instead of prohibiting grain exports altogether, the government sought to foster an increased movement of food supplies into the stricken regions. The reduction of railroad tariffs was the method adopted. Vyshnegradskii and Durnovo reasoned that the new rates would make the shipment of grain from the ports and borders profitable. They expected that the resulting flow of foodstuffs into the internal market would simultaneously reduce exports and lower prices in the afflicted *gubernii*.[70]

For a while it seemed as if these measures might produce the desired results, and in early July, Vyshnegradskii was able to report that domestic grain prices had fallen slightly.[71] Despite this small success, the situation remained serious. Grain prices were still far above those of 1890—in some places over 60 percent above normal.[72] Moreover, the European demand for grain and the low value of the ruble continued to act as a magnet for Russian foodstuffs. At the same time, demands for aid from the provinces increased steadily. Estimates made in late July seemed to indicate that the nation would suffer a serious shortage of rye and that there might not be sufficient supplies available to meet the needs of the people.[73]

Under the increasing pressure of the food supply crisis, on July 28, 1891 the government issued a ban on the shipment of rye abroad. This action ended Vyshnegradskii's policy of forced export and threatened the whole of his economic program. Such a turnabout, even a temporary one, was obviously not accomplished without considerable resistance from the Minister of Finance and his colleagues. Vyshnegradskii's foot-dragging in this matter is evidenced by the fact that the trade restrictions were not put into effect at once. In the hopes of salvaging something from the ruins of his program and as a concession to grain merchants under contract to foreign buyers, Vyshnegradskii allowed rye exports to continue until mid-August. This half-way measure had unfortunate results. In the days before the final closing of the borders, the price of rye rose sharply, to the great advantage of big landowners and speculators. The excitement on the grain markets was tremendous, and merchants strove to get as much rye abroad as possible. In the three-week "grace period" the port of Odessa alone exported almost 2 million *pudy* of grain as compared with less than 6 million *pudy* in the six months before the ban.[74]

At the same time, a steady torrent of grain poured over the border into Germany. The sight of these exports, when prices at home were so high, produced serious discontents among the population of the western *gubernii*. In the provinces of Vitebsk, Kovno, Grodno, and Vilna, disorders broke out in some fifty localities. Thousands of persons, many of them Jewish, participated in food riots. People demonstrated, hurled rocks at grain wagons, and in some cases forced the drivers to turn back from the frontier. At some railroad stations, rioters broke into sealed boxcars and removed the contents; in other places, demonstrators lay down on the tracks in order to prevent the shipment of the grain. In Vitebsk, the house of a grain merchant was attacked and looted.[75] In the end, the disturbances were quelled, and the exports continued until the ban went into effect. The amount of grain that crossed the border into

Germany was so large that more than a month later mountains of Russian grain were still standing in Koenigsberg waiting for the German railroads to move them to their destinations.[76]

The government ban on exports has been criticized by later students of the famine. Some have felt that it was unnecessary;[77] others have charged that while the concept itself was sound, the trade restrictions should have been applied much earlier and more stringently if they were to be an effective measure against famine.[78] It is probably impossible to give a definitive evaluation of the government's policy with regard to the grain trade or to know for certain the motives of the officials who devised the program.[79] The statistics available on the harvest of 1891 are not complete. Because they do not give figures on the harvest in the Caucasus, we cannot make a final estimate on the amount of grain in the country at a given time. Certainly the information upon which the government based its original decision on rye exports was far from adequate, and it may well be that the primary motive for this measure was panic.[80] But the fact that the government expanded the scope of the original restrictions in October and November, when the picture of the harvest had become much clearer, indicates that officials in the center felt that the initial measure had been of some value and that the situation warranted more of the same. The use of these restrictions as a sop to public opinion cannot be wholly discounted, but they also caused disquiet in many quarters, especially business and finance.[81] Whatever the reasons for its promulgation, the ban on exports was one of the first public admissions by the government that the nation faced a serious crisis ahead, one that could not be met by ordinary means.[82] It was the government—not Leo Tolstoi—which in effect first raised the "terrible question" whether or not Russia possessed enough food to meet the needs of the people. The discussion provoked by this query could not easily be stilled.

chapter five

THE CRISIS DEEPENS: THE PROMISE AND DEFAULT OF THE COMMITTEE OF MINISTERS

As the summer drew to a close, both government and "society" realized that the months ahead promised ever greater difficulties. Although the data on the harvest, the existing grain reserves, and the number of needy persons were not yet complete, the picture of the situation was clear enough to indicate something of the size and scope of the problem. The vast central expanse of European Russia, sixteen provinces, containing the most fertile portions of the Empire, lay stricken by drought. This enormous tract, approximately 900,000 square miles, stretched from the Ural mountains in the East, westward along and across the Volga, south of Moscow to the borders of the Ukraine. The population of the region numbered some 36 millions. The vast majority were peasants, living in small, widely scattered villages.[1] During the winter and early spring the isolation of these villagers from the outside world was virtually complete; and the task of providing those in need with the necessary supplies of food and seed would be extremely difficult. The troubles of European Russia, however, were not the only ones with which the government had to contend. Beyond the Urals, the usually fertile plains of Tobolsk province had also been ravaged by the weather.

The problem of meeting the needs of the population of the affected *gubernii* was complicated by the fact that the transportation network linking these areas to the rest of the country was far from adequate. Railroads were few especially in the east. A single line, stretching from Riazhsk to Samara, bound the whole region east of the Volga and south of the Kama rivers to the main railroad routes. The entire expanse between Riazan and Simbirsk, including the northern corner of Tambov and the southern part of Nizhni-Novgorod provinces, was without railway lines at all. The construction of the railroad along the Volga had stopped at Nizhni. Only the great waterways linked Viatka, Perm, and Kazan provinces to the outside world; but the river routes were not navigable during the late fall and winter.[2] In the autumn of 1891 the situation had been further complicated by the shallowing of the Volga. As a result, the difficulty of moving grain barges into the famine areas increased.

By the fall of 1891 it had become obvious that only the shipment of enormous quantities of grain into the stricken provinces could prevent a major calamity. It was equally clear, however, that the railroads, which would have to play a decisive part in these operations, were experiencing difficulties. Encouraged by the special freight rates, the zemstvos of the affected *gubernii* were avoiding high local grain prices by making purchases on distant markets, especially in the southwestern provinces and the northern Caucasus. The amount of grain being carried at reduced rates rose steadily throughout the summer and autumn.[3] This jump in the volume of goods being transported into the central agricultural region of Russia strained the carrying capacity of the roads, for they had not been designed to move large quantities of grain in this direction.[4] By the end of October considerable delays were being reported on key railroads;[5] collapse of the entire network threatened at a time when lives depended on it. Unless the situation improved in the near future, government intervention would be necessary.

At the same time, state officials were awakening to the fact that the relief operations were not proceeding as intended. The difficulties which had developed were not due to mismanagement on the part of the provincial administrations or the zemstvos. They resulted in part from the vast size of the task of relief and, more importantly, from serious miscalculations by officials at the center. As we have seen, initial MVD guidelines put sharp limitations on the scope of zemstvo loans.[6] Consequently, at the start of the relief campaign, many persons—men of working age, young children, and rural dwellers who were not members of a commune—were frequently denied aid.[7] The government had hoped that these people could either find work or would be provided for by charity. But these hopes had not been realized. Work was extremely scarce in the countryside, wages were low,[8] and local food prices were high. In addition, it had proved difficult to mobilize the public in a massive charitable campaign.[9] Clearly, the government would have to act quickly to fill the gaps in the relief system if it were to avert a real disaster.

Given these many difficulties, it is not surprising that those who visited St. Petersburg in the fall of 1891 found despair and confusion to be the dominant moods in government and society. Upon his return to the capital in October, State Secretary Polovtsov was informed that all the ministers were "weighed down with despair . . . , that no one [had] a clear idea what to do but all . . . [vied] with one another in proposing the most wild-eyed schemes."[10] Others, too, noted the situation. In his diary for 1892, Tertii Ivanovich Filippov, the State Controller, recalled the feeling of helplessness that gripped officials during the crisis.[11] Chaos seemed general. Orders were issued and then withdrawn;[12] some local officials refused to obey directives from the center. At least one *chinovnik* felt the muddle in the capital to be worse than the disaster in the provinces. He summed up the situation declaring: "We do not have a [real] famine, but there is a dreadful confusion in the government's orders."[13]

But the difficulties caused by the famine were not the only reason for the prevalence of a mood of despair. The measures adopted by the government itself were often counterproductive, giving an impression that things were even worse than they actually were. The ban on grain exports helped to create a panic psychology; even well-meaning officials circulated documents which could only increase disquiet. In September, T. I. Filippov, in an effort to raise funds for the relief of the needy, turned to the various departments of his Ministry with a circular which began as follows: "During a recent tour of the local budgetary institutions, I had to visit seven provinces ravaged by crop failure. Samples of the bread they are eating in these provinces and the products from which this bread is made lie on my desk and horrify . . . visitors [to my office]."[14] Filippov's circular presented unvarnished facts. But such straightforward language in official documents, usually characterized by the driest farm of expression, was bound to produce something of a "*sensatsiia*" and perhaps lead the public to draw conclusions which went beyond the realities described.

The sense of crisis and confusion was further heightened by the rumors which flew about the capital. Now the role of gossip in Russian society is a subject that deserves study in its own right. Still it is safe to say that few peoples cultivate rumors as assiduously as do the Russians, and the fruit that develops is often weird and luxuriant. The absence of a genuinely free press strengthened the Russian propensity for rumor-making, but the government compounded the problem by its failure to develop any kind of public relations program. Official statements told little about the steps taken to aid the needy, and so "society" was slow to learn of the regime's commitment to relief.[15] In addition, government documents never used the word "*golod*" (famine) to describe the situation in the countryside. Instead terms like "*neurozhai*" (crop failure), "*nedorod*" (bad harvest), and "*bedstvie*" (misfortune) were employed. The use of these milder expressions was partially justified because *golod* had highly emotional connotations, implying to many nothing less than mass starvation.[16] State officials reasoned that to use the term famine would simply heighten the mood of panic which already existed. But the government's plan backfired. The refusal of the regime to utter the word *golod* only convinced society that the bureaucrats were trying to cover up the truth.

Thus government reticence, instead of slowing down the rumor machine, further heightened speculation about what was going on in the stricken *gubernii*. Some of the legends which circulated were favorable to the regime, or at least to the Tsar, attributing to him the intention of donating 50 million rubles from his own resources to aid the needy.[17] But most gossip painted the situation in the darkest terms. Stories reported corruption on a massive scale. One rumor had it that the ban on wheat exports had been delayed until a certain high state official had been able to sell his grain abroad at a good price.[18] Another tale insisted that the governors and peasant officials were working hand in hand to steal funds earmarked for the destitute; between 30 and 65 million rubles were supposed to have been lost.[19] Even the Red Cross was slandered.[20] Estimates of the number of needy were wildly exaggerated,[21] and reports of mass deaths of children spread.[22] In December, Alexandra Bogdanovich wrote:

> They say that in Simbirsk province all the children have died; they sent children's clothes there and all [were] returned—there is no one to wear them. There is indignation everywhere. . . .[23]

Rumors also charged that in some of the stricken provinces the peasants were so desperate that they attempted to steal grain from the storehouses of the local *pomeshchiki*. In one case, it was alleged, troops were called out to protect the nobles' property, and at the order of the governor fired into a crowd of peasants, killing and wounding many.[24]

The government was disturbed by the spread of rumors about the famine, especially when such stories appeared on the pages of the major newspapers. Yet state officials did not attempt to impose a blackout of news from the countryside. During the famine the government regarded the press as a valuable source of information about conditions in the stricken *gubernii*, a useful supplement to official communications.[25] The importance of news reports from the famine region explains why the government's dealings with the press were quite restrained in 1891–92. To be sure, the MVD ordered the governors to see to it that local newspapers carried truthful accounts of what was happening, but at the same time the Ministry stressed the "unquestioned value" of accurate and detailed reportage.[26] The government's need for the information supplied by the nation's press makes clear its failure to suppress the liberal *Russkie vedomosti* even after that newspaper carried Tolstoi's inflammatory "*Strashnyi vopros*" and Korolenko's exposé on relief work in Nizhni-Novgorod.[27] But this lenient policy toward the press had some undesirable consequences for the regime. Years of tight censorship had taught the Russian public to read between the lines of their newspapers, to search for the Aesopian phrase, and in some cases to extrapolate on what had been written to the point of exaggeration. Thus accurate accounts of conditions in the famine area tended to be blown up in the public mind. For it was believed that reporters were probably soft-pedaling the crisis in order to avoid the wrath of the censors.

Against this background of crisis, rumor, and confusion, the Committee of Ministers reconvened on October 8, 1891. Its first order of business was to hear Durnovo outline the antifamine measures he had adopted during the summer.[28] But as the Minister of Internal Affairs presented his report, it must have become increasingly obvious to the perceptive members of the Committee that the steps taken to date were insufficient. The crisis which lay ahead demanded more; it called for an overall plan of attack and the coordinated work of the major governmental agencies. And it was also clear that the Committee of Ministers could play an important role in meeting the challenge posed by the famine. The Committee was in the position to act as a clearing house for information about the crisis and to effect cooperation between the several Ministries. Beyond this the Committee of Ministers might also contribute to the working out of a comprehensive scheme for coping with the disaster.

No one saw the potential of the Committee of Ministers better than

A. A. Abaza, then Chairman of the State Council's Department of National Economy. In the next months, Abaza would become the driving force behind the work of the Committee, pushing it to assume a larger role in the work of famine relief. Many times Abaza would put the ministers, especially Durnovo, on the spot, scrutinizing their actions, demanding more information, and urging bolder measures. Abaza's determination to play the gadfly was, in large part, a reflection of his general opposition to the policies of Alexander III's government. A remnant of the liberal era of Loris-Melikov, under whose aegis he had briefly served as Minister of Finance, Abaza strongly disapproved of the course state policy had taken in the 1880s. In addition to his dislike of government programs, Abaza had little regard for the leading political figures of the day. He was particularly contemptuous of Durnovo, who he felt was unfit to hold the office of Minister of Internal Affairs.

Abaza's hostility to the current regime made him revel in the role of critic. Even the dry extracts of the journals of the Committee of Ministers fail to conceal entirely Abaza's delight in embarrassing those in power. Unfortunately, however, Abaza was too negative; and beyond criticism had little to offer. Ultimately he would prove unable to lead the Committee in working out a general plan for relief. But this failure was not simply a personal one. The Committee of Ministers *as an institution* proved unreceptive to the kind of direction that Abaza tried to provide.

In its externals the Committee of Ministers resembled the ministries found in Western European states; but form belied substance. The Committee of Ministers was in no sense a cabinet created to facilitate the development of collective programs and policies. Russian autocrats, jealous of their powers, had never permitted the evolution of an institution which might become truly independent and so limit imperial prerogatives. As a result, no united Ministry with joint responsibility for its actions had ever been formed. Ministers were responsible to the Emperor on an individual basis. In addition, the heads of the various branches of government were selected with little regard for their ability to get along with their colleagues. Members of the Committee often had widely differing views on the Empire's problems, and relations between them were frequently strained as the result of palace intrigues. This lack of unity meant that the Committee of Ministers was, to use the words of M. M. Speranskii, not an institution but a form of report. It was primarily a device for keeping the Emperor and other ministers informed about current actions and problems, not a policy-making body.

The absence of any tradition of collective action was one of the major factors which would inhibit the Committee of Ministers from playing a decisive role in the famine crisis. But there were other reasons. The composition of the Committee was diverse. It included many officials besides the ministers, a fact which made the development of common policies all the more difficult. Moreover, the powers of the Committee were quite limited. The Committee as a whole was not allowed to take the initiative in bringing matters up for consideration, and of course all decisions required imperial sanction. Finally, the Committee lacked executive organs to carry out its decisions. The only machinery available to it was the apparatus of the various Ministries. Given the absence of unity in its ranks, the Committee had no guarantee that a particular minister would implement its orders in the way it intended.[29]

Yet for all the Committee's inadequacies, it was not vain to hope that the institution would move into the center of the relief campaign. Food supply had always been an area in which the Committee had been active; under previous tsars it had been instrumental in working out and supervising aid programs.[30] Beyond this, during the reign of Alexander III, the Committee of Ministers' role had been expanded and it had assumed somewhat broader policy-making functions.[31] In any case, Abaza was determined to push the Committee to action. And for a time, it appeared as if he might succeed.

Abaza began his efforts at the Committee's session of October 8th. As soon as Durnovo completed his account of the MVD's relief activities to date, Abaza demanded information on future plans. In particular, he asked Durnovo for an estimate of how much further aid would be required by the stricken areas. Abaza's question apparently caught Durnovo by surprise, for the Minister had to admit that he was not able to supply any specific figures. He simply stated that eighteen *gubernii* were now receiving assistance and that more might be expected to request help in the near future. Durnovo informed the Committee that he and the Minister of Finance had agreed to ask the State Council for permission to borrow over 30 million rubles from the treasury to meet the needs of the famine provinces.[32]

During the remainder of October, Abaza and the other members of the Committee were content to study the situation in the stricken *gubernii* on the basis of information supplied by the MVD. In general, the Committee followed Durnovo's suggestions concerning loans to the provinces; in the month between October 8 and November 5 it approved the granting of 17,518,765 rubles to areas in need.[33] During this period, the Committee concerned itself with some of the smaller details of the relief business such as the question of when loans made to the zemstvos might be repaid.[34] But these minor activities could obviously not satisfy the more energetic members of the Committee. They continued to be disturbed by the fact that there was as yet no complete and accurate picture of the requirements of the population and no general program for government relief.

This doubt and disquiet came into the open in mid-November. At the session of November 12th, Vyshnegradskii called the Committee's attention to the fact that despite the vast sums made available to the MVD (some 56 million rubles including the recently granted 32 million), only 12 million rubles remained on hand. Moreover, he noted that "at the present time . . . the food supply situation in those parts of the Empire suffering from crop failure has become considerably clearer, [and] it is impossible not to see that the above mentioned sum will hardly cover all the needs of the stricken population for food and seed either in the near future or in the coming spring."[35] Vyshnegradskii called upon Durnovo to provide at least an "approximate estimate" of the amount of money the state would have to expend on relief in the months ahead. Vyshnegradskii pointed out that the MVD's figures were necessary if the Ministry of Finance were to take them into account when drawing up the proposed budget for the next year. Absence of such data would make it extremely difficult to find the means to meet the needs of the population.[36] In answer to Vyshnegradskii's questions, Durnovo stated that he would work together with the Minister of Finance to provide the information requested. He cautioned the Committee, however, that the figures he planned to present would have only "relative significance" because the price of grain was rising steadily and the outcome of the winter sowing was not yet clear.[37]

Abaza was not willing to let Durnovo off the hook so easily. While he agreed that any estimates of need made at this point were likely to be approximate, he felt that they would still be of value. Abaza doubted that the situation in the provinces would change appreciably in the near future, and he therefore urged that the government make use of the data available to obtain as clear a picture as possible of the needs of the population. He also proposed that Durnovo be required to outline his plans for carrying out the relief operations. The Committee accepted Abaza's suggestions and ordered Durnovo to prepare the requested information.[38]

The decisions taken by the Committee of Ministers on November 12 were an important step forward. They marked the start of an attempt by Abaza and some of the other ministers to force Durnovo and his colleagues in the MVD to modify their piecemeal approach to relief and to work out some kind of overall plan of action based on comprehensive and reliable information. In the meetings to follow, Abaza would keep up the pressure on the Minister of Internal Affairs and would expand the scope of the Committee's discussions to include many other aspects of the struggle against famine.

The new mood of the Committee of Ministers was illustrated at the session of November 27. As in the previous sitting, the Committee was primarily interested in obtaining a more precise picture of the relief situation, but it was no longer exclusively concerned with the work of the MVD. Once more Abaza took the lead in the deliberations. He reminded his colleagues of the developing crisis on the railroads, and especially the delay in the shipment of grain from the northern Caucasus into the stricken provinces. Abaza stated that, in order to study the requests of the *gubernii* effectively, the Committee would like information on the measures being taken by the Ministry of Transportation (*Ministerstvo Putei Soobshchenii*) to alleviate the difficulties.[39] The Committee again followed Abaza's lead. It insisted that A. Ia. Giubbenet, the head of the Ministry of Transportation, provide regular reports on the state of the railroads and the movement of grain into the stricken provinces. Finally, Vyshnegradskii was asked to inform the Committee on a regular basis about the state of the grain trade and the price tendencies on the various markets of the country.[40] The ministers obviously hoped that by collecting data of this nature they would be in a better position to guide the work of supplying the needy areas.

In addition to information on the immediate situation in the famine provinces, the Committee of Ministers sought to enlighten itself as to some of the causes of the disaster. Thus, at the session of November 27 it also turned its attention to the problem of food supply capital and grain stores. The Committee's interest in this matter had been excited by a report from the Governor of Saratov, General A. I. Kosich, which provided data on the decline of the grain storage system in his province. Abaza suggested to his colleagues that historical background of this nature from all provinces affected by the crop failure would be extremely useful, "since such information would make it possible for the Committee to shed light on the question as to what degree the present economic crisis was due to the unsatisfactory condition of the grain storage houses and the series of years of bad harvest."[41] The Committee once again accepted Abaza's proposal. It ordered Durnovo to supplement his expected report on the size of local grain stores and capital funds as of January 1, 1891 with the kind of historical information requested by Abaza.[42]

The decisions taken on November 27 cleared the way for the Committee of Ministers to assume a dominant role in the administration of relief operations. The information which it would now receive made it possible for the Committee to oversee and coordinate the fight against the consequences of the crop failure. Armed with this extensive data, the Committee was in the position to create a general plan of attack and to insure the cooperation of the various agencies working to stave off disaster.

At the same time, however, other developments were taking place in government circles which would weaken the position of the Committee of Ministers. Because the problems caused by the famine were so extraordinary, calling for relief measures which went far beyond those envisioned by the framers of the *ustav narodnogo prodovol'stviia*, the Emperor and his advisors decided to set up a number of special agencies to take over and administer portions of the relief program.

The first of these extraordinary institutions was the Special Committee on Famine Relief, established by Imperial rescript on November 11, and headed by the Tsesarevich, Grand Duke Nicholas Alexandrovich.[43] The aim of this organization was to stimulate and coordinate charitable work in the suffering provinces. It was hoped that the Special Committee could mobilize public support for the work of relief and, at the same time, enable the central authorities to retain some measure of control over these operations. The second innovation was the decision to establish a public works program. Toward the end of November a special conference was set up to administer the works, and 10 million rubles were appropriated to finance them.[44] Finally, the railroad crisis, which had already come to the attention of the Committee of Ministers, was also handled by extraordinary procedures. On November 27, Colonel A. A. fon Vendrikh, a railway engineer and an expert on traffic operations, was dispatched to the Caucasus to correct the difficulties that had arisen on the Vladikavkaz railroad.[45]

The institution of these special procedures was not an attempt by elements in the highest circles of the administration to prevent the Committee of Ministers from assuming the lead in relief operations. It reflected the standard practice of the Russian government, when faced with problems of extraordinary dimensions, to fill in the gaps in its institutional structure by setting up temporary committees and conferences to meet specific needs. At the same time, however, the resort to extraordinary measures demonstrated that many *sanovniki* distrusted the regular channels of the bureaucracy and were convinced that if a difficult problem were to be solved it would have to be accomplished outside the established chain of command. These developments did not preclude the possibility that the Committee of Ministers could become the coordinator of all the various relief operations. But the role to be played by the Committee would now depend in large part on the assertiveness of the ministers themselves. Especially important would be the work of the Minister of Internal Affairs, who, because of his central position in the relief operations, was best able to work out a viable scheme for coordinated action.

In the meantime, the Committee of Ministers continued to act as a clearinghouse for information on the problems of food supply. The regular reports submitted by the Ministry of Transportation enabled the Committee to watch over the growing crisis on the railroads, although it could do little to influence the course of events.[46] On December 8 the Ministry of Finance presented a detailed survey of the grain trade during the month of November. Its conclusions were guardedly optimistic; the data pointed to a "cooling off" on the grain market and a slight, gradual reduction in grain prices.[47] The MVD, however, remained the main source of information for the Committee of Ministers. By means of its numerous *zapiski*, requesting approval of loans to the provinces, the MVD kept the Committee up to date on general development in the country and the problems encountered by rural officials and the zemstvos.

The ministers continued to be receptive to appeals for aid to the provinces, and generally approved Durnovo's proposals with the minimum of discussion.

Toward the end of December, Durnovo began to present to the Committee of Ministers some of the data it had requested of him in November. On December 17, he submitted a report on the status of communal grain stores for the period 1886–90,[48] and on December 24 he gave the Committee information on the capital funds held by peasant communes during the years 1886–91.[49] Simultaneously, Durnovo presented a series of documents which, for the first time, provided the Committee with an overall picture of the needs of the population in the affected *gubernii* and the means required to meet the crisis.[50] Finally, on December 26 Durnovo submitted a report which summarized the situation and outlined his program for central government action to counter the effects of the crop failure.[51]

Durnovo began his proposal of December 26, entitled "On the Adoption of Certain Measures with regard to Food Supply," by dismissing any doubts that the Empire lacked sufficient food for its people. He presented figures to show that the harvest of 1891 had provided European Russia with over 1.2 billion *pudy* of food grains for domestic consumption, or about 13 *pudy* per person. He pointed out to the Committee that, considering the amount of grain on hand, the needs of the provinces affected by the crop failure were not very large; between December and the new harvest only 70 million *pudy* of food grain and 30 million *pudy* of seed were required. The Minister of Internal Affairs stated that the main problem facing the government was to transport the available food and seed into the needy areas before the *rasputitsa*, or time of bad roads, which would occur around the beginning of March. Then rains and spring thaws would turn rural dirt roads into seas of mud, preventing the delivery of grain to isolated peasant villages. Durnovo estimated that between December 15, 1891 and March 1, 1892 the railroads would have to deliver almost 56 million *pudy* of grain to the stricken *gubernii*.[52] This would be an enormous task; but he noted that the Ministry of Transportation (MPS) claimed that the railroads could deliver about 24 million *pudy* a month.[53]

Durnovo then turned his attention to the question of the price of grain in the affected provinces. He presented the Committee with a chart which compared current prices of the major food grains with those for the period 1881–87. The conclusions were obvious and disturbing; throughout the region of the crop failure, prices were, for the most part, twice the norm. Durnovo informed the Committee that the high cost of food was due only in part to the effects of the poor harvest. He stated that "the unanimous testimony of the governors" had verified the fact that the extreme prices resulted both from the manipulation of speculators and from the fact that many landowners who possessed considerable supplies of grain were holding them back from market in the expectation of a further rise in prices. The concentration of available grain stores in "strong hands" (*krepkie ruki*) had taken place in almost all the stricken *gubernii.* In Saratov speculators held 6 million *pudy* of grain, and in Samara, 10 million. The tight market in the famine provinces had caused considerable difficulties for the zemstvos engaged in the purchase of food and seed for the needy peasants. Unable to obtain sufficient supplies on the local market, zemstvo agents had turned to other areas of the Empire where the harvest had been better and the prices were lower. This development had resulted in further complications. Zemstvo agents competed with one another, and prices, even in areas of good harvest, had been pushed upward. Moreover, the extensive grain purchases and the need for their rapid delivery had placed almost intolerable burdens on the railroads, causing delays and other troubles.

Durnovo insisted that for the relief of the population of the stricken *gubernii* to be successfully accomplished, two requirements had to be met. First, the famine provinces must "cover part of their needs with [the local] . . . supplies [of grain] which are now [being] withheld from the market;" and second, other grain purchases in areas not affected by the crop failure had to be carried out in such a way as not to produce an extensive rise in prices.[54] Durnovo stated that one means for attaining the first goal was the confiscation of private stores of grain or their forced sale at fixed prices. But the Minister of Internal Affairs was well aware of the difficulties that this approach would entail, and he noted that such measures would result in "sharp limitations in the civil rights and interests of private persons," and might produce "an unfortunate impression on the population."[55] He therefore felt that a more moderate program was in order. Durnovo suggested that he be empowered, in case of real need, to issue orders for the uncovering (*privedenie v izvestnost'*) of stores of grain in private hands and to forbid the sale of such grain without the permission of provincial authorities.[56] The Minister also proposed that the central government ban the export of foodstuffs from the provinces of Voronezh, Viatka, Kazan, Nizhni-Novgorod, Orenburg, Penza, Perm, Riazan, Samara, Saratov, Simbirsk, Tambov, Tobolsk, and Ufa.[57]

Durnovo did not put forward any new plan for solving the second major problem, the improvement of the current system of buying grain for the famine provinces. But he reminded the Committee that on December 13 he had proposed to eliminate the inconveniences and confusion caused by zemstvo purchase of grain by centralizing the whole business in the hands of a single government agency[58] which would be closely linked with the merchants of the country.[59] Durnovo noted that a number of difficulties had prevented the realization of that scheme,[60] and he now stated that the MVD would content itself with issuing instructions and proposals to the zemstvos. The aim of these documents would be to "organize the activities of all zemstvo agents . . . in accordance with their [own] mutual interests and . . . the conditions on the grain markets."[61]

Durnovo's proposal of December 26 was hardly a comprehensive plan for the organization of famine relief, but its details were neither extreme nor foolish. Nonetheless, as the Committee of Ministers quickly pointed out, the implementation of Durnovo's program might have caused as many difficulties as it attempted to solve. When the Committee of Ministers discussed the plan on December 31, Abaza and Vyshnegradskii called attention to the fact that the pressures Durnovo proposed to apply to the grain merchants would probably be counterproductive. Instead of forcing the grain onto the market, they could create a mood of panic among the merchants and the public which might force prices still higher. As for the idea of a ban on grain exports from certain provinces, not only did this proposal violate the unity of the Empire's internal market, which had existed since the eighteenth century, but it might be beyond the power of state officials to enforce. The only measure the Committee felt it could approve was the proposal to give the MVD the power to undertake large-scale grain purchases to meet the needs of the stricken provinces. The MVD would be free to handle these operations as it saw fit, and it could buy grain wherever it became available.[62]

Durnovo was visibly disturbed by the Committee's rejection of his proposals, but he made almost no attempt to defend them. His only reaction was to ask laconically: "In that case, tell me, what should be done?"[63] With this question, Durnovo attempted to turn the tables on the Committee and his chief critic, Abaza. Durnovo in effect admitted that the measures he had taken in the struggle against the famine fell short of the mark, but that aside from the program he had just outlined he was unable to come up with a comprehensive plan of action. The Minister of Internal Affairs now called on Abaza and the other members of the Committee to step into the breach. He asked them to propose alternative steps to deal with the crisis or at least to assume some kind of joint responsibility for the administration of the food supply campaign.

Neither Abaza nor the Committee as a whole responded to Durnovo's challenge. As we have seen, there was little in the tradition of the Committee of Ministers to prompt it to take up the task of policy formulation. Abaza, too, failed to put forth a plan for relief. He seemed satisfied to enjoy the spectacle of Durnovo's discomfiture. At the crucial moment the shallowness of Abaza's "oppositionism" was exposed. The thrust of Abaza's criticism had been directed against personalities; he could not go beyond the embarrassment of those who held power and responsibility. This is not to say that Abaza had not performed an important service in the months between October 1891 and January 1892. He had forced Durnovo to examine the relief program and had helped make the Committee of Ministers a center for information about the crisis. Abaza had also focused the government's attention on the railroads, whose difficulties threatened the whole food supply campaign. But Abaza could not offer the positive leadership that the situation required.

The default of Abaza and the Committee of Ministers would have important consequences for the relief campaign. It marked the end of attempts to concentrate the direction of food supply operations in the hands of a single institution. The Committee of Ministers would remain a clearinghouse for information and the source of an occasional suggestion. But, from now on, the management of relief would be fragmented. The several *gubernii* would operate independently in what they considered to be their own best interests. The initiative of the central government would, for the most part, be confined to those areas where special agencies or individuals had been empowered to act: railroad transport, private charity, and public works.

chapter six

THE RAILROAD CRISIS

In all but the most extraordinary cases, the success of any famine relief operation depends on the proper functioning of the means of transportation. For most countries experiencing food supply problems, the question is never one of an absolute lack of food but rather of acute shortages in certain localities. In Russia during the crisis of 1891–92, this general rule held true. There were sufficient supplies of grain within the borders of the Empire to feed the people, but these food reserves were at considerable distance from the starving, black soil *gubernii*. In the famine year, the major task facing state officials was to bring the food to the hungry mouths.

As we have already seen, from the very beginning of the food supply crisis, the government placed great reliance on the railroads which it saw as an absolutely vital means of combating the consequences of the crop failure. The special freight rates, introduced in June, were viewed as a way of normalizing the grain trade and bringing foodstuffs back into the afflicted *gubernii*. That these measures were effective cannot be contested. Together with the ban on exports, they produced a considerable shift in the normal direction of Russian internal trade, and millions of *pudy* of grain poured back into the black soil provinces. In the month of October alone, over 8 million *pudy* were carried at the special rates.[1] The success of the new tariffs for food grains encouraged the government to extend these advantages to the shipment of other supplies needed in the famine area, including fodder for cattle and work animals.[2]

The government sought to promote the use of these new rates by giving them wide publicity in official sources. Not only were they outlined in the *Sbornik tarifov rossiiskikh zheleznykh dorog*, the standard reference guide for these matters, but also a special booklet was published by the Railroad Department of the Ministry of Finance which provided the same information in a more convenient form.[3] Moreover, in order to enable the zemstvos and other groups working for the relief of the stricken areas to use the railroads to the best advantage, the Ministry of Transportation (MPS) telegraphed orders to the directors of the various railroads requiring that all shipments made for the purpose of aiding the population of the needy provinces be given priority over other traffic.[4] In addition, the Ministry of Finance sought to ease the task of grain purchase by providing information on food prices throughout the Empire. It regularly gathered data from local railroad officials and issued a printed bulletin listing prices on the important grain markets. The Ministry asked that a copy of this list be posted in all railroad stations.[5]

Despite the eagerness of government officials to use the railroads to the fullest in the struggle against the famine, a number of difficulties threatened to block the realization of their plans. The first problem was the weakness of the railroad network in the famine region. Few lines serviced the area, and those that did had low carrying capacities. Most of the roads consisted of a single track, and hence the volume of traffic they could handle at a given time was limited. These railroads also suffered from shortages of locomotives, rolling stock, and competent personnel. Another source of difficulty was the fact that the railroads serving the black earth area had been designed primarily to move goods from the central regions of the country to the frontiers and the ports, and not the other way around.[6] This meant that in order to meet the needs of the famine provinces, there would have to be a complete revision of shipping schedules to accommodate the altered flow of traffic. Such a task would have been troublesome even in the best of times. Under the emergency conditions of 1891–92, the job would be doubly difficult.

But the problems caused by the technical deficiencies of Russia's railroads might have been overcome had there been effective and unified governmental direction. Unfortunately, such was not the case. The Ministry of Transportation, which had overall responsibility for supervising the rail network, was notoriously inefficient and poorly led. The men chosen to head the MPS were, often as not, career civil servants or military people with little of the technical knowledge called for in the post.[7] Adolf Iakovlevich Giubbenet, Minister in 1891, was a case in point. Although Giubbenet had had some experience in the MPS before his appointment to ministerial rank,[8] he was virtually illiterate when it came to the specific problems of the railroads.[9] Moreover, Giubbenet did not seem to have the ability or the desire to master this side of affairs.[10]

In addition to the poor quality of its leadership, the MPS lacked technical expertise. The pay scales for Ministry personnel were not competitive, especially as people advanced from the lower to the higher ranks. In consequence, many officials of the MPS who had acquired a good knowledge of the railroads left the Ministry at a point in their careers when they would have been the most valuable. They sought employment with privately owned lines or in other government agencies. The low wages paid to officials of the MPS discouraged men of talent and ability from entering its ranks and demoralized those who stayed in service.[11]

Finally, the smooth operation of the railroads during the famine was hindered by an absence of centralized management. No single government agency exercised effective control over the rails.[12] Not all lines were state-owned, and those in private hands enjoyed considerable freedom of action. The situation was further complicated by the fact that the Ministry of Finance was competing with the Ministry of Transportation for dominance over the railroads and that between Vyshnegradskii and Giubbenet there existed a bitter personal feud. A major bone of contention seems to have been the matter of railroad tariffs, which in 1889 had been turned over to a special Railroad Department within the Ministry of Finance. The purpose of the new Department was to formulate a unified tariff policy for the railroads and to help eliminate the railway deficits which had been a big drain on state finances. This move angered the leadership of the MPS, however, and subsequent actions by the Ministry of Finance did nothing to cool the situation. The Director of the new Railroad Department, S. Iu. Witte, constantly impinged on the prerogatives of the MPS. He aimed to make his office the nerve center for the financial side of railroad operations and to leave only technical matters to the MPS. By 1891, thanks to the support of the Tsar and Vyshnegradskii, Witte had practically realized his goal.[13]

In ordinary times the conflict between the Ministries of Finance and Transportation and the split between the technical and financial sides of railroad affairs would not have produced serious difficulties. But during the crisis of 1891–92 this situation nearly proved disastrous. The moment demanded the closest cooperation between the Ministry of Finance and the MPS; each agency needed to know what programs the other was adopting and what problems the other faced. But this cooperation did not develop. In the early stages of the crisis no attempt was made to work out an overall program for railway operations.[14] Moreover, the lack of co-ordination between the Ministries meant that the economic measures adopted by the Ministry of Finance did not take into account the technical problems which existed on various lines. The new freight rates were introduced apparently without reference to the carrying capacity of some of the roads.[15] The Ministry of Finance then compounded this basic error by failing to alter the standard practice favoring the shipment of all loads by the shortest and most direct routes.[16]

The tariff policies worked out by the Railroad Department of the Ministry of Finance caused great difficulties because they forced a relatively few railways to carry an enormous burden of traffic. Problems developed first in the northern Caucasus. The harvest had been excellent in that region, prompting zemstvo agents and grain merchants to flock there with the aim of buying grain for shipment to the stricken *gubernii*. But moving the grain after purchase proved extremely troublesome. The shortest route from the northern Caucasus to the majority of the famine provinces was over the Voronezh line which, even in the best of times, had a low carrying capacity. The costs of using the alternate route through Kursk and Kharkov were considerably higher than those on the Voronezh line, and hence *zemtsy* and merchants favored the latter railroad. The consequences of this situation were easily predictable. The inefficient Voronezh line proved unable to digest the flow of cars coming from the Caucasus. This in turn led to a backup of shipments on the Vladikavkaz railroad. By the end of August 1891, some 7481 boxcars, most of them containing grain destined for the famine region, were delayed on the Vladikavkaz.[17] The yards at Rostov-na-Donu were literally choked with freight waiting to be passed on to the Voronezh road.

During the month of September, problems on the Empire's railways increased as more and more lines experienced shipping delays. But for a long time the government failed to act. The reasons for this hesitation are by no means clear. Some officials no doubt hoped the crisis might solve itself; but conflict between the Ministries of Finance and Transportation was probably the main reason for the slowness of state intervention. Only in October did representatives of the Ministries of Transportation, Finance, and Internal Affairs join to work out a common policy. This

EUROPEAN RUSSIA,
SHOWING FAMINE PROVINCES
WITH MAIN RAILROAD LINES

task, however, was made difficult by the same problems which plagued other aspects of relief operations—the lack of clear and precise information on the amount of grain needed in the famine-stricken provinces, when it had to be delivered, and where. The formulation of a program to deal with the situation on the railroads involved considerable debate between the various experts, and it was not until late October that a plan was ready to be put into effect.[18]

The primary purpose of the new program was to relieve the pressure on the Vladikavkaz line. It was decided that instead of shipping all the grain intended for the stricken regions via Voronezh, two alternate routes would be opened. The first alternative was to move grain along the Kursk, Kharkov, and Azov line; the second involved shipping grain by sea from Novorossiisk to Odessa or Sevastopol and then by rail into the stricken provinces. The Ministry of Finance established new tariff rates to equalize the costs of the three routes, and somewhat later the Emperor ordered the state treasury to provide 500,000 rubles to defray the expense of sea transport.[19] The new plan also established quotas for the shipment of grain by rail. According to its terms, zemstvo purchases would make up 50 percent of all shipments, those of private persons 40 percent, and those of the Army 10 percent.[20] Many more freight cars and 132 extra locomotives were made available to the Vladikavkaz line, and other railroads were ordered to prepare for an increasing volume of traffic.[21] These measures were clearly successful in easing the problems on the Vladikavkaz. In the month of November the number of carloads of grain awaiting shipment declined from 11,408 to 9382.[22] But the situation, although improved, was still critical.

During November the central authorities sought to obtain a clearer picture of the situation on the railroads and began to devise further measures to eliminate the difficulties. The Ministry of Transportation commissioned one of its engineers, a certain Gorbunov, to survey developments on the railways and to make recommendations for coping with problems. In the Ministry of Internal Affairs, I. I. Kabat, the MVD's representative on the tariff committee, also turned his attention to the problem of transporting zemstvo grain purchases. At the end of November he presented his conclusions in a special report.[23]

Kabat was not optimistic about the possibility of any radical improvement in the carrying capacity of the Russian railroads. He noted that as a result of their technical deficiencies most roads were unable to deal with the present crisis. Beyond this, Kabat warned the MVD not to base its assessment of the ability of the railroads to deliver grain to the famine region on information supplied by the Ministry of Transportation. He stated that the MPS's estimates were simply ideal norms which bore little or no relationship to realities on the railways, and he noted that on the Vladikavkaz line the rate of shipment was only about one-third of what the Ministry said it should be. Kabat wrote that the MPS was often ignorant of the reasons for the breakdown of the railroads, and he claimed that his attempt to clarify the cause of the difficulties on the Vladikavkaz line had been unsuccessful because "data on this subject were not to be found in the Ministry of Transportation."[24]

Kabat felt that the best way to ease the crisis on the railways would be to eliminate the virtual anarchy which prevailed in the area of zemstvo grain purchase. He proposed that a special commission be set up under the chairmanship of the Director of the Economic Department of the MVD and include representatives of the Ministries of Finance and Transportation. The main function of the commission would be to gather information on grain prices and transport conditions. It would then use these data to guide the zemstvos, showing them where they could buy foodstuffs at lowest prices and at the same time prevent them from making excessive purchases in areas where the railroads were experiencing difficulties. The commission was also to have the authority to intervene directly on railroads where traffic problems had developed and to set up special schedules for grain shipments, giving priority to grain headed for the neediest areas of the country. Kabat proposed that the commission be given extraordinary powers, including the right to send out its own special agents and, when necessary, to communicate directly with all agencies and officials concerned with transport problems without going through regular government channels.[25]

The central authorities did not adopt Kabat's suggestion for a special commission, but his plan to establish greater cooperation between the various ministries concerned with transport problems was taken up by the Committee of Ministers. The decisions adopted by the Committee on November 27, requiring the Ministries of Internal Affairs, Transportation, and Finance to submit regular reports on grain deliveries and grain prices, made it possible for the top officials in the government to keep a close watch on the many developments in the field of transportation. In addition, the MVD followed Kabat's suggestion that it encourage zemstvo purchasing agents to stay away from those areas where the railroads were experiencing difficulties. On November 30 the Ministry issued a circular stating that further purchases of grain in the northern Caucasus would be harmful to relief operations. It urged the governors to so inform the zemstvos and to induce them to avoid the grain markets in the Caucasus. The circular asked the zemstvos to shift their buying to other regions of the Empire, especially the southwestern and Baltic *gubernii*.[26]

Although Kabat's plan for a special commission was rejected, by the end of November it had become clear that the regular employees of the Ministry of Transportation were not equal to the task of straightening out the difficulties on the railroads. As a result, Giubbenet came under ever-greater pressure to take some kind of dramatic action. Finally, on November 27 the Minister decided to intervene in the situation more decisively. In an attempt to get a clearer picture of the problems on the Vladikavkaz line, Giubbenet dispatched Colonel A. A. fon Vendrikh, an expert on railway traffic management, to the Caucasus to survey the operation of the road. At this point, however, the Tsar himself stepped in. On November 28 the Emperor granted special powers to Colonel Vendrikh and ordered him to clean up the difficulties on the Vladikavkaz by whatever means were necessary. Under the terms of the Tsar's commission, Vendrikh was to have virtually complete freedom of action in dealing with the railroad crisis as a whole, and he was absolved of all the formal limitations imposed on the personnel of the Ministry of Transporation.[27] Thus, responsibility for managing the details of the railroad crisis passed from the regular staff of the Ministry into the hands of an individual enjoying the favor of the Tsar.

Alexander III's decision to turn the management of the railroad crisis over to Vendrikh was clearly the result of lobbying by Prince V. P. Meshcherskii, editor of the newspaper *Grazhdanin*. During the fall of 1891, Meshcherskii had been very critical of the performance of the Ministry of Transportation and had become convinced that the regular staff of the MPS could not handle the backlog of traffic caused by the famine. On the pages of *Grazhdanin*, Meshcherskii had campaigned for the appointment of a person capable of taking direct command of the troubled railroads.[28] He pointed to Vendrikh as a man equal to the task.[29] The

Prince no doubt combined his public statements with private representations to the Tsar. Meshcherskii apparently used his close personal ties with the Emperor in order to force Giubbenet to dispatch Vendrikh on a tour of inspection.[30] Having done this, it was probably not difficult for Meshcherskii to persuade the Tsar to grant Vendrikh extraordinary powers.

When Vendrikh reached Rostov-na-Donu on December 5, 1891 he found himself confronted with a task of herculean proportions; for despite the slight progress made during November, there remained a backlog of over 9000 carloads of grain awaiting shipment on the Vladikavkaz line.[31] Still, Vendrikh was not awed by the difficulties he faced, and soon after his arrival in Rostov he sent a telegram back to the capital stating confidently that he would be able to clear up the difficulties in the Caucasus in about twenty-five days.[32] But disposing of the jam-up on the Vladikavkaz would only be the beginning. The grain from the Caucasus had to be moved into the famine-stricken region over other railroads which were often in worse condition than the Vladikavkaz line.[33] Moreover, this had to be done quickly. In order to meet the needs of the population of the afflicted provinces, almost 60 million *pudy* of grain had to be delivered between mid-December and early March.

Although his immediate concern was with the problems on the Vladikavkaz line, Vendrikh realized that the difficulties in the south were intimately connected with conditions on other railroads throughout the country. He saw that only through the coordinated action of all the lines could the vital grain supplies be delivered to those who needed them. Accordingly, soon after his arrival in Rostov, Vendrikh established a Temporary Administration for Transport (*Vremennoe upravlenie perevozkami*), which included the Director of the Traffic Department (*otdel dvizheniia*) of the Ministry of Transportation, a technical engineer attached to the Ministry and representatives from various railroads.[34]

The new Administration adopted a number of measures to increase the overall carrying capacity of the nation's railroads. Perhaps the most important of these decisions was the establishment of new schedules designed to quicken the rate of traffic on those lines carrying the bulk of the grain intended for the famine region.[35] Several technical innovations were also introduced to make it easier for the roads to meet the new schedules. The first of these was the use of block signals connected by telegraph lines. This device enabled railroad officials to establish a smoother flow of traffic and paved the way for the introduction of a packet system—the steady dispatch of trains at fifteen-minute intervals. As a result, it was possible for the railroads to reduce the distance between trains by as much as 25 percent and to speed traffic accordingly.[36]

Vendrikh sought to increase the movement of goods on the railroads shipping grain into the stricken provinces by borrowing locomotives and rolling stock from other lines not directly involved in these operations. During the winter over 500 engines and 3000 cars were obtained in this manner.[37] At the same time, Vendrikh attempted to eliminate delays caused by breakdowns along the roads. To speed repairs wherever possible, he ordered the establishment of special work trains, fully equipped with tools and repair crews. They were to be kept in constant readiness at strategic points along the line for immediate use in case an accident or other difficulty occurred.[38] Vendrikh also tried to see that the tracks were kept free from snowdrifts. Soon after he assumed his special powers, Vendrikh ordered the directors of the various railway lines to see to it that sufficient supplies of shovels and other necessary equipment were obtained, and he asked the provincial governors to pass on information regarding the number of persons who might be available for snow-removal work.[39]

When Vendrikh turned his attention to the Vladikavkaz line, he encountered a number of specific difficulties. The administration of the railroad lacked adequate information on the intended destinations of many of its cars.[40] Scheduling was haphazard; grain shipments were dispatched at random, often with no reference as to when they had arrived at the railhead. At one station, Vendrikh found 800 carloads of grain which had been awaiting shipment since October.[41] Switchyards were unable to handle the enormous volume of traffic. Rostov, where three lines came together,[42] proved to be a special bottleneck, and there were great delays in moving trains through the city's freight yards.[43] Because of poor scheduling and the difficulties at the switchyards, the available rolling stock on the Vladikavkaz was poorly utilized. According to Vendrikh, the average boxcar on the line was able to carry only about 1.25 carloads of grain per month.[41]

Vendrikh sought to remedy the situation on the Vladikavkaz by a number of palliative measures. He introduced new schedules and curbed the power of individual stationmasters to decide which loads would be shipped first. In order to avoid the clogged switchyards in Rostov, Vendrikh arranged to have some of the trains heading north along the Voronezh line made up at the Bataisk station, about ten *versty* to the south of Rostov. By this means, it was possible to relieve the congestion in the main yards and move the grain more swiftly.[45] Vendrikh also tried to make the most of the alternate routes to the north, thus bypassing the already heavily burdened Voronezh line. One of the first measures he adopted after his arrival in the Caucasus was to remove all restrictions on the shipment of grain via Kursk.[46] Vendrikh did not, however, use the method of shipping grain by sea which had been proposed earlier. He felt that such a roundabout route would be too complicated and expensive and that it would do little to speed the movement of grain into the areas of greatest need.[47]

Toward the end of the year, Vendrikh achieved his first successes in dealing with the railroad crisis. During the last weeks of December and the first days of January 1892, Vendrikh was able to eliminate the logjam on the Vladikavkaz line. By December 31 the number of carloads of grain awaiting shipment had declined to about 2250; by January 5 only 637 carloads were held up; on January 9 the last of the delayed shipments passed beyond Rostov.[48] The carrying capacity of the Russian railroads as a whole increased under Vendrikh's management. In December the amount of grain delivered to the stricken provinces was 17,680,000 *pudy*, as compared with 9,225,000 *pudy* the previous month. The amount of zemstvo grain shipped by the railroads rose by more than three times.[49]

But these successes had not broken the backbone of the problem. The difficulties on the Vladikavkaz had simply been passed on to other railroads,[50] which in turn threatened to collapse under the strain. Vendrikh's haste to eliminate the backlog of traffic in the south caused a number of other problems. There were cases of shipment of grain without adequate precautions against damage and spoilage; in some instances grain was dispatched in open cars, without even so much as a canvas tarpaulin to protect it from the ravages of the weather.[51] The overall situation remained bleak. Even at increased rates of transport, the railroads were still not delivering grain fast enough to make sure that the afflicted provinces had all the supplies they needed before the onset of the *rasputitsa*. The Committee of Ministers continued to be alarmed about the problem, and Giubbenet came under increasing criticism from his colleagues.

As Vendrikh proceeded to attack the situation on the other railroads, he was confronted with a series of exasperating problems. On the Voronezh line, conditions bordered on the impossible. Equipment was in poor condition and subject to constant misuse; vital repairs were delayed. Sometimes apparatus which might have been used to good effect during the crisis was simply "lost." Vendrikh noted that at one station the existence of a valuable turntable had been completely forgotten, and the rails that led to it were covered with junk.[52] The main difficulty, however, was the poor quality of the railroad's personnel, especially those in charge of the management of traffic. Virtual anarchy prevailed on the Voronezh line. Vendrikh wrote that "[traffic] management was entirely without direction. . . . Every stationmaster gave orders on his own, striving, somehow, to get rid of the trains at his station, paying no attention to the consequences."[53] As a result of this chaos, Vendrikh decided to suspend the Director of Traffic on the Voronezh railroad, and he put one of his own agents in command.[54]

Besides incompetence of railroad personnel, Vendrikh encountered considerable opposition from managers and engineers on the various lines throughout the period of his work. This in itself was not surprising, for the cliquish, caste mentality of railroad officials and technical people was well known to all who worked on the railways.[55] Such experts naturally resented having to take directions from an outsider; but their displeasure was increased by the nature and tone of Vendrikh's own activities. Working under considerable pressure himself, Vendrikh demanded that those under his command carry out his instructions without delay. He showed little sympathy for the problems others had to face and he seemed unaware that the railroads were understaffed and that the personnel were greatly overworked.[56] Vendrikh's own manner tended to be gruff, even rude. It was often impossible to carry out his orders due to a lack of time and equipment.[57]

For the most part, the resentment felt by railroad personnel did not prevent them from executing the orders of the Temporary Administration with the minimum of delay.[58] But some conflict was inevitable. A major clash took place when the managers of the Moscow-Kursk railway balked at Vendrikh's order to speed up operations and increase the receipt of cars from other railroads. Vendrikh pressed the issue, and the Director of the Moscow-Kursk line responded by blocking traffic on the railway, claiming that the extra cars which had been pushed onto the road could not be accommodated by existing station facilities. At Vendrikh's orders, the Director was removed from his post; traffic soon returned to normal and even increased.[59] Similar conflicts occurred on other railroads, and Vendrikh often resolved them by resort to equally high-handed methods. By such means Vendrikh was able to force a gradual increase in the volume of traffic on the railways, but discontent among railroad personnel grew. A steady stream of complaints filtered back to the Ministry of Transportation, and tension developed between Vendrikh and Giubbenet.

Meanwhile, the speedup in the movement of grain on the railroads was creating its own difficulties, not the least of them being the problem of removing grain from the railheads once it had been delivered to the needy *gubernii*. This task was the province of the zemstvos, but the volume of grain unloaded at the depots was so large that it strained the resources of local institutions to the limit. Peasants and horses capable of moving the grain were not easy to find and, as a result, the stations in the famine region became clogged with cars waiting to be unloaded. Storage facilities at the depots were rapidly exhausted. The problem was further complicated by the fact that part of the grain purchased by the zemstvos had not been shipped in bags. This loose grain had to be put in a warehouse, and could not be stored on the platforms at the stations. Despite the difficulties, some means of storage were usually found, even if the grain had to remain in the boxcars in which it had been shipped. But sometimes, especially during January and February, the situation became desperate, and railroad workers simply dumped grain into the snow, trusting that the cast-iron stomachs of the Russian peasants would enable them to consume the food no matter what its condition.[60]

Vendrikh experienced his greatest difficulties on the Syzran-Viaz'ma line. This railroad, the only link with Samara and the other trans-Volga *gubernii*, suffered from all the weaknesses that plagued the other lines. Ill-equipped from the start to carry a huge volume of traffic from west to east, its problems were compounded by ineffective leadership and a general lack of competent workers and station personnel. At some stations, twelve-hour shifts by key individuals were not uncommon; and at one depot a member of the staff combined the functions of stationmaster, telegraph operator, baggage agent, and ticket clerk.[61] The locomotives and rolling stock were in deplorable condition, and Vendrikh found that at a given time as many as 40 percent of the engines might be out of service.[62] Not surprisingly, a number of accidents and collisions occurred on the line in late December and early January. In one such misfortune, fourteen persons were injured, nine seriously.[63]

The most crucial problem on the Syzran-Viaz'ma line, however, was one so elementary as to seem ludicrous—an absence of adequate supplies of water for the locomotives. The drought of 1891 had made the maintenance of water supplies very difficult, but according to Vendrikh the management of the Syzran-Viaz'ma had been negligent. Moreover, it failed to inform him of the crisis until the matter had gotten completely out of hand.[64] The effect of the collapse of the water supply system on the movement of grain into the famine areas was disastrous. Traffic on the Syzran-Viaz'ma line ground to a halt; on January 11 only three trains pulled out of Morshansk headed for Penza. On January 12, 13, and 14 not a single train moved eastward along the line, and the number of cars received from other railways dropped sharply.[65] The tie-up on the Syzran-Viaz'ma threatened to undo the modest gains made during December, and to render impossible the goal of delivering 60 million *pudy* of grain to the starving region before the onset of the *rasputitsa*.

In order to combat better the difficulties plaguing the Syzran-Viaz'ma line, Vendrikh shifted the Temporary Administration's base of operations to Penza. There he decided that his first task would be the solution of the water supply crisis. Vendrikh's methods were primitive, but successful. Since water was lacking, he decided to make use of the ample snow available along the road. Vendrikh ordered the construction of special wooden trestles to help move the snow and ice to the stations. Once the snow was delivered, it was carried to the engines and tenders by means of a series of hampers. When the snow was used in the locomotives, they had to be heated prodigiously before a head of steam could be raised; and this produced considerable wear and tear on the equipment.[66] The hardships experienced by railroad personnel were also enormous, for the task of supplying the trains had to be accomplished in the dead of winter in temperatures of as much as thirty degrees below zero. It proved necessary to maintain these difficult operations for a month and a half, but in the end, Vendrikh's efforts bore fruit. Traffic on the Syzran-Viaz'ma began to increase gradually;[67] by mid-February the situation was well in hand and the backlog of cars on the line had been eliminated. In March the railroad was operating on a practically normal basis.[68]

While Vendrikh labored in Rostov and Penza, the railroad crisis was causing political repercussions in the capital, and Giubbenet's position as Minister of Transportation was becoming increasingly untenable. Giubbenet was attacked from all quarters. Railway officials and technicians complained bitterly about Vendrikh's high-handed methods.[69] They demanded that the Minister intervene and curb the powers of Vendrikh and the Temporary Administration. At the same time the functioning of the nation's railways was criticized in the Committee of Ministers. At the session of January 7, Giubbenet was chided by Durnovo and by other members of the Committee who expressed concern that the job of supplying the needy provinces would have to be accomplished by other means.[70] The Emperor himself openly criticized the performance of the MPS[71] and placed ever greater reliance on Vendrikh with whom he had established direct communications, bypassing regular channels.[72]

In the meantime, Giubbenet's enemies moved against him. Prominent among the intriguers were Prince Meshcherskii and Vyshnegradskii. Meshcherskii had long been disturbed by the chaos on the railroads and within the Ministry of Transportation, and he was angered by Giubbenet's resistance to Vendrikh's activities. The Prince was convinced that until Giubbenet was removed nothing could be done to end the transportation crisis. Vyshnegradskii's attack on Giubbenet was politically motivated. The Minister of Finance saw in Giubbenet's discomfiture a chance to deliver the *coup de grace* to a rival and to expand his own power over the MPS. Vyshnegradskii hoped to replace Giubbenet with his protege, S. Iu. Witte. By giving the Director of the Railroad Department the post of Minister of Transportation, Vyshnegradskii believed that he could bring the MPS into harness with his own Ministry, thus ending a tedious conflict. Meshcherskii, too, was prepared to back Witte as successor to Giubbenet. He regarded Witte as an extraordinarily capable person, a type desperately needed by the regime. Thus these two powerful individuals joined to bring Giubbenet down. Together they played on the Tsar's discontent, skillfully exploiting the tensions that had developed between Vendrikh and the Minister of Transportation.[73]

The struggle for control of the MPS reached its climax in the first weeks of January 1892. The crucial question at issue was the fate of Vendrikh and his mission. The opponents of Giubbenet supported Vendrikh's efforts, while the Minister of Transportation and the regular staff of the MPS wished to end what they considered an abnormal and unhealthy situation. The conflict over Vendrikh's activities grew so intense and bitter that on January 14 the Committee of Ministers ordered the creation of a special conference to look into the continuing crisis on the railroads and the attempts to deal with the problem.[74] Vendrikh was asked to return to the capital for a few days to present his case.[75]

The pro-Giubbenet forces apparently hoped to use the conference as a means of unseating Vendrikh.[76] But their plans fell through. The conference composed of Witte and General N. P. Petrov (Director of the Railroad Department of the MPS) and chaired by the Deputy Minister of Transportation, G. A. Evreinov, supported Vendrikh. As a result of the conference, Vendrikh's position was strengthened; he received additional powers and was assigned a number of assistants to help him in his work.[77] The outcome of the conference was a crushing blow to Giubbenet, who resigned at once.

For the next month, Evreinov took over as acting head of the Ministry of Transportation, but he too ran afoul of Vendrikh. The fatal clash came as the result of Vendrikh's decision to dismiss certain railroad personnel whose performance he found unsatisfactory. Vendrikh's proposal was approved by the Emperor, who passed it on to the Ministry with a simple command: "Carry out at once." But Evreinov hesitated and requested further explanation, for he realized that the dismissal of the men in question would deprive them of their pensions. The Tsar retorted that Evreinov should carry out his orders first and then wait for an explanation.[78] Evreinov did not immediately resign as the result of the Tsar's displeasure, but any hopes he had held to succeed to Giubbenet's position were clearly dashed. In mid-February the struggle for control of the Ministry of Transportation ended. Thanks to the good officers of Meshcherskii and Vyshnegradskii, Witte was selected to fill the post.[79]

With Witte now at the head of the Ministry of Transportation, Vendrikh's days of power were numbered. Soon after taking over the MPS, Witte began to undermine Vendrikh's position, spreading rumors of his incompetence and attacking his methods of managing the railroads.[80] This marked a considerable shift from Witte's stand a month earlier when presumably he had supported Vendrikh against his critics. Witte's change of view is understandable, however, when seen against the background of the intrigues which had advanced him to ministerial rank. Vendrikh had been a useful weapon in the struggle for mastery in the MPS, but he was also a potential rival. Vendrikh had apparently been considered for the post of Minister of Transportation,[81] and as long as he enjoyed a special relationship with the Tsar[82] he could pose a threat to Witte's new office.

Witte thus proceeded to maneuver Vendrikh out of the picture. He realized, of course, that he would have to move cautiously, and his first inclination was simply to give Vendrikh enough rope to hang himself.[83] Soon, however, Witte succeeded in ending Vendrikh's special status and placing him under firmer ministerial control. Witte suggested the possibility of greater control over Vendrikh's work in one of his first reports to the Emperor, and on February 24 His Majesty agreed that from then on Vendrikh would be subject to Witte's authority and guidance.[84] At about the same time, Witte undertook the defense of one of the railway engineers who had been removed from his post at Vendrikh's request.[85]

Meanwhile, the success of Vendrikh's own mission was rendering the continuation of his extraordinary powers unnecessary. Even in January, despite the difficulties and opposition he encountered, Vendrikh had managed to produce a small increase in the delivery of grain to the famine-stricken region.[86] The major breakthrough, however, came in February. During that month, 23,403,908 *pudy* of grain, well over half of which had been purchased by the zemstvos, were delivered to the suffering provinces.[87] By mid-February the Committee of Ministers, which in January had seen the bleak side of things, switched to a more optimistic view. At the session of February 11 the ministers expressed confidence that the situation was well in hand,[88] and on February 25 the Committee stated that grain deliveries were exceeding the estimated minimum needs of the affected provinces.[89]

The satisfactory resolution of the difficulties on the railroads enabled Witte to press for the termination of Vendrikh's special authority. During the session of the Committee of Ministers on February 25, Witte spoke of the need to reestablish a more normal system of traffic management. Clearly demonstrating a willingness to sacrifice the peasantry on the altar of industry, Witte noted that the emphasis on the shipment of grain had caused a disruption in the delivery of other vital goods. Coal was needed soon at many metallurgical factories, and Witte warned that unless the situation were corrected, there might be a decline in the production of steel and pig iron.[90] In order to get the operation of the railroads on a more regular schedule, Witte proposed a ten- to fifteen-day moratorium on the loading of grain for shipment. This program would be put into effect at the beginning of March after the bulk of the required grain had been delivered to the stricken provinces, and exceptions could be made at the discretion of the Ministry of Transportation. The Committee ratified Witte's suggestion with little discussion.[91]

Vendrikh continued to wield his special powers through the end of March, but as soon as Witte felt his own position becoming sufficiently firm, he approached the Emperor about ending the abnormal situation on the railroads. According to Witte's own account, the Tsar responded favorably to the suggestion that Vendrikh might be removed. The Emperor stated that Vendrikh had been given extraordinary authority because Giubbenet had proved unable to cope with the crisis on the railroads. But, the Emperor continued, now that Witte, who was well versed in railroad matters, had assumed the post of Minister of Transportation, Vendrikh could be safely removed.[92]

On April 18 Witte issued the order ending Vendrikh's extraordinary authority in the field of railway transport. In this document, Witte noted that Vendrikh's own reports showed that the major problems on the railroads had been solved, and he publicly praised Vendrikh for his services. He wrote:

> I consider it a pleasant duty to express to Colonel fon Vendrikh my sincere gratitude for [his] energetic, zealous and valuable activity in carrying out the tasks I assigned him in increasing the transport of grain and coal shipments. The result of [fon Vendrikh's labors] . . . has now made it possible to terminate the extreme procedures necessitated by the extraordinary circumstances of the past winter.[93]

Privately, of course, Witte had expressed considerable doubt as to Vendrikh's effectiveness during the railroad crisis. Later, in his memoirs, Witte stated that while Vendrikh had been of some use ("*prinosil pol'zu*") in the work of eliminating the great backlog of cars on the roads and had shaken railway personnel out of their state of somnolence, his extreme methods and his harsh personality had tended to confuse the situation.[94] Witte's skeptical view was shared by others who knew the railroads well. Izmailov, writing a few years after the event, felt that Vendrikh's Special Administration had complicated matters by attempting to take too much power upon itself. Vendrikh and his colleagues had tried to manage a railway network of some 4670 *versty* virtually on their own, leaving only the most insignificant tasks to the regular officials.[95]

But while these criticisms of Vendrikh are probably justified, it should be remembered that the size and importance of the assignment he faced was tremendous. The job of unsnarling the notoriously inefficient Russian railroads and of shipping almost 60 million *pudy* of grain in the space of three months necessitated dictatorial methods. The added pressure of knowing that human lives depended on the success of his mission could only have increased Vendrikh's harshness in dealing with recalcitrant railway personnel. No doubt when the job was completed, Witte and the officials of the Ministry of Transportation had considerable difficulty bringing the roads back to normal operating procedure; undoubtedly there was considerable ill will and confusion among the staffs of the various railroads which had experienced Vendrikh's control. Still, the main task had been accomplished: the vital supplies had reached the famine provinces. Without Vendrikh's efforts it is doubtful that the needs of the stricken *gubernii* could have been met, and the struggle of the zemstvos and local administrations to feed the hungry might have been doomed to failure.

chapter seven

THE SPECIAL COMMITTEE ON FAMINE RELIEF

The establishment of the Special Committee on Famine Relief in November 1891 was one of the most important events of the famine year, but the significance of this decision has been considerably distorted by historians. The generally held opinion is that the setting up of the Special Committee was a shamefaced admission on the part of the Russian government that it had failed in its struggle against the famine and was now forced to turn to the educated public for assistance.[1] But those who share this view are clearly ignorant of the relief measures adopted by the central authorities during the summer of 1891. There is no doubt that the Special Committee was established with an eye to public opinion, yet it was hardly a concession to an aroused "society" eager to rush into the struggle against famine but hitherto prevented from doing so by the government. Indeed the founding of the Committee was an attempt to awaken society, to encourage private initiative, and to expand the focus of charitable efforts.

From the very beginning of the famine crisis, the government was aware that private charity would have to play an important role in the relief of the needy. The existing food supply system did not provide coverage for all inhabitants of the countryside; only the members of peasant communes were eligible for food supply loans. But many nonpeasant households had also been affected by the disaster and would need assistance. Moreover, the initial decision of the MVD to limit the size of food loans and to grant them only to persons incapable of working meant that a sizable portion of the population of the stricken *gubernii* would require nongovernmental relief. In making its plans for combatting the famine, the government counted on private initiative to assume a large share of the burden of helping the afflicted population.

As we noted in chapter 4, the government sought to encourage charitable work during the summer of 1891. In an attempt to fill the gaps that existed in the structure of zemstvo relief, the authorities permitted the establishment of local committes which were to gather contributions and render assistance to the needy. At about the same time, the Red Cross and the Holy Synod began operations in the famine area. The Synod ordered the formation of bishops' committees to oversee the distribution of relief through the institutions of the Church. The Red Cross established a series of *uezd* and local bodies (*popechitel'stva*) under the direction of its provincial organizations.[2] These *popechitel'stva* were empowered to collect contributions, but more importantly they were designed to draw local landowners and peasants into the work of relief.[3] In addition to the work of these semiofficial organizations, many private persons set about to aid the distressed. Merchants' committees as well as other private groups were formed, the most famous of which was the Moscow Committee under the chairmanship of the Grand Duchess Elizaveta Fedorovna. Despite these favorable developments, however, by the beginning of winter charitable relief had not become a truly effective weapon for dealing with the crisis. In many provinces charitable committees had developed slowly, and the network of private relief was far from complete.[4] Even in the capitals, the public response to appeals for help had not been overwhelming. Moreover, the sacrifices of those who gave to aid the needy were canceled out in part by the activity of grain speculators and other unscrupulous persons who sought to take advantage of the situation.[5]

One of the reasons for the delay in the growth of charitable efforts was the fact that the work of private persons and groups lacked coordination. In a single *uezd*, for example, representatives from the local bishop's committee, the Red Cross, the governor's committee, as well as local nobles and outside volunteers might all be at work. Although the field was vast and the need was great, some duplication of effort was hard to avoid. Beyond this, public distrust of the government still lingered. Many persons felt that the MVD's regulations concerning private charity were designed to hinder relief work, and there were reports that government officials were harrassing individuals seeking to aid the distressed. These fears were somewhat overblown. Cases of official interference did occur, especially at the local level, but such incidents were, on the whole, quite rare.[6] In this situation, there was a need for some kind of action by the government which would at once allay the distrust of those eager to engage in private charitable work and at the same time help put non-governmental relief on a firmer basis, avoiding duplication and conflict.

The idea of a special relief committee, headed by a member of the Imperial family, was discussed in government circles for some time before any definite plans were drawn. One of the first proposals for such an organization came in a letter written by Count I. I. Vorontsov-Dashkov to the Emperor in late August. After an extensive description of the distress in the countryside, Vorontsov called on the Tsar to aid his subjects:

[The people] need moral support, which can only come from you, Your Majesty. If they were to learn that by your order a committee for the relief of the hungry had been established under the chairmanship of the Empress or the Tsesarevich, they would bear their misfortune more calmly. This news alone would support their moral strength [which has been] crushed by the impossible situation in which this famine year has placed them.[7]

The Emperor did not respond at once to Vorontsov-Dashkov's suggestion, but there is good reason to believe that he was sympathetic to the idea. During his father's reign, the Emperor had served as the head of just such a committee for the relief of famine victims in Arkhangel'sk province.[8] In October, Durnovo also took up the idea and suggested it in a letter to the Tsar.[9] The idea was quickly approved and by the end of the month plans were being made to establish the committee.[10] In mid-November the arrangements were complete. On November 17 the Emperor issued the following rescript to his son:

The crop failure of the present year has put the population of several provinces of the Empire in a difficult position with regard to food supplies. The misfortune affects not only that portion of the agricultural population which, on the basis of existing legislation, is entitled to food supply relief, but also a large number of persons who do not belong to local village communes.

Supplying these persons with sufficient food and also generally protecting the needy from grievous losses as the result of the crop failure, cannot but be an extremely important concern of the government. Watching with heartfelt sympathy the development of various forms of public spirited aid to the needy, I feel that now is the proper moment to provide the noble efforts of private charity, based on the principles of Christian love, with the guidance and the necessary unity of action [which] correspond to the importance of the cause. With this in view, I have founded a Special Committee for the relief of the needy in the areas affected by the crop failure [and] I have chosen Your Imperial Highness as Chairman of this Committee.

Asking the blessings of God on the work of public service which stands before you, I hope that you will draw the strength to complete [the task] from the deep feelings of love for your family and the Motherland which inspire you.[11]

The precise duties of the new Committee were defined in a special order signed by the Tsar the following day. The chief goal of the organization was to aid private charity by seeing that it achieved the unity of action necessary for its success. The Committee was also to collect contributions and distribute them among the various local charitable institutions. Even more important, however, was the Committee's role as a mediator between official bodies and charitable organizations. According to the order, the Committee was to "take measures [to secure] the concordance of charitable activity with the orders of local officials and the institutions concerned with food supply and public relief."[12] Besides the heir apparent, the staff of the Committee included Durnovo, Pobedonostsev, and General Kaufman, head of the Red Cross. Other persons could be included at the will of the Emperor, and the chairman was empowered to invite anyone who, in his judgment, might be of use to the Committee to participate in its work.[13]

The establishment of the Tsesarevich's Committee was greeted enthusiastically by Russian society, for it placed the Imperial seal of approval on the activities of charitable groups whether or not they operated under the aegis of the Special Committee. *Russkie vedomosti*, which had been rather critical of government efforts so far, summed up the mood of the liberally minded public:

Thus, the Special Committee, under the chairmanship of the august Heir to the Throne . . . is called to solve one of the most important problems in the struggle with the national disaster. With the establishment of the Committee, private charity receives a new impulse, . . . the various local institutions for the relief of the needy [find] a center uniting, directing and supervising [them], the population of the stricken region [obtains] the hope of appropriate relief.[14]

But although the opening of the Special Committee made possible a more fruitful cooperation between government and society, it did not eliminate all friction and distrust. Several examples illustrate this fact. In November, at about the same time that the Special Committee was established, the Free Economic Society decided to collect funds for the relief of the poor and also to study the causes of the famine. In connection with the latter task, the Society sought to obtain information from the files of the MVD. On November 29 the Secretary of the Society wrote to A. I. Zvegintsev, an official of the Ministry who had just completed a tour of the afflicted provinces, asking him to provide an account of conditions in the countryside.[15] Zvegintsev replied shortly thereafter. He stated that while he was in sympathy with the work of the Society and would be willing to help it in any way he could, he was not at liberty to discuss his impressions. These had been the subject of a report to the MVD which could not be released without ministerial permission.[16] The archives do not indicate whether or not the Society pursued the matter further, but no copy of Zvegintsev's report was found among the related papers in the *fond* of the Free Economic Society. The reluctance of the Society to push for such information may have been the result of the conviction that the reaction of the MVD would be unfavorable.[17]

A further indication of government distrust of private charity was the reaction of the MVD to the arrival in Russia of two English Quakers who came with the intention of surveying the situation in the famine provinces and undertaking efforts to aid the sufferers. The men in question, Messrs. Brooks and Fox, had been encouraged in their venture by Olga Novikova, the sister of General A. A. Kireev, and they came expecting a friendly reception in official circles. They were quickly disappointed, largely due to the efforts of Durnovo. The Minister of Internal Affairs apparently feared that the Quakers' investigation of conditions in the famine area might produce a scandal on the order of the one resulting from the publication of George Kennan's book, *Siberia and the Exile System*.[18] Pobedonostsev and Vorontsov-Dashkov welcomed the Quakers, but their good offices were not enough to enable Brooks and Fox to be presented to the Emperor.[19] The British ambassador was also uncooperative and refused to arrange an interview with the Emperor, lest it appear that the British government approved of the Quakers' mission. At the beginning of December, however, the Friends set forth into the famine provinces without official endorsement,[20] and no attempt was made to stop them. They returned to the capital at the end of the month[21] and soon sailed for England. They came again to Russia in 1892 and conducted a highly successful relief operation.[22]

But these few instances of friction between the government and private charitable groups did not hamper the Special Committee when, at the end of November, it set about its tasks. By the time of its first sessions, the Committee's staff had been considerably augmented. Count Vorontsov-Dashkov had been asked to serve along with M. N. Ostrovskii, the Minister of State Properties, Count P. S. Stroganov, and V. K. Pleve, who assumed the function of manager of the Committee's business (*deloproizvoditel'*). The young Chairman, Grand Duke Nicholas Alexandrovich, was carrying out his first major official assignment, and he attended to the Committee's affairs with the utmost seriousness. He listened attentively to all matters under discussion but generally refrained from expressing his own opinions. When debate occurred on a particular subject, he usually held aloof from the discussion and in the end sided with the majority.[23] Nicholas was by no means the driving force behind the Committee. Pleve was in charge of the day-to-day management of affairs; he prepared the agendas[24] and passed on reports to be considered at the various sessions. Vorontsov-Dashkov also played an important part in the Committee's operations. He proposed many of the programs undertaken by the Committee, and he assumed the task of organizing and executing a number of these plans.

The Special Committee held its first meeting on November 29, 1891. Its first step was to survey all the charitable organizations in the stricken provinces that would be under its general supervision. Also included in this survey were other charitable groups operating on nationwide scale, such as the Moscow Committee and the St. Petersburg Bishop's Committee. The members of the Special Committee feared that the loose structure of private charity was limiting the effectiveness of relief operations and was making it difficult to see where funds were actually going. In order to eliminate this confusion and disorder, the Committee asked Pleve to gather all available information on the organizations and individuals engaged in private charitable work. Pleve was to see to it that all charitable contributions in the hands of governors and local groups were placed under the control of the Special Committee. He was also ordered to draw up a plan for the introduction of a common system of bookkeeping in all local charitable institutions.[25]

The Committee was concerned that the various local charitable groups might end up duplicating each other's efforts and blunt the effectiveness of nongovernmental relief work. It was therefore proposed to bring all organizations operating under the direction of the Special Committee into one structure. In each province, one committee, under the general control of the Special Committee, would replace the separate bodies run by the bishops, the governors, and the Red Cross. These new organizations would include representatives from all charitable groups. A similar merger of charitable institutions would take place at the *uezd* and local levels. The plan to unite private relief operations in this manner found wide support within the Committee. The only opposition was expressed by Pobedonostsev who argued that Church committees should continue to act independently. He was overruled on this point, however, and the unified scheme was adopted.[26]

The Committee then turned to the question of the public appeals for aid which were to appear in the press. The Committee noted that as a result of the publication of requests for aid which had contained "exaggerated and even false information about the famine," the MVD had issued an order (dated November 11) forbidding such appeals unless they were authorized by the appropriate government institutions. The Committee approved this measure but observed that "in the task of aiding the stricken population, the work of persons knowing local conditions and . . . [guided] by a feeling of Christian love . . . produces the most desirable results." The members of the Committee therefore opposed any *total* ban on private requests for aid.[27] They requested the MVD to maintain its restrictions on unauthorized appeals for funds, but asked that further limitations on private initiative be avoided. The Committee urged that those engaged in private relief efforts be given moral and material support, and pledged that all its agencies would extend cooperation to local private groups.[28]

Toward the end of the first session the members of the Committee made a general survey of their task. They felt that the primary responsibility of the Committee was to those elements of the population not eligible for zemstvo and government loans, and that as a rule it should seek to prevent persons already receiving other forms of relief from getting aid from charitable institutions. The members of the Committee further stated that the main focus of its operations would be on those seventeen provinces most hard hit by the crop failure. Both of these rules, however, were not designed to be hard and fast. Exceptions could be made regarding individuals receiving aid from other sources, and the Committee could arrange for the relief of the population in areas not blighted by crop failure. The members singled out the city of Odessa as an area eligible for emergency aid, because, as a result of the ban on grain exports, large numbers of workers were unemployed and needed charitable relief.[29]

Having established its basic procedures and program, the Committee decided to send representatives into the various provinces to help organize and supervise the work of its local organs. Those chosen for this task were persons who were well known in government circles and who had demonstrated both loyalty to the state and a concern for the distressed. At a meeting on December 13 the Committee drew up a set of instructions to govern the operations of these representatives. According to the instructions, their first task was to gather information on the structure and activities of existing charitable institutions in the provinces and to see that these organizations were merged into a single committee under the chairmanship of the governor. The representatives of the Special Committee were then to survey the situation in their provinces finding out which areas were most needy and what, if any, defects existed in the work of local charitable institutions. The representatives were to look into the state of local contributions and to suggest what means might be taken to increase these donations. They were also ordered to pay special attention to the medical situation and to the state of provincial grain supplies. They were to make suggestions regarding any other programs that might be undertaken.[30] The Committee soon found, however, that these instructions were not an adequate guide for the work of its representatives, and at the end of January 1892 supplemental orders were issued. These new rules stressed the Committee's determination that its operations not interfere with individuals who were engaged in their own relief work. The representatives were also ordered to visit the neediest areas of the provinces to which they were assigned, and they were authorized to make immediate grants of money or grain to local relief workers in order to satisfy the pressing needs of the population.[31]

When the representatives of the Special Committee arrived in the provinces, they usually found a rather varied situation with regard to local charity. In some *uezdy* and districts private relief was well developed, while in other areas it was virtually nonexistent. Many factors accounted for these differences, but the most important element was usually the character of local leadership. An energetic governor could be of great assistance in encouraging private efforts, and similarly an indifferent or hostile governor could seriously retard the growth of the relief network. Perhaps even more important was the activity of those engaged in work at the *uezd* or village level. Here the initiative of a single person, a marshal of the nobility, a *zemskii nachal'nik*, or a private citizen could be extremely effective in organizing and coordinating relief efforts. In one of his reports to the Special Committee, Count A. A. Bobrinskii, the representative in Tambov province, described the significance of local workers:

> Most important charitable work in the province is in the hands of the *uezd* committees, and where these committees are led by an energetic marshal of the nobility, the needs of the population are clarified quickly and decisively, and aid is administered reasonably. Private charity, acting virtually independently of the committees, has special significance in the province. In *uezdy* where the marshals of the nobility participate personally in the work, private charity joins hand in hand with the committee; [it] supplements zemstvo loans, [and all] merge into a harmonious whole.[32]

Not all regions were blessed with energetic and effective local leadership, however, and some representatives of the Special Committee were forced to create a network of charitable institutions themselves. Iurii Stepanovich Nechaev-Mal'tsev, the Committee's representative in Kazan, was faced with such a situation. Arriving on the scene at the beginning of January, he found local charitable groups in disarray:

> The work of [these local] institutions did not have any coordination. Aid was distributed without any system, in a random manner, and the granting of funds to [local] relief committees had an accidental character. Thus charity could not effect all those [who were] truly needy. . . .[33]

Nechaev-Mal'tsev set about to remedy the situation by putting Kazan charity on a firm organizational basis. He brought about the formation of a provincial committee uniting the various disparate groups, and he drew up rules governing its operations.[34] He then established *uezd* committees to act as transmission belts for orders from above and requests for aid from below. At the district level, every *zemskii nachal'nik* was required to set up at least one local committee (*popechitel'stvo*). These bodies were to include local priests, *volost' starshiny*, judges (*sud'i*), and any other persons who might benefit the work of the organization. The local committee was in charge of the actual distribution of the relief funds passed on by the *uezd* and provincial committees or collected in the district. All villages under the protection of the local committee were divided among the members of that body for special supervision. The members were to visit the villages assigned to them and to draw up a list of the needy which was to be presented to the district committee with comments on the type and amount of relief required. The district *popechitel'stvo* was obliged to present a monthly report to the *uezd* committee and to keep a detailed record of receipts and expenditures.[35]

The structure of charitable relief which developed under the aegis of the Special Committee varied, of course, from province to province, but it was generally similar to the system in Kazan. This arrangement placed a tremendous burden on the *zemskie nachal'niki* and the public-spirited members of the local committees. They had to travel many miles to visit all the widely scattered villages for whose welfare they were responsible. They were forced to haggle with peasant officials about the lists of the needy, and they had to break down whatever barriers of distrust separated them from their charges. The task of the land captains was complicated by the fact that most of them had just begun their term of office. They hardly had time to become familiar with their districts, when they were forced to take charge of relief operations of enormous proportions. Besides their work in organizing private charity, many land captains had to oversee the distribution of zemstvo loans at the local level, because the zemstvo apparatus did not reach into the peasant villages. Thus, the management of charity and zemstvo relief, which were supposed to be two distinct operations, often merged at the district level. The lack of local personnel made the task of aiding the poor extremely difficult and increased the possibility of error and abuse.[36]

Local relief took various forms, depending on the needs of the population, the resources available to the *popechitel'stvo*, and the capabilities of its members. The most unimaginative type of relief was the distribution of grain and seed to the needy. In many areas, however, charitable help was administered differently. Fodder was purchased for the peasants' horses and cattle to help tide them over the hard winter. Child care centers were set up in many villages, and school lunch programs were developed. One of the most widespread forms of charitable relief was the soup-kitchen, or *stolovaia*. This method, which was popularized by Leo Tolstoi and his family, came to be used in all the stricken provinces and proved to be extremely effective. The main aim of the soup-kitchen was to provide warm food and a more balanced diet than would be had if the peasants were simply handed grain or flour. But this system had other advantages. At the *stolovaia* the peasants ate together under one roof; this helped to raise the morale of the needy and to develop a feeling of community solidarity in the face of crisis.

While the representatives of the Special Committee struggled to strengthen charity in the provinces, the main body was hard at work with other aspects of relief operations. On the whole, the Committee's primary occupation was to survey the requests for aid presented by governors, representatives of the Committee, and local people engaged in charitable efforts. The Committee generally accepted the estimates of need made by local officials, and it was loath to intervene in the operations of provincial and *uezd* bodies. When requests for money came from individuals carrying out relief work on a private basis, the Committee was more cautious. If the person making the request was known to it, or when the request was sponsored by its local representative, the Committee usually obliged. When the petitioner was unknown, the Committee was likely to refer his request back to the local charitable committee.

The Special Committee did, however, undertake a number of programs which transcended provincial boundaries or appeared to be beyond the powers of the local groups. At Vorontsov-Dashkov's suggestion the Committee attempted to improve and simplify the process of obtaining and shipping the large quantities of grain it needed for the relief of the stricken provinces. It decided to set up a conference of persons who were especially knowledgeable about the grain trade and with their help to work out a plan for the purchase of the required food and seed. Fifteen officers from the War Ministry were assigned to the Committee to assist it in implementing its plans concerning the acquisition and shipment of the grain.[37]

The plan for grain purchase was presented to the Committee on January 3, 1892. It proposed to entrust the procurement of the needed food supplies to the governors or to large commercial organizations commissioned by the Committee. Delivery of the food to the stricken areas would be supervised by specially selected agents. Once it reached the famine provinces, the grain would be disbursed and stored in local storehouses. From these points it would be distributed to the various agencies engaged in charitable work. The Special Committee approved the scheme and assigned 3 million rubles to finance grain purchases. Vorontsov-Dashkov was placed in charge of these operations.[38] Whether or not the plan accepted by the Committee was fully successful cannot be said for certain. But there were few complaints about the slowness of the delivery of grain purchased by the Committee or its agents. The railroad crisis no doubt affected the rate of the shipment of the Committee's purchases, but a special effort was made to speed their delivery. One of the first orders Colonel Vendrikh issued after he assumed his extraordinary powers in the field of railway transport was that the boxcars carrying grain intended for use by the Committee bear special markings and be moved ahead "*vne ocheredi.*"[39]

The members of the Committee realized that they could not limit their work to provisioning the peasants for the winter months. They quickly saw that the Committee must do something to shore up the peasant economy as a whole, and to prevent it from collapsing under the blows of adversity. Once again, Vorontsov-Dashkov came forward with a valuable suggestion. Noting that the crop failure had caused many peasant households to sell the horses which would be needed for spring planting, he proposed that the Committee purchase up to 15,000 horses for sale at reduced prices to peasants who had lost their work animals. The Committee accepted the idea and put Vorontsov-Dashkov in charge of the business.[40] The Minister of the Imperial Household reacted quickly and dispatched State Councilor Freifel'dt to Samara, Simbirsk, and Kazan provinces in order to survey the needs of the peasants. When he had completed this part of his mission, Freifel'dt proceeded to Orenburg, where he studied the possibility of purchasing horses from the local non-Russian population. He then reported to Vorontsov-Dashkov that about 30,000 horses were available for purchase. They could be obtained and transported into the famine region at a cost of about 50 rubles per head. Vorontsov-Dashkov urged his colleagues to authorize the purchase of these animals, and they agreed, assigning 1.5 million rubles for this purpose.[41] By mid-February 30,000 horses had been obtained,[42] and at subsequent sessions of the Committee its members evolved a general program for the distribution of these animals. It was decided to give out horses to those peasants who merited them on the basis of their economic self-sufficiency. The peasants who received the horses were required to pay 25 rubles a head over a period of four years, during which they could not dispose of the animals. [43] The distribution of horses by the Special Committee proved to be one of its most successful ventures; in the end over 42,000 horses were given out in eleven provinces.[44] The success of the program in 1892 led to the adoption of similar measures during the famine of 1898.[45]

Another program directly sponsored by the Special Committee was the encouragement of women's handicrafts in the stricken provinces of Nizhni-Novgorod and Voronezh. The idea was originally suggested by M. N. Ostrovskii, Minister of State Properties. He proposed that 10,000 rubles be allocated for the handicraft program, and asked that S. A. Davydova, the widow of an army officer, be placed in charge.[46] On December 20 Davydova appeared before the Committee to present her view of the situation and her assessment of the problems involved in the program. Davydova suggested that the women's handicraft project be limited to three provinces, Nizhni-Novgorod, Voronezh, and Kazan. She felt that such works could be most easily organized in Voronezh since initial steps had already been taken by charitable workers there. In Nizhni-Novgorod, too, the problems would be relatively simple, but Davydova felt that the situation in Kazan would present serious difficulties. In that province there was a large Moslem Tatar population whose work habits and customs were different from those of the Russians.[47]

The Committee approved Davydova's plan and issued special instructions governing the details of her activities. She was required to work closely with local officials, especially the governors and marshals of the nobility; but more importantly, she was to enlist the cooperation of persons at the local level who could continue the work once she had gone on to other areas. Davydova was ordered to keep accurate records of expenditures and to report to the Special Committee regularly on her progress.[48] Davydova received 48,000 rubles,—10,000 from the Ministry of State Properties and 38,000 from the Special Committee. During the first five months of 1892, Davydova traveled some 12,000 *versty* and succeeded in setting up handicraft work (mostly weaving and knitting) in 143 villages. Her efforts helped to provide supplemental income to over 4600 persons.[49] Although the results of Davydova's work were modest, the Committee was pleased. At the suggestion of Ostrovskii, it decided to continue these *kustar'* operations in 1893.[50]

The Special Committee also assumed the task of distributing the large quantities of grain and other foods which came from abroad. The Russian government was initially quite sensitive about receiving aid from other countries, and the Ministry of Foreign Affairs stated that national pride would not permit the acceptance of gifts from foreign governments. It was announced, however, that the assistance of charitable groups in other countries would be welcomed. Thus, on December 20 the Special Committee declared that it would accept the grain that had been offered by the governor of the state of Minnesota, because this food had been gathered through the efforts of private charity.[51] Throughout the winter and spring of 1892 the Committee received a series of large shipments of American grain paid for by contributions raised in the United States. The food was sent to the famine region in boxcars bearing the sign of the Special Committee and distributed to the needy in accordance with lists drawn up by the British-American Church in St. Petersburg.[52] The American representatives who accompanied the grain were received warmly (unlike the poor English Quakers) and were rendered every honor and courtesy. They were allowed to visit the interior of the country and observe local conditions firsthand. The whole affair produced good feelings on both sides and resulted in some accounts of the famine which were not at all unfavorable to the Russian government.[53]

The operations of the Special Committee were always on a rather modest scale. Between its founding and the termination of its activities in March 1893, the Committee gathered about 13 million rubles and disbursed over 12 million. The bulk of its funds (more than 8 million rubles) came from the proceeds of two charitable lotteries established by Imperial permission. Actual donations to the Committee itself were small, under 2 million rubles; another 2.5 million rubles flowed into the Committee's coffers from other institutions.[54] Most of its funds were spent to provide food for the population of the stricken *gubernii*, either in the form of grain purchased by the Committee or in the form of money granted to the provincial and local committees. But well over 3 million rubles went to support the economy of the peasant villages by providing seed and animal fodder, encouraging local handicrafts, and purchasing horses to replace those lost as a result of the disaster. Limited medical aid to the needy was also given out.[55]

While the sums dispensed by the Special Committee were small when compared with the huge grants made directly by the central government, the significance of its work was large. Its activities touched the lives of thousands of peasant households, bringing a more intimate form of aid than the zemstvos were able to provide. The establishment of a village soup kitchen under the auspices of the Tsesarevich's Committee was a more tangible sign of the Emperor's concern for his subjects than the monthly distribution of zemstvo grain loans. Moreover, the founding of the Special Committee and the influence of its representatives helped smooth the way for the growth of charitable activity independent of any government agency. Orders issued by the Special Committee stressed the need for ending restrictions on private relief operations. The representatives of the Committee joined with public-spirited citizens in the provinces, rendering them assistance and cooperation wherever possible. The example set by the Special Committee helped to eliminate whatever tensions existed between private relief workers and government officials. Beyond this, the work of the Committee contributed to the revitalization of Russian public life. Under its auspices, a number of persons who were regarded as politically suspect were permitted to take an active part in relief work.[56] This fact, which caused some consternation in official circles, did not go unnoticed by "society." For a moment at least, there seemed to be the possibility of some kind of reconciliation between the government and the liberal public which had become increasingly alienated from the regime as the result of its reactionary policies in the late 1880s.[57]

chapter eight

PUBLIC WORKS

The system of food supply aid established by the *ustav narodnogo prodovol'stviia* did not provide for a program of public works as a means of fighting the effects of crop failure, but past Russian governments had often adopted such measures. Public works were used as a technique of famine relief during the reign of Catherine II, and had again figured prominently in the era of Nicholas I.[1] By the end of the reign of Alexander II it had become obvious that works projects were among the best means of helping the needy population in times of distress, but nothing was done about putting public works on a regular basis. The government did not advance beyond the programs initiated by Nicholas I, and during the disastrous Samara famine of 1873 no attempt was made to provide employment for peasants in the stricken province.[2]

The crisis of 1891 once again pushed the idea of public works into the foreground. The vast ocean of peasant poverty, the drying up of traditional sources of employment, and the expense involved in state relief all pointed to the need for some kind of works project. Accordingly, toward the end of July, the question of public works began to be discussed in the Ministry of Internal Affairs. At about the same time, Durnovo raised the issue with Vyshnegradskii. The Minister of Finance supported the idea of setting up public works, and stated the government might loan money to the zemstvos for that purpose. The question was then brought to the attention of the Emperor, and on August 29 he authorized the loans suggested by the Minister of Finance. The money advanced to the zemstvos was to be used primarily to finance the building and repair of roads; it could be drawn from the credits already assigned to meet other food supply needs.[3]

Two provinces, Kazan and Kharkov, immediately requested public works loans, and during the summer, the MVD granted 650,000 rubles to

Kazan and 465,000 rubles to Kharkov for the purpose of road construction. The Ministry of Internal Affairs then turned to the governors of the other famine-stricken provinces with the suggestion that works be established in their *gubernii* as well. The zemstvos of Nizhni-Novgorod, Penza, Samara, Saratov, Simbirsk, Tambov, and Voronezh responded, making requests for sums totaling about 10 million rubles. After a close examination of the zemstvo proposals, however, the MVD found that many of the provincial requests were unacceptable. The zemstvos of Penza, Samara, Saratov, Simbirsk, and Tambov were cool to the idea of loans, and proposed instead that the cost of public works be borne by the treasury. The requests from Nizhni-Novgorod and Voronezh had been made before the technical details of their projects had been worked out. Moreover, some of the zemstvos clearly misunderstood the limited character of the plan for public works, and had asked that relief be provided by means of extensive railroad construction in their provinces. The defects in the zemstvo proposals slowed the MVD's timetable for the introduction of public works in the stricken *gubernii*, and meant that the Ministry's plan to provide supplemental employment to the needy population could not be immediately implemented.[4] By November 1891 only 650,000 rubles had been assigned for public works in the seventeen most hard-hit provinces. Despite this setback, however, the Ministry continued to feel that provincial officials were in the best position to advise it as to the feasibility of various works schemes. Thus, in early November, Durnovo began to sound out the governors of the famine-stricken *gubernii* about the possibility of their coming to St. Petersburg to attend a conference on the organization of public works.[5] Most of the governors favored the idea of such a conference and wired their acceptance right away.

In a report dated November 18, 1891 Durnovo brought the Emperor up to date on the situation regarding public works and put forth some new suggestions. The Minister of Internal Affairs posited several explanations for the failure of the initial scheme to finance works by means of loans to the zemstvos. The first reason was that "the zemstvo institutions in the provinces affected by the crop failure are in a transitional period with regard to their structure and activities, [and are], as the result of the composition of their executive organs, not fully capable of managing large economic undertakings of a technical nature."[6] The second reason was more practical. Durnovo argued that the zemstvos were unwilling to assume the obligation of large loans which would have to be paid back, and which, in view of the weakened economic situation of the peasantry, might prove to be an intolerable burden.[7]

Despite the problems which had hindered the establishment of a viable program of public works, Durnovo stated that the question was still one of the utmost importance. Fifty million rubles had already been granted to the zemstvos of the stricken provinces to finance food and seed purchases, and it was clear that additional sums would be needed in the near future. But the Minister argued that exclusive reliance on zemstvo relief could have a pernicious effect on the moral character of the peasants by undermining their will to work. Durnovo noted that many peasants who had gone to other provinces in search of employment had returned home when they learned that zemstvo loans were being distributed.[8] In view of these facts, Durnovo insisted that a program of public works must be put into operation as soon as possible. He also maintained that the government must be prepared to finance these works by means of direct grants from the treasury instead of loans. Most important of all, the Minister argued, the central authorities must seek to strengthen their ties with provincial institutions and find "means of combing governmental initiative [with] local economic activity."[9]

Durnovo suggested that the problems of public works be examined from all sides. He proposed that the question of financing the works be discussed by a special ministerial conference composed of the Minister of Internal Affairs and the Minister of Finance, under the chairmanship of A. A. Abaza. As for the implementation of the works in the provinces, Durnovo felt that this required the participation of the zemstvos under the "guidance" of the central authorities. He proposed to assist the zemstvos by permitting them to draw on whatever relevant technical skills the various ministries might possess.[10] Durnovo suggested that the details of the works program be studied at yet another conference of persons who knew local conditions well and who had experience in the management of like operations. Such a conference would be primarily composed of zemstvo personnel and provincial officials, but might include other persons whose experience and knowledge would be of particular value. One such person would be General Mikhail Nikolaevich Annenkov, who was then in charge of the construction of the Transcaspian railway. Durnovo stated that he hoped Annenkov would be able to take an active part in both the organization and the management of the proposed works.[11]

Later developments made it clear that Durnovo wished to have Annenkov become the manager of the works program once it got under way. Durnovo favored Annenkov for a number of sound reasons. First, the General possessed considerable knowledge of public works. He was an enthusiastic exponent of Russian railroad construction and was then in charge of building a major line in Transcaspia. Moreover, the fact that Annenkov was a military man made him acceptable to the Emperor and would thus help gain Imperial support for the works project. Finally, Annenkov had excellent connections in government circles and was on good terms with the other officials Durnovo intended to involve in the supervision of the public works. Annenkov's efforts to secure foreign financial backing for Russian railroad development made him acceptable to Vyshnegradskii. Annenkov's ties to Abaza were of a personal nature; the General's sister, Elena Nelidova, was Abaza's mistress.

The Emperor approved Durnovo's proposals on November 18, and on the following day the Minister of Internal Affairs contacted Vyshnegradskii and Abaza, informing them of the Tsar's decision to have them participate in planning the public works program.[12] The ministers moved quickly to put the Emperor's decision into effect, and on November 22 the ministerial conference composed of Durnovo, Vyshnegradskii, and Abaza met to examine the financial problems involved in the establishment of the works. The Minister of Finance opened the discussion by pointing to the economic difficulties the government would face in the coming months. He maintained that the extraordinary expenditures of the current year and the anticipated deficit for 1892 would "swallow all the resources gained by means of the last three [foreign] loans,"[13] and he warned his colleagues that in the present circumstances, floating another loan would be extremely difficult.[14] Vyshnegradskii argued that a line must be drawn with regard to further relief operations, and he suggested that only 20 million rubles more be made available for this purpose during 1891. Part of this money should be used for public works and the remainder for direct aid to the population. If the demands for relief exhausted the sums available in the treasury, Vyshnegradskii urged that the needs of the distressed be met through the expansion of private charity. He cautioned Durnovo and Abaza against excessive reliance on direct grants from the treasury. This, he felt, could lead "to the development of the extremely dangerous idea of 'the Tsar's rations,'" with the implication that the government was responsible for the care of all needy persons.[15]

Durnovo and Abaza were not prepared to support Vyshnegradskii's stand on limiting relief expenditures. While recognizing the need for caution, they felt that 10 million rubles would be needed for public works alone. The Minister of Finance was overruled, and the conference turned to the question of financing the works program. It decided that the works should be paid for by a direct grant from the treasury and not by means of a loan to the zemstvos. As for the management of the works, the conference concluded that special rules and procedures would have to be established in order to speed the introduction of the projects into the stricken provinces. The task of drawing up these regulations was assigned to the Ministry of Internal Affairs.[16]

The essential groundwork completed, Durnovo moved to give life to the public works project. On the day after the meeting with Vyshnegradskii and Abaza, he cleared the way for the conference of governors and provincial representatives. Durnovo wired the governors of Nizhni-Novgorod, Penza, Samara, Saratov, Simbirsk, Tambov, and Voronezh, asking that they or their delegates come to the capital in the near future in order to discuss the establishment of a public works program in their provinces.[17] On November 26 the Minister of Internal Affairs wrote to General Annenkov requesting him to join in these deliberations.[18] On November 28 Durnovo presented the Emperor with an account of the decisions taken at the meeting with Abaza and Vyshnegradskii and with his own proposals for the general management of the works project.

In his report, Durnovo stressed to His Majesty that the program must be begun as soon as possible because "in the adoption and execution of public works, speed is the prime requisite for success."[19] To insure that the works would be started quickly, Durnovo suggested that those who were to administer the project be freed from the general rules of financial accountability which applied to other government undertakings.[25] Durnovo proposed to assign the general supervision of the public works program to a Special Conference (*Osoboe Soveshchanie*), chaired by Abaza, which would include the Ministers of Finance and Internal Affairs, the state controller, and General Annenkov. This Special Conference would have the final say on any proposals for public works, and it would be free to assign sums as it saw fit. Its accounts would not be subject to the scrutiny of any other government organ. According to Durnovo's plan, General Annenkov would be in charge of the technical and financial details of the works, and he would supervise the management of the project. Annenkov would be under the control of the Special Conference, and he was to be governed by instruction drawn up by the Minister of Internal Affairs.[21]

The Tsar approved the decisions taken at the ministerial conference on November 22 and the proposals made in Durnovo's *doklad*. Ten million rubles were assigned to finance the works, and the MVD was told to go ahead with the meeting of the governors and their representatives, now scheduled for the first week of December. The Ministry of Internal Affairs drew up an agenda and a list of proposed works for the consideration of the governors and provincial delegates. According to the MVD's plan, the governors' conference was to take up such questions as the number of workers to be employed, the organization and management of various projects established in each *guberniia*, and the relation of provincial officials, especially the governors, to the works. The conference was also to examine the problem of whether or not to make participation in the works obligatory for those receiving public assistance.[22]

The conference of governors and provincial representatives convened on December 2, 1891, under the chairmanship of Durnovo. At the opening session the delegates quickly agreed to eliminate from consideration as public works such ambitious projects as railroad construction and water control. In the view of the majority of the conference, the present task of the government was "to give immediate relief to the needy population by providing the peasants the opportunity for employment on [public] works,"[23] and not to introduce programs of long-range regional development. The delegates realized that the scope of the works project was limited, because only 10 million rubles would be available to finance these operations, and they therefore felt that the primary focus of the program should be on forestry and the repair and construction of roads.[24] Since the list of works proposed by the MVD consisted almost entirely of roadbuilding and forestry, the conference approved the Ministry's plan with a minimum of discussion. The only major quarrel arose when Governor Terenin of Simbirsk objected to the construction of a highway in his province because he felt that the costs of upkeep would be too great. The majority of the delegates, however, sided with the MVD, and the Governor was overruled.[25]

The next major issue the conference took up was the question of the organization of the works themselves.[26] The discussion quickly focused on the problem of control of the project. Governor Terenin suggested that the management of the works be decentralized and placed in the hands of provincial committees selected by the governors. General Annenkov sharply disagreed with Terenin and promoted the idea of central control and one-man direction of the project. Annenkov was prepared, however, to permit the governors and the zemstvos to assume responsibility for many of the purely economic aspects of the problem such as providing food and housing for the workers and seeing to it that they were transported to their place of employment. Other delegates, among them A. S. Gatsiskii of Nizhni-Novgorod, tended to back Terenin and insisted that the role of the governors in the management of the works should not be too greatly restricted. Finally, even Annenkov agreed that central control should not be carried to the extreme, and he accepted the suggestion that the person in charge of the works maintain regular contact with the governors of those provinces where works were to be opened. As for the role of the zemstvos, the general feeling of the conference was that they should not be required to assume too much responsibility for the public works because they were already overburdened by other aspects of relief operations. After permitting this discussion to go on for some time, Durnovo intervened and shut off debate before the conference could reach any final decision. He assured the delegates that he would take their views into account, but he insisted that the regulations governing Annenkov's powers with regard to the works would be drawn up by the MVD at a later date.[27]

The last problem the governors' conference examined before it disbanded was the issue whether or not to make work compulsory for those receiving aid from the government. The delegate from Nizhni-Novgorod, A. S. Gatsiskii, agreed in general with the idea that participation be made obligatory where this was possible, but he insisted that the rules governing the works should be flexible enough to allow for exceptions. Durnovo himself supported Gatsiskii's stand, noting that in Tambov there had been cases of peasants refusing to work when they learned that zemstvos loans were being given out. Despite the arguments of Gatsiskii and the Minister of Internal Affairs, the majority of the conference rejected the idea of forced labor, and it was decided that the whole program be kept on a voluntary basis.[28]

The testimony of the provincial representatives convinced Durnovo that the proposed public works could be carried out successfully, and he now proceeded to put the finishing touches on his plan. When the conference broke up, Durnovo drew up regulations which would govern the activities of General Annenkov, the director of the project. Under these rules, which closely resembled those suggested by Durnovo in his *doklad* of November 28, Annenkov was given wide powers over the management of the works. But he was subject to the overall supervision and control of a Special Conference chaired by Abaza. All plans for the works, together with the financial estimates, had to be submitted to the Special Conference for its approval, and once the required authorization had been obtained, no changes would be made in the program without the Conference's permission. In the provinces, Annenkov was to manage virtually all aspects of the program. Where it proved impossible for him to assume direct control of a particular project, Annenkov was empowered to appoint a person to take charge, but the General was to remain finally responsible.

The regulations specified that, in organizing the works at the local level, Annenkov and his agents were to cooperate closely with the provincial governors. Together they were to make arrangements concerning the number and type of workers to participate in the project, how they were to be provisioned, and what wages they were to be paid. At all times, Annenkov was to keep the Minister of Internal Affairs and the Special Conference informed as to the course of the works. He was to submit a monthly report to Durnovo and, at the completion of a given project, to permit a special commission chosen by the MVD to examine the results. The regulations required Annenkov to communicate with the central authorities by means of regular MVD channels; any requests made by the governors were to be called to the attention of the Ministry. Finally, Annenkov had to present a general account on the financial aspects of the works to Durnovo within six months of the termination of the entire project.[29]

Durnovo presented the proposed regulations determining Annenkov's powers and the results of the conference of governors and provincial representatives to the Tsar on December 12. They obtained immediate approval; the way was now clear for the final planning and implementation of the public works project.[30] On December 18 the Special Conference on Public Works, composed of Vyshnegradskii, Durnovo, T. I. Filippov (State Controller), and chaired by Abaza, met for the first time. The Conference turned at once to the discussion of the kinds of works that should be adopted. It decided that the most desirable works would be those "whose costs consisted chiefly of wages . . . [and] did not demand large expenditures on materials." The other major consideration should be that the works begun be of real public significance "so that the loss incurred by the state would not be without results, but would produce something of value for the future."[31] The Conference felt that road-building and repair would be an excellent means both for providing work to the needy and for improving local transporation. It appropriated 1.45 million rubles for this purpose, figuring the costs of such operations at about 5000 rubles per *verst*.[32] Other works projects were considered, among them the construction of granaries, church schools, and grain elevators. The idea of granaries was rejected, largely because it was felt that the whole system of food supply was going to be reviewed by the MVD and that an investment in village storehouses at this time might be wasted if the basis of the system was radically changed. The Conference favored the building of church schools, especially in the areas with large non-Russian populations; it postponed until another session the consideration of whether or not to undertake the construction of large grain elevators.[33]

The Conference then turned to a discussion of the possibility of financing large-scale forestry operations. This idea was presented by General Annenkov who had been invited to attend the opening session of the Conference. His basic plan was to take some 3.175,000 rubles from the funds put aside for public works and use this money to pay for the cutting of timber in state forests. Annenkov then proposed to sell the lumber, arguing that the gross receipts from such an operation would be over 6 million rubles, with a profit of 3 million rubles for the state. By this method, he insisted, the government could not only provide employment for the needy but would obtain considerably more revenue than could be expected if the business were farmed out to private contractors. Annenkov noted that once the forestry operations were completed, the initial 3,175,000 rubles could be plowed back into other public works while the profit would flow into the treasury to help defray the overall costs of relief.

The Conference approved Annenkov's suggestion, but noted that the proposed forestry operations would not provide the population with any more work than if the matter had been left to private hands. Two reasons prompted the Conference to support the project. First, the scheme "made it possible to provide work for the most needy persons and, in general, to direct the business [of forestry] in the interests of the population and not simply with a view to commercial profit." Second, Annenkov's plan enabled the government to "turn the sums spent on forestry back into new works for the benefits of the needy population without increasing the expenditures from the treasury."[34] Still, the Conference's reluctance to adopt Annenkov's scheme reflects a basic tension within the government between officials who favored government intervention in all spheres and those who wanted to give a greater role to private enterprise.

Having obtained the Conference's support for the lumbering operation, Annenkov outlined some of the details of his plan. He proposed to conduct most of the work within the confines of the stricken *gubernii*, but he felt that to guarantee the commercial success of the business he would have to open forestry operations in some areas not affected by the famine—namely, Novgorod, Tver, and Vladimir provinces. The Conference authorized this measure although it realized that some funds meant for relief would go to those who were not in need. It hoped that this defect in the program would be offset by making it possible to bring workers from the famine provinces into areas where the harvest had been good and food was plentiful.[35]

In subsequent meetings, the Special Conference hammered out the details of other works projects. The Conference appropriated 2.2 million rubles for the construction of grain elevators in the famine area, although it decided against a proposal, made by the Minister of Finance, to use the project as a means to test the feasibility of a national system of elevators.[36] The Conference also decided to spend 2 million rubles of public works funds to help build a highway along the Black Sea from Novorossiisk to Sukhum. This measure actually ran counter to the rules governing the management of public works which stated that works were to be concentrated in the areas affected by the crop failure. The Conference justified this deviation from the original plan, however, by noting that the excellent harvest in the Caucasus had induced many workers in the famine-stricken provinces to go south looking for work and cheap grain. This development, the Conference felt, had created the need for some kind of public works in the area. Not only should work be provided for refugees from the famine provinces but peasants in the afflicted *gubernii* should be encouraged to come to the Caucasus. Such a program, the Conference argued, "would be of significant benefit to the needy population both in terms of the amount of work that could be given to it and the convenience of providing for [the workers] in an area where the delivery of grain did not present difficulties."[37]

With the general plan for the works approved and the bulk of the available sums appropriated,[33] Annenkov proceeded to set up the machinery for administering the works at the local level. To maintain central control over these operations, Annenkov established a Main Administration (*Glavnoe upravlenie*) in the capital. This body had its own chancellery and special sections to manage technical matters of bookkeeping.[39] In the provinces, local departments of the *upravlenie* were founded. They were headed by a special representative (*upolnomochennyi*) of Annenkov, chosen at the suggestion of the governor of the province or the Minister of Internal Affairs. These representatives had the right to discuss with the governors any problems which concerned the organization of public works, but they were ultimately responsible to Annenkov. Each of these agents had his own staff of technical people and other workers who were to look after various details of the works projects.[40]

During 1892 and the first half of 1893, Annenkov and his colleagues struggled to put the plans developed by the Special Conference into effect. Despite their honest efforts, however, the program proved unsuccessful. Indeed, of all the government measures undertaken to mitigate the effects of the bad harvest, only the public works can be regarded as a true failure. A catalog of all the shortcomings of the project is not needed here; ample details are provided in Maksimov's study. Still, some general reflection on the causes of this failure may prove instructive.

The first major weakness was the timing of the operations. The detailed plans for the works were not drawn up until the first months of 1892 and, as a result, the project was not in full swing until the summer and fall. Thus, the main crisis, caused by the crop failure of 1891, had passed before the needy population could really benefit from the establishment of the works. Furthermore, many of the works were hastily chosen and poorly organized. As we noted earlier, a number of them were not located within the boundaries of the stricken provinces. Much of the construction work, such as the building of church schools and grain elevators, did not benefit the poor, unskilled peasants, but helped, instead, skilled craftsmen—masons, carpenters, and the like—who had far less need for government aid than the starving village dwellers.[41] Beyond this, the impact of the works was decidedly limited because the number of workers involved was quite small (perhaps 100,000), and only a fraction of these received steady work.[42] Of the 15 million rubles actually spent on the works, less than half (about 6 million rubles) went to the workers in the form of wages.[43]

Some of the managers of the works devoted little attention to the living and working conditions of those they employed. Works were often established at great distance from the places where the workers lived, and they had to travel miles before they could get to the job. When the peasants arrived at the work site, they often found conditions to be extremely hard, and in some cases there was no work to be had. One observer described the fate of workers who sought employment on the Novorossiisk-Sukhum highway as follows:

> People would be delivered by the several hundreds and deposited on the coast. . . . A while later, they would be taken away again because there was no work [at hand]. There was no place to deliver [these workers]; all the jobs had already been taken by those who had arrived previously. As there was no work, there was no bread. [The peasants] had to scrape by, to sell their clothes and go into debt. . . . There were cases where people, having wasted the time on travel, and having sat around for several months in the expectation of work, got only a month or two's [employment] and could earn [only] ten or fifteen rubles.[44]

In many cases, the payment of workers would be delayed, and peasants would be forced to go two and three days without food. Given such conditions, it is not surprising that many persons employed on the works became sick.[45]

Perhaps the biggest weakness in the public works program proved to be the choice of Annenkov as its director, for despite his good intentions and enthusiasm for the project, the General badly mismanaged the whole affair. Not only was he responsible in large part for the shortcomings listed above, but he also consistently violated his instructions concerning the administrative and financial aspects of the business. Annenkov failed to establish proper control over the activities of his agents at the provincial level, and this often resulted in unnecessary expenditures of money and labor. In many cases, the General did not secure the cooperation of the governors, provincial officials, zemstvos, and charitable groups before working out the details of the various projects. Annenkov's biggest mistake concerned the management of the forestry operations which, as we noted above, were expected to produce about 3 million rubles in profit for the state. Under the General's inept direction, however, the anticipated profit was never realized, and, as the result of poorly conceived commercial arrangements, the sale of the lumber failed to cover the costs of the labor. In the end, instead of a profit, the state had to absorb a considerable loss. In all, the public works cost over 4 million rubles more than had been expected.[46]

Eventually, Annenkov's blunders came to the attention of the central authorities. When the famine crisis had passed, the General's work as director of the public works program was subjected to a long and detailed investigation lasting from August 1893 to December 1895. Personal dishonesty was neither charged nor proven; only Annenkov's shortcomings as an administrator were really at issue. A board of inquiry consisting of the state controller and the Minister of Justice found that the General had abused his authority and had undertaken a number of works without obtaining the required permission. These unauthorized works had cost about 3.5 million rubles. Beyond this, Annenkov's mismanagement of the sale of the lumber cut in the state forests was found to have resulted in a loss for the treasury. As a result of the findings of the board of inquiry, Annenkov was censured by the Committee of Ministers; but although he was liable for criminal prosecution, no action was taken against him. At one point, he was ordered to repay to the treasury a sum of more than 100,000 rubles— a small portion of the money lost due to his mismanagement of the works—but in the end even this penalty was cancelled.[47]

There is no question that General Annenkov was to a large extent responsible for the poor results of the public works project, but he was not the chief cause of the disaster. The failure of the works program illustrates the major problem which confronted the Russian government during the famine—the lack of adequate administrative machinery for coping with the crisis. The basic idea of public works was a sound one, and the measure had been used to advantage in the past. But because the existing system of famine relief did not provide for works as a regular part of relief operations, there was no plan on hand ready to be put into effect, and no apparatus for managing the project. As a result, everything had to be worked out in a very short time. The works could not be handled through the regular channels of the administration. The entire business had to be turned over to a small group of *sanovniki*, and a single person was made responsible for all the various aspects of the program. Even an administrator who possessed the greatest talent was doomed to make mistakes in such a situation. The choice of Annenkov only compounded the difficulties.

chapter nine

RELIEF IN THE PROVINCES: THE WORK OF GUBERNIIA INSTITUTIONS

We have now surveyed the most important relief operations conducted by the central government during the famine of 1891–92, but the picture of the struggle against the disaster is far from complete. The real focus of relief work, especially after the autumn of 1891, was in the stricken *gubernii* themselves. To understand fully how the task of feeding the hungry was actually carried out, we must examine the work of provincial institutions. But the study of local relief operations is an extremely difficult business. The amount of source material is enormous. Besides the numerous *dela* relating to provincial relief held in the central archives, there are published zemstvo records for almost all the *gubernii* and *uezdy* affected by the crop failure. The provincial archives would, no doubt, contain additional materials, including reports submitted by *zemskie nachal'niki* and local relief committees. To sift through this volume of documentation could be the work of a lifetime, and thus, for the purposes of this study, the scope of the investigation must be limited. Relief operations in three provinces—Nizhni-Novgorod, Kazan and Tambov—have been singled out for closer examination.

These three provinces have been chosen because they illustrate many of the problems found in other parts of the stricken area. Kazan, Nizhni-Novgorod, and Tambov were all predominantly agricultural *gubernii* (although Nizhni-Novgorod had well-developed handicraft industries) and in normal times they were self-sufficient as far as grain production was concerned. Growing impoverishment of the peasantry was also a common factor. The size of peasant allotments was generally small (from three to five *desiatiny*), and a series of bad harvests had recently undermined the well-being of the villagers. Local grain reserves had steadily diminished in the years preceding the disaster. When the crop failure occurred, peasants in all three provinces had to turn to the zemstvos and the central government for assistance. But while the economic conditions in the three *gubernii* were similar, the responses of the provincial administrations in each province were very different. In the course of relief operations in Kazan, Nizhni-Novgorod, and Tambov, a number of unique local problems and conflicts developed. These difficulties are worthy of close study because they throw light on larger problems facing the Russian state.

The next two chapters will not attempt to survey all aspects of relief at the provincial level; instead they will focus on the work of the most important institutions which sought to combat the effects of the crop failure. The primary concern will be to examine the functioning and interaction of these institutions—to find out to what degree the provincial adminstrations, the zemstvos, and local relief organizations were able to cooperate in a common cause. We shall first discuss the role of the governors, paying special attention to their relations with other agencies trying to aid the stricken population. Then we shall look at the work of the zemstvos and provincial food supply conferences and their roles as coordinators of relief operations. In the following chapter we shall study relief activities at the lowest level, concentrating on the work of the *zemskie nachal'niki* and the district *popechitel'stva*. In the course of our discussion we shall also attempt to present some statistical data which will help to determine the scope and the effectiveness of the provincial relief.[1]

The governors stood at the very center of the provincial operations, and it would hardly be an exaggeration to say that they shaped the course of the struggle against famine in their *gubernii*. As we have noted earlier, the law stated that the function of the governors with regard to food supply was primarily supervisory.[2] But the power and prestige of their office, and the central role played by the administration in provincial life generally, made it only logical that the governors would emerge as a dominant force in a time of real crisis. The part played by the governors in the struggle against the famine of 1891 was further enhanced by the fact that local resources were not sufficient to meet the situation, and as a result aid had to be requested from the center. The governors, as agents of the MVD, became the vital link between the Ministry and the zemstvos; they presented the requests of these local bodies to the Ministry and gave their own evaluation of the situation.[3] They also transmitted the orders from the MVD to the zemstvos. The obligations of the governors increased steadily over the summer as a result of ministerial circulars concerning the establishment of provincial food supply conferences, the organization of private charity, and the management of zemstvo relief. The governors were active at the provincial level, often well before the intervention of the MVD, stimulating the activity of the zemstvos and private relief workers. Some governors sought to encourage local merchants to assist in grain purchases, a task which was vital to the success of the campaign against famine.

The scope of the governors' responsibilities was great because there were no organs or officials in the provincial administration capable of taking over some of the burdens the governors carried. In theory, the governors were supposed to be assisted in their work by a vice-governor and a provincial *pravlenie* composed of various local *chinovniki*. But the tradition of one-man rule was such that the functions of these officials were minimal at best.[4] During the famine crisis most governors tended to work with little reliance on the other institutions of the provincial administration. Thus the outcome of relief operations depended in large measure on their personal capabilities. Where the governor proved energetic and able, relief usually proceeded effectively. Where the governor was of a phlegmatic nature, seeking to avoid action and perhaps even minimizing the actual needs of the province, serious difficulties often developed.[5] The importance of the governors' leadership in organizing and directing relief work is illustrated when we compare the relative weakness of relief operations in Kazan with the greater success of those in Nizhni-Novgorod.

Although Kazan was one of the most hard-hit areas of the country and had been given ample warning of the possibility of a crop failure,[6] Governor Poltaratskii and the zemstvo did little to meet the impending crisis until prodded by the MVD.[7] When the provincial assembly met in early July, a split developed between the *uprava* and the majority of the delegates as to the amount of aid that should be requested from the center. The *uprava* felt that the estimates of need prepared earlier by the *uezd* assemblies were excessive, and made a number of cuts in the proposed relief budget.[8] The provincial assembly, however, concluded that the reductions made by the *uprava* were too severe, and decided to increase the size of the request. In the end, the Kazan zemstvo asked for a loan of 5 million rubles.[9] It is not certain where Governor Poltaratskii stood in the dispute between the zemstvo assembly and the provincial *uprava*, but in all likelihood he supported the views of the latter body.[10] In any case, the initial grant to the Kazan zemstvo (made July 11, 1891) was small—only 1.7 million rubles.[11] Over the summer, the zemstvo made additional requests for aid, and the central authorities responded. By October the province had received a total of 3 million rubles.[12]

During the summer, Governor Poltaratskii did little to moblize the province to meet the coming crisis. He felt that the situation was less serious than reports indicated and, accordingly, he did not take steps to encourage or direct zemstvo activity. For the most part the Governor restricted his involvement to paper shuffling, leaving the zemstvos to operate without any guidance from the administration. He often failed to inform the zemstvos of developing problems. Thus, when one of the *zemskie nachal'niki* sent him an urgent telegram requesting a more rapid delivery of seed grain, Poltaratskii delayed four days before passing the request on the *uprava*.[13] The lack of central direction from the Governor led to a number of cases of mismanagement. In many areas, seed loans were not given out on time. As a result of these mistakes, as much as one-third of the winter fields in some of the northern *uezdy* remained unsown.[14]

The weakness of the food supply operations in Kazan led to serious criticism of the provincial administration and the zemstvos. Some of these complaints were sent directly to the MVD, while others appeared in the press. Starting in the fall of 1891, Governor Poltaratskii found his work increasingly scrutinized by central officials. In mid-October the MVD called upon Poltaratskii to answer questions concerning reports that there had been delays in the delivery of seed to needy peasants.[15] Later in the month, the Governor had to make a more detailed defense of the relief policy adopted by the province.[16] The state of famine relief in Kazan also became the concern of the Department of Police. On October 31 the Department wrote Poltaratskii stating that it had received information that as the result of insufficient food loans, the peasants in the *guberniia* "[had] begun to plunder the grain storehouses belonging to the nobility and [that], in general, cases of robbery in the province [had] increased to a great degree." The letter also stated that cases of death from starvation had been reported to the Department.[17] Subsequent inquiries from the Department of Police also sought information about deaths caused by the famine, and the alleged demoralization of the agricultural population.[18]

But aside from their admonitions and requests for information, there was little officials at the center could do to bring about a change in the management of relief in Kazan. Once again, the independence of the governors and the inadequacy of the regular MVD apparatus as a means of controlling their actions were clearly demonstrated. In all cases, Poltaratskii denied that there was anything fundamentally wrong about relief operations in his province,[19] but he remained under a cloud. Government concern for the situation in the *guberniia* was revealed by the fact that the first representative of the Tsesarevich's Special Committee to be dispatched to the provinces was sent to Kazan. At the same time, the inadequacy of relief work created indignation among certain elements in the province, and an attempt was made on the life of the Governor. On January 4, 1892, a young man fired three shots at Poltaratskii, wounding him slightly.[20]

By the beginning of 1892 the situation in Kazan had not improved to any noticeable extent. When N. A. Troinitskii, the Director of the Central Statistical Committee of the MVD, toured the Volga provinces he found the zemstvos in Kazan still unprepared to meet the situation and the administration uninformed and lacking direction. In his report to the Ministry he wrote:

> The Governor is too cautious and is sometimes insufficiently firm with regard to the activities of the economic institutions of the province, allowing them complete freedom and limiting himself exclusively to formal proposals and demands. As a result of this [policy] he knows less than he should [about relief work], and the activity of even *uezd* institutions has achieved an independence which, in my opinion, cannot be tolerated . . . particularly with regard to food supply operations.[21]

Troinitskii charged that the Governor had failed to provide the zemstvos with the proper leadership, and as a result the provincial *uprava* was often unsure how to act or whom to turn to for advice.[22]

About one month after his first report on the situation in Kazan, Troinitskii had obtained an even clearer view of the problem. He had had the opportunity to tour the province and to observe the conduct of relief work at the local level. In two reports submitted to the MVD at the end of February 1892, Troinitskii reiterated his opinion that Governor Poltaratskii's ineffective leadership was a stumbling block to the proper management of local relief. Troinitskii argued that the provincial administration had to play a much more decisive role in supervising and unifying the work of the *zemskie nachal'niki*. These officials, he noted, were not completely familiar with the districts under their control (they had only assumed office on July 1, 1891), and they were often unwilling to accept the leadership of the zemstvo institutions.[23] Troinitskii urged that the Governor be encouraged to undertake a tour of the famine-stricken areas of the province, and he pointed out that since Poltaratskii had visited three of the affected *uezdy* in late November and early December, he had not budged from the city of Kazan. Troinitskii felt that if the Governor were made to confront the situation at first hand, he would take immediate steps to overcome the difficulties.[24]

Shortly after Troinitskii's reports to the MVD were filed, Poltaratskii made an inspection of seven *uezdy* of the province (Spasskii, Tetiushskii, Sviazhskii, Tsivil'skii, Iadrinskii, Kozmodem'ianskii, and Cheboksarskii). His aim was to gather information about the state of the *uezdy* and the conduct of relief. In each *uezd* he summoned the local marshal of the nobility, the chairman of the zemstvo *uprava*, the *zemskie nachal'niki*, the *ispravniki*, and tax inspectors to help him get a clearer picture of the situation. Poltaratskii found great differences in the way aid was given out in various areas, and he noted that the competence of local institutions varied markedly. The Governor sought to encourage greater unity and efficiency in the administration of relief, but at the same time he urged local officials to hold food supply loans and other forms of aid to a minimum wherever possible.[25] After the Governor returned from his tour of the famine region, relief work in the province seemed to improve. At least this is what we can infer from Troinitskii's final report which closed on a complimentary note. Troinitskii stated that when the Governor became more aware of the difficulties in the province he moved to correct the situation. When complaints came to his attention he sent out members of his staff to investigate and took remedial action when necessary.[26]

Despite the ample criticism of the conduct of relief operations in Kazan, Poltaratskii never admitted that any fundamental errors had taken place in his province. In July 1892 he vigorously defended the work of the administration and the zemstvos against the attack leveled by Iu. S. Nechaev-Mal'tsev in his report to the Special Committee. Nechaev charged that not only had local charity been poorly organized at the time of his arrival in the *guberniia* but that zemstvo loans were also inadequate. He claimed that, before December 1891, loans to the needy did not exceed five or ten *funty* of grain per "eater."[27] Poltaratskii insisted that zemstvo relief had been sufficient to meet the needs of the population, and he stated that the zemstvos would have been able to undertake a wider relief program only if they had had more funds at their disposal.[28]

Poltaratskii's denials of any mismanagement of relief measures in his province cannot gainsay the weight of the evidence, which seems to favor the critics of his administration. It is safe to say that had the Governor been more alert and energetic, relief operations might have begun at an earlier date, and some of the confusion which developed, especially at the local level, might have been avoided.

Governor N. M. Baranov of Nizhni-Novgorod presented a marked contrast to the phlegmatic Poltaratskii. If any one word describes Baranov, it is "energetic;" and in the initial stage of relief work, this energy proved extremely valuable. As early as May 1891, Baranov watched the developing agricultural crisis in his province with increasing concern. At the end of the month he began to gather detailed information on the situation. He also informed the Ministry of Internal Affairs that signs pointed to the possibility of serious food supply difficulties in the *guberniia*. By June 6 Baranov was convinced that a crisis was at hand, and he moved decisively to mobilize the province for a struggle against hunger. On that day Baranov sent letters to Messrs. Bugrov, Blinov, and Bashkirov, three of the most important grain merchants in the province. The Governor told them of the situation in the *guberniia* and asked them each to deliver 5000 sacks of rye flour to wharves near the most hard-hit areas. He stated that the merchants would be paid out of funds which would soon be made available to the zemstvos.[29] At the same time Baranov sent telegrams to the marshals of the nobility and *zemskie nachal'niki* in the affected districts, telling them that grain would soon be available to meet the crisis.[30] Baranov also informed the chairman of the provincial zemstvo *uprava*, A. V. Bazhenov, of his actions, and ordered Bazhenov to call the *uezd* and provincial zemstvos into session.[31]

While the zemstvo machinery began to get under way, Baranov strove to lay the groundwork for the upcoming relief operations by means of administrative channels. In a circular to the *zemskie nachal'niki* of the province, the Governor called on these officials to gather detailed information on the needs of their districts, and he warned them to be vigilant lest the peasants misuse the loans they would be given. Baranov urged the *zemskie nachal'niki* to work together with the chairman of the local *upravy* wherever possible so as to achieve the necessary unity of action in the struggle against famine.[32] In order to facilitate the purchase of the grain needed to head off the disaster, the Governor turned to the local merchants' committee (*birzhevoi komitet*), asking its help in preventing speculation.[33] Finally, Baranov contacted the central authorities, bringing them up to date on the situation and requesting money to finance grain purchases. These early measures were strikingly successful. When the provincial zemstvo assembly convened on July 1, Baranov was able to present it with over 100,000 *pudy* of rye flour and a government credit of 1 million rubles.[34]

Baranov's actions in the first month of the famine crisis helped to get relief in Nizhni-Novgorod province off to a good start. During July almost 150,000 peasants received food supply loans.[35] But there was another side to the Governor's activity which, if it did not hinder the success of relief operations, certainly complicated relations between the administration and the zemstvos. This was Baranov's desire to bring the entire food supply campaign under his personal control and to exclude, as far as was possible, the zemstvos from the work of relief.

Baranov's first step in the direction of realizing this goal was his proposal to the MVD asking permission to set up a special committee to supervise food supply operations.[36] Then, on June 25, the Governor submitted a report to the Ministry which was highly critical of the zemstvos and called for a new system of administering relief in the *guberniia*. Baranov began his report with a general attack on zemstvo competence with regard to the economic side of relief work. He charged that

> . . . with the onset of need, whether large or small, the zemstvo assemblies are [both] superficial [and] . . . late when they determine the amount of aid [required]. And when, by means of their petitions [the zemstvos] extract [the money] from the government, they buy grain . . . wherever and by whatever means come to mind. . . . [This bread] is given out both to the needy and to *kulaks* engaged in the grain trade. Very often, grain requested for seed is delayed until after sowing; some [of this grain] is eaten by those who receive it, but the greater part is either drunk up in the taverns or sold to speculators at an unusually low price.[37]

Baranov called the attention of the MVD to what he regarded as "the complete inability of the zemstvos to manage the local economy," and he warned the Ministry that "once again to give the zemstvos millions from the Treasury would be a great sin against both the government and the population in whose name those millions were requested." Baranov proposed to take the management of relief out of the hands of the zemstvos and to entrust it to a special committee under his chairmanship. This committee would be composed of the marshals of the nobility, the *zemskie nachal'niki* and *uezd upravy* of the afflicted areas, the big grain traders of the province, and the heads of the *udelnaia kontora* and *kazennaia palata*.[38] Baranov requested an immediate decision on this matter from the MVD; and on June 28 he wired Durnovo stating that he would delay informing the zemstvo about the government's grant of 1 million rubles until he had heard from the Ministry.[39]

The MVD reacted cautiously to Baranov's proposal. It approved the Governor's initial plan to set up a committee to supervise the zemstvo's activities and to cooperate with it in the work of relief,[40] but the Ministry was cool to any measures which would exclude the zemstvos from the picture altogether. On July 1 Durnovo addressed a confidential letter to Baranov discussing the proposal the Governor had made on June 25. The Minister found Baranov's scheme to be "in direct contradiction to the existing laws governing food supply and the many interpretations [of those laws] made by the Committee of Ministers and approved by the Emperor." He reminded the Governor that the zemstvos could be relieved of their lawful functions only in cases of complete inactivity or gross malfeasance. Since Baranov had failed to present any evidence of zemstvo mismanagement, Durnovo stated that he could not agree to any diminution of zemstvo powers. The Minister requested Baranov "not to delay the transfer of the sums . . . assigned into the hands of the zemstvos," and he concluded his letter by expressing confidence that as a result of the friendly cooperation between the zemstvos and the provincial administration, "the present food supply difficulties . . . [would] be solved with complete success."[41]

Durnovo's rebuff put an end, for the moment at least, to Baranov's plan to take personal control of relief operations in Nizhni-Novgorod province. But the Governor still might have sought to dominate the struggle against the famine by means of his own special committee had he not encountered resistance from the provincial zemstvo, which met in extraordinary session on July 1. In his speech to the opening meeting of the assembly, Baranov told the delegates that he had already established a special temporary committee composed of administration and zemstvo personnel. This committee, he continued, would examine all requests for aid and, after having evaluated them, pass its conclusions on to the MVD. Baranov stated that his committee would work to insure the fruitful cooperation of the government and the zemstvos in putting relief programs into effect.[42]

But although Baranov assured the delegates that the establishment of his special committee was in no way designed to limit the role of the zemstvo in the work of relief, the assembly remained suspicious. A proposal from the *uprava* to set up a special zemstvo commission to handle the very problems which Baranov would have assigned to his own committee was greeted with general approval.[43] On July 3 the assembly authorized the establishment of the commission proposed by the *uprava*, and ordered that its membership include not only zemstvo people but also *uezd* marshals and representatives from the *kazennaia palata* and the *udelnaia kontora*. This body was to work in conjunction with the *uprava* in managing all aspects of relief work in the province.[44]

The decisions of the extraordinary zemstvo assembly put Baranov in a difficult position. The formation of a rival zemstvo food supply commission rendered the Governor's committee superfluous and threatened to bring about an embarrassing clash between the administration and the zemstvos. Moreover, the zemstvos' right to control food supply operations was guaranteed by the *ustav narodnogo prodovol'stviia* and supported by the MVD. There was nothing Baranov could do but yield. On July 5 he accepted the offer extended by the zemstvo commission to join in its meetings, and he announced that he would disband his own committee.[45] On the same day, Baranov wrote to the Ministry of Internal Affairs informing it of his actions and stating that

> . . . if I see a guarantee of a firm link between the [zemstvo] . . . commission and the local marshals of the nobility, the *zemskie nachal'niki*, and the *ispravniki*, I propose . . . to turn over to said commission the remainder of the grain I acquired and [the responsibility for the execution] of all temporary measures I adopted to feed the hungry.[46]

Despite his defeat at the hands of the assembly, Baranov remained on fairly good terms with the zemstvo during the summer months, at least to the extent of giving its requests for state aid considerable support. In his statement accompanying the zemstvo requests, Baranov, like most governors, argued that the estimates of need were probably exaggerated and certainly were based on insufficiently accurate data. Still, he felt that it would be foolish to reject the demands of the zemstvo out of hand. With regard to the zemstvo's request for a grant of 8,229,000 rubles, made at the July session of the assembly, Baranov proposed that the government accept the estimate at face value, but that it dole out the money in several moderately sized installments.[47] The MVD proved unwilling to grant more than a portion of the sums requested;[48] but Baranov kept up his pressure for more funds, incurring the displeasure of Vishniakov in the process.[49] When the zemstvo met in emergency session in August, the Governor informed the delegates of the MVD's reluctance to grant all that had been requested.[50] The Governor no doubt hoped that the zemstvo might modify its demands; but when the assembly stood firm, he presented its decision to the MVD. Baranov informed the Ministry that he did not fully support the zemstvo requests; but during the summer the Governor used his office to obtain almost 1 million additional rubles to finance relief work.[51]

Although Baranov maintained good relations with the zemstvos, he did not abandon his plan to centralize relief in the hands of the provincial administration. On September 28 the Governor again turned to Durnovo with a long letter, calling the attention of the Minister to the danger of famine and attacking the current system of managing relief operations. After outlining the perils of the present situation, Baranov launched into an attack on the zemstvos. He began by noting that the creation of these institutions in 1864 was a first step on the road from a monarchy to a republic, and if little progress had been made in that direction during the intervening thirty years, this was because, among zemstvo personnel, there were "fewer conscious revolutionaries than [there were] idlers, thieves and drunks."[52] Still, Baranov argued, the zemstvo had had considerable impact on life in the countryside:

> Its services [have been] great. The ruin of the villagers, the collapse of the provincial roads, the destruction of the grain storage houses, the corruption of the people by the example of endless thievery and disrespect for authority, etc. The present famine is also one of the contributions of the zemstvo because, to a large degree, it was brought about by the recklessness of zemstvo management.[53]

Baranov felt that the influence of the zemstvo had corrupted other institutions in the province, such as the marshals of the nobility, and had reduced their effectiveness in dealing with such problems as famine relief.[54]

Baranov argued that the powers currently granted to the governors were insufficient to meet the present crisis. In this report he portrayed the *nachal'niki* of the provinces as tragicomic figures, hemmed in by legal restrictions, and impossibly burdened with endless, bureaucratic busywork.[55] To remedy this situation, and to make possible the effective conduct of relief operations, Baranov proposed decisive action by the administration. He called for the establishment of a temporary governor-generalship for the famine-stricken provinces along the Volga. This institution would control all relief work in Kazan, Nizhni-Novgorod, Samara, Saratov, and Simbirsk provinces and would dominate both the zemstvos and private charity. Baranov admitted that such a measure would be a violation of existing statutes, but the times were serious and the lackluster performance of the zemstvos called for radical measures.[56] The Governor likened the struggle against famine to a military operation, and he argued that no Minister of War would attempt to conduct a campaign without first having secured complete unity of command.[57]

What the MVD's immediate reaction to Baranov's proposal was, is not certain.[58] But in the end, his idea for a temporary governor-generalship in the Volga provinces was rejected.[59] The Ministry of Internal Affairs preferred to play by the rules laid down by the *ustav narodnogo prodovol'stviia*. Durnovo no doubt recognized that Baranov's plan offered certain advantages, particularly the chance for the greater centralization of relief work. At the same time, the MVD also saw that a move by the government which ignored the prerogatives of the zemstvos could stir up a hornet's nest of opposition. It might alienate the zemstvo leadership and the liberal public to the detriment of the antifamine struggle as a whole. Moreover, such a step would politicize the food supply campaign, thus making impossible the strictly administrative approach to the crisis which the regime favored.

While rejecting Baranov's grandiose scheme, however, the MVD may have given the Governor an indication that it would support efforts on his part to achieve greater unity and administrative control of relief work at the provincial level. At any rate, Baranov decided to act. In early November, he reestablished his own food supply commission, making it the center of relief operations in the province. Under the Governor's direction the commission assumed powers far greater than those wielded by similar bodies in other *gubernii*.[60] The role of the Nizhni-Novgorod zemstvo was greatly reduced, and it was forced to assume the position of a spectator, occasionally fulfilling the duties assigned to it by the commission. The MVD, if it did not specifically authorize Baranov's move, did nothing to force the Governor to rescind his actions.[61]

Baranov's "*coup*" of November 1891 placed him at the head of all food supply operations in the province. During the winter and spring months, his views and personality left their mark on all aspects of relief work. Whether or not the Governor's move resulted in a more efficient relief campaign cannot really be answered (although the suggestion was hotly denied by the champions of the zemstvo cause). What can be said, however, is that Baranov, despite his enormous powers, was not able to secure the complete unity of action which he felt was so vital to the success of the struggle against famine. In the first months of 1892, the Governor had to cope with the resistance of a group of *zemskie nachal'niki* and other officials in Lukoianovskii *uezd* who had their own, very definite ideas of how relief should be managed. It was only with the very greatest difficulty that Baranov was able to end their opposition and bring them into line with his policies.[62]

The reason for Baranov's campaign against the zemstvo deserves some analysis and explanation. There is no doubt that the Governor was genuinely concerned that the zemstvo would not be able to rise to a challenge like the one posed by the famine; and like many bureaucrats, he had little patience with the zemstvo's involved process of gathering statistics on the needs of the province and the long debates in the assembly analyzing and approving the requests for aid.[63] Even through the Nizhni-Novgorod zemstvo had one of the best statistical departments in the country, Baranov distrusted the fruits of its research and favored the information acquired through administrative channels. But the Governor's distrust of the zemstvo does not seem to have been based on any political grounds. With the exception of his reference to the zemstvos as a first step on the way to a republic, Baranov's reports do not paint those institutions as a danger to the state, nor do his statements imply any disloyalty on the part of zemstvo personnel.[64]

Baranov's struggle against the zemstvo seems to have been caused, in large part, by the Governor's personal ambition, his striving for publicity, and the favor of his superiors. Many years after the famine, V. G. Korolenko accurately described this aspect of Baranov's personality. The Governor was, in Korolenko's words, "a flashy sort of person, not deep, but energetic, active, decisive, prepared to take any chance if it would turn attention to himself, a real gambler by nature, willing to risk his career."[65] Baranov's service record bears out Korolenko's evaluation. The Governor began in the naval service and saw action in the Turkish war of 1877–78 where he commanded the steamer *Vesta*. On the basis of his own account of his action against the enemy, he was raised in rank, decorated with the Order of St. George (fourth class), and assigned as *Fligel ad'iutant* to the Emperor. In May 1879 he was appointed temporary Governor-General of St. Petersburg.[66] Soon after Baranov's appointment, however, it was discovered that the statements he had written concerning his exploits during the war were false. He was put on trial before a naval court, found guilty, and forced to retire from the service.[67] Despite this disgrace, Baranov bounced back. Barely three months after he left the navy, he was appointed to a post in the army with the rank of colonel. In September 1880 Baranov was chosen Governor of Kovno province, and in March 1881, in the wake of the assassination of Alexander II, he was appointed *gradonachal'nik* of St. Petersburg.[68] Baranov was active during the suppression of the *Narodnaia Volia*, but toward the end of 1881 his star began to fade. He was shunted off to be Governor of Arkhangel'sk, and in 1882 he was moved to a similar post in Nizhni-Novgorod province.

Having tasted the heady wine of great power, it is understandable that Baranov was eager to curry favor with the central authorities. He no doubt saw in the famine an opportunity to further his career. By his attack on the zemstvo, Baranov hoped to gain the support of the MVD which was, in general, suspicious of these institutions. When he proposed the special governor-generalship for the stricken provinces, it is hard to imagine that Baranov did not see himself in that post. After his bid to become "dictator" of the famine region failed, Governor Baranov tried another tactic to gain the attention he sought. Using the Nizhni-Novgorod food supply commission as his sounding board, he became a prominent spokesman for massive aid to the needy. The Governor gave wide publicity to the work of the commission and succeeded in acquiring a reputation as a leader in the struggle against famine. He even came to be regarded as something of a "liberal" in view of his willingness to employ politically suspect persons as representatives of the commission.[69] This latter tactic may have helped the conduct of relief work in Nizhni-Novgorod and in the country as a whole, but it did not win Baranov any promotions.[70] He continued in his post as governor of Nizhni-Novgorod until 1897.[71]

Neither the slowness of Poltaratskii's response to the famine nor the "energy" which characterized Baranov's activities was typical of the performance of the governors during the crisis of 1891–92. In the main, the actions of most governors fell somewhere between these two extremes. Most took an active part in the work of relief, touring their provinces and seeking to encourage the efforts of the zemstvos and private charity. On the whole, relations between the *guberniia* administrations and the zemstvos were correct if not cordial. Although the governors often disputed the accuracy of the zemstvos' estimates of need and preferred to work through the provincial food supply conferences, they seldom attempted to squeeze the zemstvos out of the business of famine relief. When conflict occurred between the zemstvos and the administration, it usually happened at the *uezd* and district level. Direct clashes between the governors and the provincial assembly or *uprava* were rare.

Few governors sought to dominate the relief operations in their provinces the way Baranov did. The majority would probably have assumed a position close to that expressed by Governor Rokasovskii of Tambov in his analysis of the proper way to organize relief:

> Such a huge task . . . as the providing of food for the mass of needy persons in the whole province, could be accomplished only by the widescale decentralization [of relief]. The guiding organ was the special food supply conference, composed of representatives of the state and the zemstvos . . . under the chairmanship of the governor. Then, to aid the economic institutions in the task of famine relief, the *zemskie nachal'niki* were drawn into the work. To the provincial and *uezd* zemstvo *upravy* belonged the management and disbursal of the millions of rubles assigned for the food supply operation. [These institutions were responsible for] . . . the delivery of the grain . . . to the areas stricken by the crop failure, in accordance with the needs of the *uezdy*, . . . the demands of the government and the decisions of the provincial zemstvo assembly.[72]

This more cautious approach to the problem of organizing relief work found general acceptance throughout the famine region. For although it lacked the advantages that stricter centralization might have provided, it avoided the possibility of a bitter clash between the administration and the zemstvos. Moreover, the MVD and most governors felt that it would be impossible to cope with the crisis by bureaucratic means alone, and favored a plan whereby all elements in the province would be allowed to play a part in relief work under the general supervision of state officials.

When we turn to an examination of the work of the provincial zemstvos in the struggle against the famine, we find considerable variation both in the scope of their activities and in the energy with which they approached the task at hand. These differences were, in no small part, the result of decisions made by the governors, but they were also caused by the peculiarities of the local situations and the capabilities of the leadership of the zemstvos themselves. Despite the many differences, however, all provincial zemstvos assumed a number of obligations in the work of relief. The first and probably most important task was the gathering and evaluation of data on the state of the harvest, the condition of the population, and its needs in terms of seed and food for the coming year. On the basis of the figures they obtained, the zemstvos then requested loans from the central authorities to finance relief operations. Once the money had been received, the zemstvos together with the provincial food supply commissions would decide how it would be used to meet the needs of the population. The zemstvos also assumed the responsibility of purchasing the bulk of the grain required by the province. Most of these purchases had to be made at some distance from the affected *gubernii* because the crop failure had produced high prices on local grain markets. Finally, after the purchases had been made, the zemstvos undertook to arrange the delivery of the grain to the stricken areas in their provinces and exercised general supervision over its distribution to the needy.

The gathering of statistical information on the state of the province and the needs of its people was necessarily a difficult task. The problem was further complicated by the fact that speed was essential if the zemstvos were to be able to begin relief operations in time to head off disaster. The process of assessing the needs of the provinces for food and seed began almost as soon as the danger of a crop failure became apparent, usually in June but sometimes as early as the end of May.[73] The initial figures came from the *volost' pravleniia* and were usually based on estimates made by the local communes. These data were collected and evaluated by the *uezd upravy* and passed on to the *uezd* assemblies for further examination. The *uezd* assemblies in turn drew up their own estimates of the needs of the population, and submitted them to the provincial *upravy*. The *guberniia upravy* scrutinized these figures once again, and when the provincial assemblies met, they were presented the requests of the *uezdy* together with a *doklad* expressing the provincial *uprava*'s views of the situation. The provincial assemblies rarely accepted the reports of the *upravy* straight away. In most cases, special commissions were set up to examine the figures once more and to make their own recommendations to the assemblies.

The care with which the estimates of need were examined by the provincial assemblies was fully justified because the requests made by the *uezd upravy* were often exaggerated and were derived from the sketchiest kind of information. The methods used by local people to determine the amount of seed and food the population would require during the coming year varied considerably. The procedures employed were often quite complex, but few were notable for their precision. The requests for seed were usually based on estimates of the size of the spring harvest. But since, in many cases, the survey of the spring fields was made at a time when the outcome of crops was far from certain, the accuracy of local estimates was suspect. The food supply needs of an *uezd* were often determined by first calculating the *nedobor*, the difference between the normal grain consumption of the peasants and the amount of food the harvest was expected to provide. Once the *uezd's* deficit in terms of grain had been estimated, this figure was corrected by subtracting the quantity of food available in local storage houses from the total amount of extra grain required. Information on the amount of employment that might be available to the population was also used to supplement this basic figure. But even these rough estimates were not always forthcoming from the *uezdy*. At the time of the first extraordinary sessions of the provincial assemblies (July 1891), certain *uezdy* could present only partial data on the needs of the population, and some gave no information on how their figures were obtained.[74] It is not surprising then, that the provincial *upravy* and assemblies reacted with some skepticism to the initial figures from the *uezdy*, and in most cases reduced them considerably.[75] Little wonder, too, that the governors and the MVD remained dubious despite the corrections made by the provincial assemblies.

Most of the zemstvos realized that their projections of the needs of their provinces were only approximate, and they were aware that these estimates would have to be further refined. The zemstvos therefore accepted without much protest the sums assigned by the MVD to meet the immediate requirements of the provinces for seed grain, even though the government grants were usually smaller than the zemstvos had requested. At the end of the summer, when the central authorities demanded new and more accurate figures on the amount of food loans that would be needed, the zemstvos met again in emergency sessions to make new requests.[76] New data were received from the *uezdy* and again were subjected to careful scrutiny. At the regular yearly sessions of the provincial assemblies (usually held in December), the revised estimates of need were again discussed and supplemental requests were made. Many zemstvos met in special session during February to review the situation and correct the figures once more.

Even after the zemstvo figures had been checked and rechecked, there remained considerable doubt as to their accuracy. During the famine year, this question was vigorously debated, both within the government and outside it. The MVD, as we have noted, was initially skeptical about zemstvo requests for aid and preferred to accept the more modest estimates of need provided by the governors. Later, the Ministry adopted a more flexible stand, and on some occasions granted aid in excess of the original zemstvo requests. Among the educated public, the discussion of the accuracy of zemstvo figures brought "liberals" and "conservatives" into conflict, the former siding with the zemstvos and the latter backing the views expressed by the MVD.[77]

The distance of eighty years does not help the historian to make a definitive statement about the accuracy of zemstvo requests. The main difficulty preventing any final judgment on this question is that we have no other statistics on the needs of the population with which to compare the zemstvos' estimates. As a result, we are forced to calculate the accuracy of zemstvo figures on the basis of how closely they approximated the government's final grants. This is hardly a satisfactory method, since it would seem to support the rather dubious contention that, in the end, the government gave out the proper amount of aid. Still, the ultimate figures on government loans are not totally useless as a yardstick against which to measure the precision of zemstvo estimates. The MVD was continually being brought up to date on the situation in the countryside, and once it had become convinced of the seriousness of the situation, it was prepared to go to considerable lengths to prevent starvation among the peasantry. Thus, while the amount of relief the government finally granted did not meet the full requirements of the stricken population, it can be taken as a kind of "minimal norm" for the needs of the famine area.

Using this rather inadequate guideline, we can evaluate the results of the investigations made by the three zemstvos for which we have gathered detailed information. It would seem that the zemstvos of Nizhni-Novgorod and Tambov overestimated the minimal needs of the population, although their approximations were rather close.[78] On the other hand, the Kazan zemstvo appears to have seriously underestimated the requirements of the local peasants, especially in the initial phase of relief operations.[79] These rather uneven results—an overestimation in one province, an underestimation in another—were probably typical of zemstvo calculations as a whole. The final statistics on relief operations show that, overall, the zemstvos purchased more grain than they could actually use. When the food supply campaign ended, the zemstvos of the seventeen famine-stricken provinces had a surplus of slightly under 6.5 million *pudy* of grain.[80] But the fact that three provinces—Saratov, Tambov, and Voronezh—were responsible for the bulk of this surplus (over 4.6 million *pudy*), would seem to point to the relative accuracy of most zemstvo estimates.[81]

It is interesting to note that the most sophisticated methods used by the zemstvos to calculate the needs of the population could not prevent error. Even the Nizhni-Novgorod zemstvo, which had an excellent statistical bureau and had worked out a rather complex system for arriving at its estimates,[82] missed the mark although by less than other zemstvos. Several factors help to account for these discrepancies. First, many zemstvos made their original estimates before the MVD had issued its guidelines on the size of food and seed loans which provided for grants somewhat smaller than those projected by the zemstvos. Second, the task of gathering accurate information on the needs of the population was complicated by the peasants' insistence that loans be given out to all the members of a given commune. This view often crept into the figures prepared at the *volost'* level, especially at the early stages of the relief campaign, and led to considerable distortions in initial estimates. Finally, the problem of determining the size of the loans required from the central government was made even more difficult by the steady rise in grain prices throughout the famine region, something that could not be estimated with any certainty at the time the first requests for aid were made. The sharp jump in prices threw off many calculations, and may account for the fact that a number of zemstvos requested less money from the government than they actually needed.[83]

Once the estimates of need were made and the funds began to be received from the MVD, the zemstvos turned their attention to the task of purchasing the grain required by the population. This work presented enormous problems, for which the zemstvos were poorly equipped. The first difficulty was a general lack of experience in the area of the grain trade. Moreover, the conditions under which grain had to be purchased were different from those of more normal times. In the past, food supply crises had tended to be localized. The quantity of grain which had to be purchased was small and could usually be obtained within the affected province or close by. In such cases, the *uezd upravy* ordinarily took on the responsibility of buying the needed supplies. In 1891, however, the picture was radically altered. The almost total crop failure in the black earth region and the accompanying sharp rise in prices forced the zemstvos to look far afield for the grain they required. In this situation, the provincial *upravy* generally took over the task of procurement. Zemstvo personnel and specially commissioned agents were dispatched to distant markets. In the end, over half of all grains purchased to meet the needs of the population of the seventeen most hard-hit *gubernii* was bought outside the borders of the provinces involved.[84]

The structure of the zemstvos did not make the task of grain purchase easy. The government's past unwillingness to permit the zemstvos to establish a nationwide organization now proved a major stumbling block to the success of relief operations. The lack of a centralized directing agency to coordinate grain purchases meant that each zemstvo had to act independently, with only the interests of its own province in mind. This state of affairs led to competition and conflict between zemstvos, of which the Viatka episode[85] is perhaps the most striking example. A more usual form of competition among zemstvos was found on the various grain markets of the country where the rivalry between the representatives from different provinces produced a sharp rise in the price of food stuffs. The central government offered little guidance to the zemstvos, especially in the early phase of relief work. Toward the end of 1891, however, the MVD began to take steps to eliminate the virtual anarchy on the nation's grain markets. It started to issue circulars advising the zemstvos on where they might purchase grain profitably and encouraging them to buy food supplies close to home, preferably within their own provinces.[86] The Ministry tried to foster greater cooperation among the zemstvos. In the Caucasus, I. I. Kabat, an agent of the MVD, set up a syndicate of zemstvos representatives. The syndicate put a ceiling on the prices zemstvos would pay for various grains, and dispatched agents to purchase grain in other areas of the Empire.[87] For the most part, however, the zemstvos continued to operate on their own; but sometimes they obtained the help of local institutions in provinces not affected by the crop failure.[88]

Despite the many difficulties they faced, the zemstvos and their agents succeeded in acquiring huge quantities of grain. But the problems of the zemstvos did not end there, because the delivery of the grain to the needy areas proved extraordinarily troublesome. Not the least of the obstacles facing the zemstvos was the railroad crisis, in large part brought about by the zemstvo grain purchases themselves. The snarl of traffic on the railways threatened to delay the arrival of the grain to such a degree that it might prove impossible to distribute it to the peasants before they actually began to starve. It took the direct intervention of the central government to remedy this situation.

Even after the grain arrived in the provinces, the problems involved in delivering it to the population were enormous. In numerous instances, grain was dumped at the railheads without bags to put it in and containers had to be found before it could be carted away. During this phase of the operations, a shortage of manpower hindered zemstvo efforts. In many *uezdy*, as a result of insufficient food, the population was not in a condition to assist in the work of transporting grain to their villages.[89] In other areas, the menfolk had left the villages to seek work in the cities or in provinces where there had been better harvests. All that remained behind were old people, women, and children. Even where there were men available, it was hard to find persons equipped to carry out the task of moving the grain to where it was needed. As a result of the poor harvest, a large number of peasants had sold their horses and those animals that remained were often too weak to pull large loads. Enough men and horses were usually found to complete the task however. There were, of course, delays in the delivery of grain to the villages, but these seem to have been the exception rather than the rule. In the majority of cases, what delays there were do not seem to have worked unbearable hardships on the population.[90]

The zemstvos' management of the grain purchases for the needy came under sharp attack during the famine crisis. Their critics argued that the zemstvos' unorganized buying techniques led to confusion, unnecessary price rises, and difficulties on the railroads. It was also charged that since the zemstvos were inexperienced in the grain trade, they were often cheated and sold grain that was unfit for human consumption.[91] In both cases these criticisms were partially justified. There is no question that the zemstvos' grain purchases were unorganized, but this was hardly their fault since the establishment of regular communications between provincial zemstvos had long been forbidden. As for the quality of the grain they purchased, there were, of course, instances where the zemstvos bought food that was spoiled or contained large amounts of impurities. But these cases were rare, and on the whole the peasants were able to make use of the grain they received with no difficulty.[92]

One aspect of the zemstvos' role in making grain purchases deserves censure. This was the failure of the zemstvos to make a proper assessment of the amount of grain available for purchase locally and their tendency to buy large quantities of grain in other famine-stricken provinces. The final statistics on grain purchases and relief, compiled by the Central Statistical Committee of the MVD, show this clearly. Kazan, for example, purchased almost 3.5 million *pudy* of grain in other provinces affected by the crop failure; Samara obtained over 1 million *pudy* this way. Perm acquired 750,000 *pudy* of grain in famine *gubernii*, while Penza bought over 500,000 *pudy* in similar circumstances. At the same time, the zemstvos in many famine provinces ignored available food supplies at home and let agents from other provinces take advantage. Thus Saratov, one of the hardest hit provinces, exported over 1 million *pudy* of grain to meet the needs of other *gubernii*; Samara exported about 750,000 *pudy*, and Tambov and Kursk 500,000 *pudy* each.[93]

Had the zemstvos in these provinces been better aware of the conditions on the local grain markets, they might have been able to avoid some of the cost and delay involved in shipping in grain from other areas. But here again the weakness of the zemstvo machinery, and not the indifference of zemstvo personnel, was the major cause of the problem. The lack of a small zemstvo unit at the *volost'* or village level made it difficult for zemstvos to follow the operations of the *kulaks* and the *skupshchiki* and so keep track of where local supplies of grain were being held.

In summing up our survey of zemstvo activity in the work of relief, we should note that despite the many criticisms leveled at their actions, in only one case did the government feel it necessary to relieve a provincial zemstvo of its obligations with regard to food supply and turn the whole matter over to the administration. The exception in this regard took place in Samara. There the provincial zemstvo seriously underestimated the amount of need in the province and, as a result, the original grants from the MVD were much smaller than required. The purchase of grain was badly organized, and the zemstvo exercised little control over its agents. The distribution of food to the needy was poorly administered; removal of grain from the railheads was very slow.

When these insufficiencies came to the attention of the MVD in early November, it dispatched a special representative, A. I. Zvegintsev, to make an on-the-scene investigation. Zvegintsev's report, submitted to Durnovo on November 14, 1891, was highly critical of the Samara zemstvo and bore out many of the charges of mismanagement that had been made earlier. Zvegintsev stated that the zemstvo had failed to make clear the degree of need among the population and had been derelict in establishing accurate lists of those who should receive loans. He also noted that the members of the provincial *uprava* failed to pay adequate attention to their tasks and neglected vital aspects of relief work.[94] As a result of this report, Durnovo turned to the Emperor with the recommendation that the Governor of Samara, A. D. Sverbeev, be empowered to assume control over relief operations, working when necessary through the *zemskie nachal'niki* and the zemstvos. The Emperor approved the measure, and on November 20, 1891 Governor Sverbeev was ordered to take charge of food supply matters in the province.[95]

Administrative control of famine relief in Samara continued until the crisis had passed, but whether state officials proved more competent than the *zemtsy* is open to question. To be sure, the number of persons recieving aid rose sharply in December and in the months that followed. By the end of the relief campaign, more people had been given food loans in Samara than in any other province.[96] But Samara's death rate was also the highest of all the famine-stricken *gubernii*, 56 percent above normal.[97] The increased mortality undoubtedly reflects the seriousness of the situation in the province and may have been caused in part by the inadequacy of early zemstvo measures. Still, the death rates show that the government, too, was unable to tame the famine completely.

In most *gubernii* the food supply conferences were dominated by the administration, and, naturally enough, reflected the views of the governors.[98] Their primary functions were to supervise zemstvo operations and to coordinate the work of these institutions with the efforts of the representatives of the administration, especially the *zemskie nachal'niki*. In the main, the conferences did not control food supply operations in the provinces, but rather sought to provide a channel for information and a forum for discussion of the problems of relief. The conferences regularly reviewed the estimates of need drawn up by the zemstvos and local relief workers, and they kept track of the general course of events. Besides evaluating the strengths and weaknesses of relief work in the provinces, the conferences were very important in the process of obtaining supplemental grants from the central authorities. Because the conferences met fairly regularly (at least once or twice a month), they could present the MVD the latest estimates on the condition of the province, the needs of the population, and the course of relief operations. Moreover, because the administration played a major role in the work of the conferences, their decisions and recommendations undoubtedly were more "credible," from the point of view of the *chinovniki* at the center, than were opinions of the zemstvos.

The Nizhni-Novgorod food supply commission was an exception to this rule. Thanks to the influence of Governor Baranov, this institution came to dominate all aspects of relief in the province. Not only did it exercise surveillance over the work of the various organizations working to aid the needy but it also sought to map out a complete strategy for the struggle against the famine. Its concerns included food supply, medical aid, public works, and even private charity. Unlike most food supply conferences, the Nizhni-Novgorod commission set up a firm organizational structure which reached into the *uezdy* and districts. In each *uezd* a local food supply commission was established to coordinate the work of the zemstvos and the *zemskie nachal'niki* and to act as a liaison between the central body and the relief workers in the scattered villages.

To give a detailed account of the work of the Nizhni-Novgorod food supply commission would be to write a complete history of relief operations in that province. This would add little to the description provided in the writings of V. G. Korolenko.[99] However, one fact which has already been mentioned deserves to be stressed. Despite Governor Baranov's hostility to the zemstvos and his intention to use the commission as a means of curtailing their power and authority, he was not entirely successful. He was, to be sure, able to limit the scope of zemstvo activity, and make the *uprava* subordinate to the will of the commission. But his attempt to challenge the moral authority of the zemstvos, especially the validity of their statistics on the harvest and the needs of the population, failed.[100] Indeed, the Nizhni-Novgorod food supply commission became something of a two-way street; and Baranov, having successfully subdued the zemstvos, became a convert to the zemstvo position on the degree of need of the population. This brought the Governor into conflict with the nobility and the *zemskie nachal'niki* in Lukoianovskii *uezd* who disputed the zemstvo estimates that sought to reduce food and seed loans to an absolute minimum. In the end, Baranov, who began by intending to use the commission to subordinate the zemstvos to the administration, wound up by leading a campaign against a group of local officials in the name of zemstvo statistics! To understand how such a strange development—the open conflict between a provincial governor and officials normally subject to his control—could take place, we must turn to an examination of the conduct of relief operations at the lowest level.

chapter ten

RELIEF IN THE PROVINCES: THE WORK OF LOCAL INSTITUTIONS

The conduct of relief work at the local level was the key to the success of the entire food supply campaign. No matter how officials at the center formulated overall policy, and no matter what measures provincial institutions adopted to implement the decisions taken in the capital, it was local relief workers who had to make the crucial decision: who will eat. The St. Petersburg *sanovniki* who worried about establishing general guidelines on seed and food loans and the *guberniia* officials and provincial zemstvo personnel concerned with grain purchases were dealing with abstract problems or, at best, only with things. At the village level, relief workers came face to face with famine. They had to confront, almost daily, the spectacle of real need—bloated bellies, pinched faces, pleas for aid. They knew that the measures they adopted could mean the difference between life and death for scores of persons.

Three institutions shared the burden of managing local relief: the *uezd* zemstvos, the *zemskie nachal'niki*, and the charitable committees (*popechitel'stva*) which on occasion handled both public and private relief. But the law did not define with any precision the roles that each of these institutions were to play during a food supply campaign and, as a result, there were considerable differences in the way relief was handled in various districts. As with the governors, a great deal seems to have depended on the personalities and capabilities of the people involved. In areas where the *zemskie nachal'niki* were particularly vigorous, they might concentrate relief in their own hands. Similarly, an unusually active zemstvo *uprava* might assume the leadership during the crisis, especially when the land captains proved unable to handle the job completely. In some cases, the head of a local charitable committee might assume the task of giving out zemstvo as well as private relief.[1] Normally, a kind of division of labor was worked out, but some overlapping of functions and duplication of effort inevitably occurred.

The first and most important problem that confronted local relief workers was that of compiling accurate lists of the persons in need of aid. The first lists were made during the summer and early fall on the basis of *prigovory* (declarations) drawn up by the village communes and approved by the *volost'* administrations.[2] Later, the rolls were verified by a representative of the zemstvo and/or the *zemskii nachal'niki* of the district, usually by means of an on-the-spot check of the economic situation of the persons applying for relief. Sometimes the members of local charitable bodies got into the act, and the status of the needy might be investigated by as many as three separate groups of outsiders. It is not surprising that this process resulted in considerable discontent among the peasants.[3]

Yet from the viewpoint of those engaged in local relief work, this constant checking and rechecking seemed necessary. It was often extremely difficult for someone who was not of the peasantry to penetrate behind the veil of village life. The peasants were distrustful of strangers, and for the benefit of visiting officials would often claim that all the inhabitants of their villages were equally needy. Many peasants were seized by panic, and sought to hoard grain and hide it away.[4] Peasants often had vastly inflated notions as to the amount of aid they were going to receive from the government, thus increasing their eagerness to be included on the relief rolls. In November, a report published in a Nizhni-Novgorod newspaper noted that

> The fantasies of the peasants concerning government aid have reached such an extent that they expect all kinds of relief. Thus, for example, in Lukoianovskii *uezd* they are saying that with the onset of winter every peasant "soul" will be given one and a half *pudy* of salted fish, and every house [will receive] a *pud* of kerosene. In Arzamasskii *uezd* a rumor is circulating among the peasants that the Emperor has sent out a grant of thirty rubles for every "soul."[5]

Despite repeated warnings from provincial officials, such legends continued to proliferate.

Even after the basic lists of the needy had been drawn up, periodic inspection of the rolls proved necessary. During the winter and fall, many new cases of real need came to light. In a number of provinces the ranks of those requiring government and private assistance swelled steadily as peasant grain stores became exhausted and as many of the workers who left the villages to seek employment elsewhere returned empty handed. Accurate relief rolls were especially important because the funds available to local relief workers were generally limited. Despite the generosity of the central government, which granted about 150 million rubles to aid the victims of the famine, the sums available were not sufficient to satisfy completely the requirements of all those affected by the disaster. Early in the relief operations, the MVD had placed strict limits on the size of the loans to be given out by the zemstvos. The Ministry insisted that government aid was not designed to provide completely for those in need but was intended to help the peasants to weather the worst effects of the crop failure.[6] Those providing charitable relief were also hampered by lack of money; for although there was great clamor in Russian "society" about the need to help the famine stricken, the actual sums collected were not large, especially when compared to the size of government aid.[7] Thus, all those engaged in the work of helping the peasants were obliged to decide which of the many persons in need most required assistance. This situation caused moral and psychological agonies for many relief workers. The problem was described by Konstantin Arsen'ev, who visited Tambov province during the crisis:

> The necessity of *choosing* from among the needy, the necessity of *refusing*—this is the most terrible aspect of the situation of those selfless people who have assumed the burden of managing a rural soup kitchen. At a village soup kitchen in Kamenka, I myself saw two women tearfully, unceasingly beg for the enrollment of their family among those receiving aid. But to grant their request was impossible because there were several tens of households in the village which were in the same condition. There remained only to comfort . . . [the women] with a vague hope for the future, i.e., the opening of a new *stolovaia*.[8]

Given this situation, relief workers were understandably intent on excluding from the rolls anyone who might possibly be able to provide for himself. This concern was the primary motive for the repeated verifications of the relief lists. But these generous aims were not the only cause of such actions. Many zemstvo workers and land captains carried out revisions of the rolls with the intention of cutting public assistance to a minimum. In some cases they were encouraged in their economy by the provincial authorities.[9]

Once relief lists had been compiled, local workers had to supervise the division of the loans among the needy. The actual task of distributing the grain was usually carried out by the *volost'* administrations and village officials. The rules governing the disbursal of zemstvo loans varied in detail throughout the famine region. Essentially, however, the procedures adopted were almost identical to the following ones, used in Sviazhskii *uezd* of Kazan province:

> The lists of persons who are eligible to receive loans are drawn up, as required, in duplicate each month. Opposite the name of each householder on the rolls is noted the size of the loan he is assigned that month. The [zemstvo] *uprava* sends [these] lists to the *volost'* administrations [stating] that on a certain day [they are] to draw from a certain storehouse the amount of grain belonging to a [particular] commune . . . and to give it out on loan in accordance with the list. At the same time, . . . these orders are brought to the attention of the *zemskie nachal'niki*. . . . When the loans are received from the storehouse, the village *starosty* must be present in their capacity as representatives of the commune. Upon receipt of the grain, they [must] sign the back of requisition attesting to the fact [that they have been given] the required amount and that it is of good quality. . . . The grain which has been received is divided up either by the *volost' starshina* or his assistants . . . in the amounts stated on the lists of the *uezd uprava.* The signatures gathered from the communes [show] that the commune which has received the loan is obliged to return it under the terms of collective responsibility.[10]

The distribution of the loans among the peasants entitled to receive them was usually accomplished without great difficulty, but in some villages irregularities occurred. These generally took the form of giving out the grain to all peasants in a commune instead of just to the needy ones. The zemstvos and the land captains tried to put a stop to such practices, but there were many cases where the deceptions practiced by the communes went unnoticed.

The size and nature of zemstvo loans varied considerably during the course of the struggle against the famine. In the summer of 1891, grants were usually made in the form of seed to insure that the winter fields would be sown. At this time, the amount of food grain given out was small; in the period between July 1 and October 1, only a little more than 800,000 *pudy* were disbursed. During these months, about 1,270,000 people in the stricken provinces received food loans averaging slightly less than thirty *funty* per month.[11] Food relief operations in the countryside began in earnest during October, and thereafter the number of persons receiving loans rose steadily. By March 1892 well over 11 million people were being given aid. For the next three months food loans continued to be assigned to about the same number of persons.[12] Generally, the local relief workers followed the MVD's guidelines concerning the size of loans, and monthly grants averaged about thirty *funty* per "eater." Toward spring, however, many zemstvos requested permission to enlarge the loans in view of the increased work load the peasants would assume during the spring planting. The MVD was receptive to the idea, and permitted the zemstvos to be more flexible in the administration of relief. In the months from February to May 1892, the size of food loans generally exceeded the norms originally set by the Ministry.[13] With the coming of spring, over 27.7 million *pudy* of seed grains were given to the peasants.[14] Additional relief in the form of food for horses and other livestock was also dispensed. By the end of the food supply campaign, the zemstvos and government agencies had disbursed over 103.2 million *pudy* of grain.[15]

Although the *uezd* zemstvos, the *zemskie nachal'niki*, and the various charitable workers shared the task of managing local relief, almost all accounts of the famine year tell us that the greatest burdens were assumed by the *zemskie nachal'niki*. This should not be suprising, for as we noted elsewhere in this study, the zemstvos, which were legally in charge of food supply operations, lacked any direct institutional link to the villages.[16] On the other hand, the post of land captain had been created primarily to provide the state with a means for more direct intervention into the lives of the peasants. It was only natural then that during the crisis caused by the famine the *zemskie nachal'niki* would be used to help fill the gaps in the existing zemstvo structure. At an early stage in the food supply campaign, the MVD ordered the governors to draw these officials into the work of relief.[17] But a number of problems threatened to limit the effectiveness of the *zemskie nachal'niki*. First, the office itself was new (it had come into being in 1889), and many land captains had assumed their posts in the very year of the famine. They were usually inexperienced and often had not had sufficient time to become familiar with their districts.[18] Moreover, the powers of the *zemskie nachal'niki* and their relationships to other institutions in the countryside had not been clearly defined through practice. As a result, the land captains had considerable freedom of action in dealing with the crisis, and they often assumed functions which were not theirs strictly according to law. On a number of occasions this produced tension between the *zemskie nachal'niki* and the zemstvos, and even caused clashes with the regular *guberniia* administration.

Because the scope of the land captain's activities was so large and his powers so considerable, it is understandable that the personality of the individual official had a great deal to do with the success of relief operations in his district. As Count A. A. Bobrinskii noted in his report to the Special Committee,

> The *zemskie nachal'niki* play an important role in giving out [zemstvo] loans. Of course much depends on personality. Where the land captains are energetic and active, . . . the people always know a person to whom they can turn and know that there is a *nachal'nik* living nearby who is concerned with the needs of the population and will not permit the peasants to be ruined.[19]

It goes without saying that a land captain who was inattentive to his duties or abused his authority over the peasants would have a detrimental effect on the food supply campaign. But on the whole, the consensus of governors, MVD officials, representatives of the Special Committee, and zemstvo personnel was that the *zemskie nachal'niki* were extremely useful and that they rendered great service by cooperating with all elements engaged in the struggle against the famine. A typical evaluation of the work of the land captains was that given by Baron Rokasovskii, Governor of Tambov. He wrote:

> It is impossible not to recognize that only the existence of a responsible administrative [unit] close to the people, in the persons of the land captains, made it possible for the zemstvo to manage the difficult task of determining the needs of the population . . . [and] correctly and justly distributing the food and seed loans. The institution of the *zemskie nachal'niki* rendered a no less valuable service to the province in the matter of private charity. . . . In their districts, [the land captains] were the center and guiding spirit of [charitable work], and wherever possible assisted in the just disbursal of aid to the needy.[20]

There were, of course, many well-documented cases of *zemskie nachal'niki* making improper use of their powers and hindering the work of others. But generally, an appeal to a higher authority—usually the governor—would result in bringing the offending official into line.[21] The power of the governor to control the action of the land captains was, however, rather limited. The *zemskie nachal'niki* were appointees of the crown, not of the governors, and the latter could not remove them at their pleasure.[22] Thus, in the event of a conflict between a governor and the land captains of a given area, these local officials could defy the governor in much the same way as Governor Anis'in of Viatka was able to defy the

Ministry of Internal Affairs. Instances of serious conflict were rare, but the food supply campaign of 1891–92 saw one such incident. This occurred in Lukoianovskii *uezd* of Nizhni-Novgorod province, and became something of a *cause célèbre* during the famine year.

The "*lukoianovskaia istoriia*" did not simply involve the *zemskie nachal'niki*; the nobility of the area, including the *uezd* marshal, and even some zemstvo personnel also took part in the resistance to Governor Baranov and the Nizhni-Novgorod food supply commission. But the role of the land captains was especially important because they were in charge of the actual management of relief in the *uezd*. Until their opposition to the provincial administration had been broken, food supply operations could not proceed along the lines laid down by the Governor and his supporters.

The whole episode had its beginnings in a clash between the provincial zemstvo *uprava* and the Lukoianovskii *uezd uprava* over the amount of grain that would be needed to feed the population of the area during the winter. The provincial *uprava* argued that Lukoianovskii *uezd* would require 613,000 *pudy* of food grain, while the *uezd uprava*, supported by the local marshal of the nobility and the land captains, felt that 300,000 *pudy* would suffice.[23] The *uezd* food supply commission, which was dominated by the local nobility, backed the view of the *uezd* officials. The land captains, who controlled the distribution of local relief, tried to keep loans to a minimum. When one *zemskii nachal'nik*, a certain Boboedov, disagreed with the policy of the other *uezd* officials and increased the size of the loans being given out in his district, he was subjected to considerable harassment by his colleagues.[24]

In November and December, Governor Baranov supported the view of the *lukoianovtsy* and urged that relief loans be kept small; at one point he even suggested that the *uezd*'s estimates of need were excessive.[25] But the leadership of the provincial zemstvo continued to stand by the figures compiled by N. F. Annenskii and the statistical bureau of the *guberniia uprava*. They bitterly contested the attempt made by elements in the provincial food supply commission to revise the estimates downward.[26] In the meantime, however, a number of factors worked to change the Governor's mind about the situation in Lukoianovskii *uezd*. Reports submitted by persons who had toured the stricken areas (including Lukoianovskii *uezd*) pointed to mistakes and confusion in the handling of local relief. The most influential of these documents was that authored by I. P. Kutlubitskii, a permanent member of the provincial council (*prisutstvie*). Kutlubitskii found that in many districts the lists of the needy were inaccurately drawn, and there was no unified procedure for administering relief.[27]

In a somewhat later report to the provincial charitable committee, Kutlubitskii dealt specifically with the situation in Lukoianovskii *uezd*. "Extremely serious doubts must be raised concerning the estimates of the food supply [needs] of the *uezd*," he wrote. "They are based . . . on no precise norms, no firm data." Kutlubitskii stated that when the figures on the needs of the population were calculated, local relief workers had failed to take into account the possibility that the number of those requiring assistance might rise sharply. But just such a jump in local need had taken place in the last few months. Kutlubitskii also charged that the land captains of Lukoianovskii *uezd* had been slow to start local relief, and he noted that food loans had not been given out on any scale until December.[28] Kutlubitskii's negative view of the situation was supported by A. I. Zybin, who had toured Lukoianovskii *uezd* to survey the operation of charitable relief.[29]

The Governor's concern about the relief operations at the local level had been growing even before he had received the reports of Kutlubitskii and Zybin. As early as the first week of January 1892, Baranov had taken steps to secure greater unity in the management of food supply operations by appointing one man in each *uezd* (usually the marshal of the nobility) to assume general supervision of all relief work.[30] Toward the end of the month, the Governor sent a confidential letter to the *zemskie nachal'niki* stating that in case of emergency they could raise the size of the peasants' monthly grants above the thirty-*funt* norm established by the MVD.[31] Somewhat later, having heard the disturbing reports of those who toured Lukoianovskii *uezd*, and having heard that the local officials were actually denying the existence of real need among the peasants, Governor Baranov wrote to the Marshal of the Nobility, M. A. Filosofov, asking for clarification as to the actual situation in the *uezd*.[32]

Filosofov quickly responded to Baranov's inquiry. In a letter to the Governor he insisted that although there was real need in the area, the 300,000 *pudy* of food grain requested by the *uezd* zemstvo and food supply commission would suffice to meet the requirements of the population. Filosofov stated that the provincial zemstvo's assessment of the situation was incorrect, and he charged that the inaccurate statistics compiled by the zemstvo were the cause of all the criticism of relief work in the *uezd.*[33] Filosofov denied that there were any problems which local officials could not handle. He opposed permitting outsiders to come in to the *uezd* and set up free soup kitchens, even if they were working under the auspices of the provincial charitable committee. He felt that such measures would have a detrimental effect on local relief.[34]

Underlying Filosofov's view on how to conduct relief in Lukoianovskii *uezd* was his fear that disturbances among the peasantry might develop. He felt that the police functions of the local administration were every bit as important as the management of food supply operations. "Besides carefully attending to the reduction of [local] need," he wrote, "my task and that of my co-workers . . . is also to maintain order among the population and to paralyze the fermentation which is visibly being induced by underground activists who are making use of the favorable conditions in . . . [our] locality."[35] Filosofov was not able to buttress his argument by pointing to any overt cases of revolutionary activity, but he stated that he "instinctively felt" the presence of underground intrigue and insisted that measures had to be taken to prevent disturbances. The *uezd* marshal advised the Governor that the visits of outsiders to the area were undesirable, and he argued that Kutlubitskii's tour had upset the peace and quiet of the *uezd.*[36]

Filosofov's letter clearly illustrated the mood of those in charge of relief in Lukoianovskii *uezd*, and it demonstrated their reluctance to cooperate with the provincial institutions which were managing the food supply campaign. The message was not lost on Baranov, and he decided to take steps to remedy the situation. At a meeting of the provincial charitable committee on February 26, 1892, the Governor raised the issue of the refusal of the *lukoianovtsy* to open free soup kitchens in the *uezd.* Sensing Baranov's support for their efforts, the members of the charitable committee asked the Governor to enjoin the local officials from hindering the establishment of the soup kitchens. At Baranov's suggestion the charitable committee dispatched A. I. Guchkov and K. G. Rutnitskii to make a new survey of conditions in Lukoianovskii and other *uezdy.*[37]

Shortly after these developments, Baranov, who had now been completely converted to the zemstvo position on the needs of Lukoianovskii *uezd*, tried to persuade local officials to get in line with these views. In early March he penned an angry letter to M. A. Filosofov, vigorously attacking the conduct of relief in the *uezd*. The Governor complained that local officials were not keeping the provincial food supply commission up to date on the situation in the *uezd*, and that they had failed to supply reliable information on the needs of the population. He pointed out that until such information was forthcoming, the provincial bodies were morally and legally bound not to accept the estimates presented by the local people.[38] Baranov reminded Filosofov of the many reports pointing to the great need of the peasants and to the total collapse of their economy, but he noted that these facts were not at all reflected in the figures presented by the *uezd*.

But the question of the estimates of need was secondary. Baranov insisted that the main problem was that the giving out of aid to the peasants did not conform even to the norms set up by the *lukoianovtsy* themselves. The Governor noted that because current food loans were so small, only one-fifth of the grain the *uezd* had obtained for relief purposes had been disbursed by the middle of February. Moreover, one-half of all loans made in the *uezd* had been granted by one land captain, Boboedov. These figures, Baranov argued, showed the peasants in the other districts of the *uezd* were getting far from adequate care.[39] The Governor charged that the tight-fisted management of relief in the area had one of two causes. Either the *lukoianovtsy* intended to give out even less than the 300,000 *pudy* of grain they had originally requested, or they proposed to wait until the peasants had sold off all their property and had been completely ruined before stepping in to prevent actual starvation. The Governor stated firmly that neither of these alternatives was acceptable to the provincial administration.[40]

Baranov was unsympathetic to Filosofov's view that serious political disturbances threatened the province, and he noted ironically that it was hard to discuss such a problem on the basis of instinctive feelings. The Governor insisted that it was not necessary to explain the existence of "nervousness" among the population by conjuring up the "terrible spectre" of revolution. The real danger, Baranov wrote, was not the possibility of civil disorder but the failure of officials to meet the needs of the people. "In this terrible year of national disaster," he continued,

> . . . the most dangerous things are those which cause the people to despair and lead them to distrust the actions of officials. . . . No kind of propaganda could have such

a disastrous effect as the growth of the feeling among the people . . . that the Tsar's servants are not carrying out the will of the Tsar . . . but are more concerned with the interests of people who need cheap labor and who [find it] profitable to keep the peasants on the verge of starvation.[41]

Baranov hoped that his criticism of the *lukoianovtsy* would bring them into line with the positions taken by the provincial zemstvo and the food supply commission, but even before he could dispatch his letter he received news which indicated that the resistance of the local officials would continue. As a protest against the policy of the provincial administration in general, and especially the setting up of *stolovye* in his *uezd*, Filosofov wrote to the Governor announcing that he was resigning from his post as chairman of the *uezd* charitable committee. Filosofov proposed to hand this job over to A. L. Pushkin, a land captain who had distinguished himself by his "hard line" with regard to peasant demands for aid. This action was a direct affront to Baranov. The Governor firmly believed that charitable and zemstvo relief at the local level should be under the direction of a single person, and he had intended that the marshals of the nobility carry out this function. He saw Filosofov's resignation as an attempt to thwart this plan.[42] At this point, Baranov decided to bring the power of his office to bear on the situation. He parried the thrust of the *lukoianovtsy* by sending in his own man, V. D. Obtiazhnov, to take over the management of relief in the *uezd*.[43]

Obtiazhnov was not immediately able to eliminate all the obstacles hindering the development of relief in the *uezd*, but he did expand the scope of food supply operations considerably. In March the number of persons receiving food loans in Lukoianovskii *uezd* almost doubled (from 42,541 to 71,625), and the size of the average grant increased.[44] The opposition of local officials to the Governor and his agents continued, however, and in mid-April, Baranov complained to Durnovo about the situation, stressing the need to take decisive action against certain recalcitrant *zemskie nachal'niki*.[45]

In the meantime, the *lukoianovtsy* had found a powerful supporter in Prince Meshcherskii, the reactionary journalist. His newspaper, *Grazhdanin*, published a number of attacks on Baranov and his followers, and defended the position of the local officials. Especially damning was the charge—in this case a true one—that Baranov was permitting V. G. Korolenko and other persons under police surveillance to take an active part in relief work in Lukoianovskii *uezd.* As a result of these disclosures, Baranov's activities were reviewed by the MVD and Durnovo wrote the Governor questioning the advisability of letting such persons as Korolenko participate in the "ticklish business" of managing relief.[46] Baranov defended his actions and continued his attack on the *lukoianovtsy.*[47] He complained of the Ministry's lack of trust and requested permission to resign his post.[48] Baranov's stand caused the Minister to modify his position somewhat. On May 6, 1892, Durnovo hastened to assure Baranov that he was not under any kind of suspicion and urged him to stay on as governor.[49]

Durnovo's letter of May 6 undoubtedly strengthened Baranov's determination to continue the struggle against the *lukoianovtsy*. He was also compelled to push on by the steady stream of reports which complained of the dire conditions in the *uezd* and the obstructionism of local officials. Typical of this kind of information was a letter the Governor received from A. I. Guchkov. In the company of Obtiazhnov and another relief worker, A. Boldyrev, Guchkov had made an extensive tour of one of the districts of Lukoianovskii *uezd.* His impressions were disquieting indeed. "There is indescribable chaos in the work of relief," Guchkov lamented. "Everywhere [there is] the tyranny of the *starshiny*, *starosty* and clerks (*pisarei*); everywhere [there is] abuse, unjustified fits of passion [and] oppression."[50] The Governor responded quickly. Four days after receiving Guchkov's letter, Baranov announced to a meeting of the food supply commission that he had decided to relieve the *zemskii nachal'nik* of the district in question, a certain A. G. Zheleznov, of his authority over local food supply operations. The Governor stated that he was turning control of relief work in the district over to Guchkov.[51]

The Governor's show of force broke the backbone of the Lukoianov resistance, but sporadic opposition continued for a while longer. When Guchkov went to take over his new duties, he found Zheleznov unwilling to render any assistance. The land captain refused to supply written information on the economic conditions of the local peasantry, and he declined to turn over copies of the government orders and circulars which Guchkov needed to guide his work. After a long hassle, Zheleznov agreed to supply the required materials, but he continued to hinder Guchkov's work in other ways. Zheleznov encouraged the peasant *starosta* who was in charge of grain distribution to refuse to carry out Guchkov's orders.[52]

But Guchkov remained undaunted, and despite Zheleznov's opposition he was determined to forge ahead. In a letter to Baranov, written soon after he had assumed his post, Guchkov exuded confidence. He felt that he was succeeding in his struggle to repair the damage caused by past mismanagement, and he was generally optimistic about the future.[53] Unfortunately, we have no other documents on Guchkov's management of relief in Zheleznov's district. But the fact that Guchkov and his problems were not discussed at the meetings of the food supply commission would seem to indicate that things moved along fairly smoothly after he took over.

Having surveyed in detail the resistance of the Lukoianov nobility to the idea of expanded relief operations in their *uezd* and their defiance of Governor Baranov's authority, it might be useful at this point to attempt a brief analysis of their motives. The views of the *lukoianovtsy* are better understood when we consider the location of the *uezd*. Lukoianovskii *uezd* was in the southeastern corner of the province, far from the influence of Nizhni-Novgorod or any other large provincial town. In such a backwoods "nest," a conservative mentality, favoring the maintenance of patriarchal customs and hostile to any change, was likely to persist long after such views had ceased to be fashionable in other parts of the *guberniia*.

The conservative outlook of the Lukoianovskii *uezd* nobility undoubtedly influenced the way in which the local *zemskie nachal'niki* viewed their duties in the field of famine relief. During the crisis, their emphasis was certainly more on law and order than it was on welfare. As Filosofov's letter to Governor Baranov indicates, the Lukoianov nobles were concerned about the possibility of peasant disturbances, and they felt the need for constant vigilance. Moreover, in their devotion to the Tsar the *lukoianovtsy* were eager to save the state a kopek wherever possible. To be sure, government officials, notably Vishniakov, had encouraged such economies in the early phases of relief operations, but the Lukoianov group clearly carried "fiscal responsibility" to the extreme. The conservative outlook of the *lukoianovtsy* also helps to account for their distrust of outside relief workers who came into the area to aid the peasants. The attitude of the *lukoianovtsy* toward the agents of the provincial food supply and charitable committees was similar to the feelings of whites in the American South with regard to civil rights and antipoverty workers. These outsiders seemed a threat to the old ways, for they might infect the peasants with radical ideas. But local pride was also hurt. The nobles of Lukoianovskii *uezd* undoubtedly would have echoed the statement so often uttered by southern officials: "We treat our nigrahs [read peasants] good! We can handle our problems ourselves."

Economic self-interest may also help to account for the behavior of the *lukoianovtsy*. Their *uezd* was in the black-soil region; the possibility of profit from the land was high, and agricultural labor played an important part in the economy of the area. During the famine crisis, it was implied by Baranov and others that the *lukoianovtsy* opposed extensive relief because they wanted to ruin the local peasantry and thus insure a ready supply of cheap agricultural labor in the years ahead. But while this possibility may have crossed the minds of some of the Lukoianov officials, the desire for cheap labor was probably not a major factor in deciding their policy. The number of workers available in the *uezd* was already plentiful. The peasant population was the largest in the province, the size of their land allotments the smallest. Thus there was little incentive for the local nobility to further impoverish the peasants. For the foreseeable future there would be no shortage of willing hands. Moreover, if, as the result of the famine, the peasants were forced to sell all their work animals and tools, the value of their labor on the nobles' estates would be greatly reduced.

Provincial and *uezd* political conflicts probably had the greatest influence on the actions of the Lukoianov group. In the years before the famine, a bitter struggle had developed between the conservative nobility of the area, headed by the local Marshal M. A. Filosofov, and the *uezd* zemstvo which was then dominated by more liberal elements. The conservatives enjoyed the support of Governor Baranov, and in the elections which had preceded the famine year they had managed to gain control of the *uezd uprava*. The victorious conservatives installed new men who were subservient to the nobility. After their triumph, the Lukoianov conservatives were determined to keep the zemstvo from playing an important role in the life of the *uezd*.

When the famine occurred, and it became clear that the provincial zemstvo intended to see that the zemstvo organization as a whole would make a major contribution to the relief campaign, the *lukoianovtsy* were alarmed. They feared that the conduct of relief operations might revitalize the local zemstvo and strengthen its influence in *uezd* affairs. With this danger in mind, Lukoianov conservatives began a campaign to further discredit and demoralize the *uezd* zemstvo. (In this their actions paralleled those of Governor Baranov, who was simultaneously engaged in an attempt to undermine the authority of the provincial zemstvo.) In November, at about the same time as the Governor made his move to take over greater control of relief operations in the *guberniia* as a whole, the *lukoianovtsy* achieved a further triumph in their struggle with the local zemstvo. They intrigued against the chairman of the *uezd uprava*, N. D. Valov, whom they themselves had put in office but who now seemed insufficiently pliant, and charged him with corruption. They brought their case to the Governor, and Valov was suspended from his post. He was replaced by A. V. Priklonskii who had been an outspoken critic of past zemstvo performance.[54]

In their struggle with the *uezd* zemstvo, the Lukoianov group felt that they were pursuing a course of action approved by their superiors and which was in the best interests of the provincial administration and the Tsar. Thus when, at the beginning of 1892, Governor Baranov changed his position on relief, supported the zemstvo's assessments of the needs of the province, and criticized the conduct of relief work in Lukoianovskii *uezd*, the conservative nobility of the area felt betrayed. In a very real sense, the *lukoianovtsy* had been Baranov's creatures and had worked under his protection. Now a strange "reversal of alliances" left them isolated. The sight of Baranov joining forces with the zemstvos and attacking the views he had once supported, filled the *lukoianovtsy* with confusion and indignation. It was this mood, far more than economic interests or conservative political opinions, which caused their stubborn and bitter resistance to the Governor and the food supply commission.

The stormy history of Lukoianovskii *uezd* was hardly representative of the general course of relief operations throughout the country. In most areas, the work proceeded successfully or at least without dramatic incidents. Of the activities of the hundreds of local volunteer groups and charitable committees which dotted the countryside, we have only a general idea. Memoir literature on the work of these smallest relief bodies tends to be rather anecdotal, and if documentary evidence has survived at all, most of it is probably buried in provincial archives. The *fond* of the Special Committee on Famine Relief, however, contains the records of one charitable committee which managed relief in Iambirnskaia *volost'*,

Shatskii *uezd* of Tambov province. There is nothing which indicates that the experience of this committee was "typical" of any larger process, but, on the other hand, many of the problems which came up in Iambirnskaia *volost'* must also have been encountered in other areas. At any rate, a brief survey of the documents we have helps us to feel the fabric of the times and brings us a little closer to the many public-spirited persons who labored on the lowest level to ameliorate the conditions of their distressed fellow citizens.

The Iambirnskoe *popechitel'stvo* came into being in October 1891, after the *zemskii nachal'nik* of the district received orders to set up *volost'* committees to administer charitable relief under the auspices of the Red Cross and the governor's committee. The land captain asked one of the residents of the district, Alexander Sergeevich Norman, to head up a committee in Iambirnskaia *volost'*. At the same time, the *uezd* zemstvo asked Norman to oversee the distribution of zemstvo loans as well. Alexander Sergeevich agreed and immediately set to work organizing a local committee to assist him in his task.[55]

We know little about Norman. He was probably a landowner, and he was clearly a man of education, energy, and courage. The difficulties he faced were considerable. The population of the *volost'* was some 6500 souls, a large portion of which might be in need of assistance. The number of people Norman could rely on was small, for as he noted, "persons of the educated (*intelligentnye*) classes [were] not to be found in the *volost'*."[56] In this situation, Norman sought to make use of whatever local talent there was. He staffed his committee with four priests, one merchant, and a number of peasant landowners. At the first meeting of the committee on October 13, 1891, Alexander Sergeevich gave his co-workers a pep-talk. He sought "to explain to the members of the committee their duties and [what] a great value their modest service would be to the state and the motherland, and by this to inspire them to greater efforts."[57] Norman's words had the desired effect. The committee members attended to their tasks seriously and rarely missed meetings. Norman could always count on the attendance of at least fifteen or seventeen members at every session.[58]

The first major task assumed by the committee was the drawing up of accurate lists of those in need. At the meeting on October 13 it was decided to divide the requests for aid among the various members of the committee so that they could be examined in greater detail.[59] The process of verifying the lists took up the better part of a month, and at the session of November 6 it was decided that a total of forty-six families were needy enough to require charitable aid. The committee resolved to give small grants (here a total of thirty-seven *pudy* twenty *funty*). But it noted that the needs of the *volost'* were rapidly increasing, and it stated that the grain which had been received for relief purposes had already been distributed. The committee turned to the land captain of the district and requested an additional grant.[60]

The task of compiling the relief rolls did not stop with the drawing up of the initial list in October. The process of verifying the needs of the population was a continuous one. At every meeting of the committee the lists were examined and reexamined. Whenever it turned out that a person on the rolls had the means to provide for himself, his name was crossed off; at the same time, however, other names were added to the list. The procedure proved to be long and involved; meetings where the rolls were examined sometimes lasted as long as seven or eight hours.[61] In addition, Norman himself often met with other members of the committee on an informal basis to take up cases of need which arose between regular sittings.[62] This often resulted in an increase in the number of persons receiving aid.

The members of the committee strove to make their lists as fair as possible and to give aid only to those in need. On the whole, they were able to operate freely without outside interference, but they were required to follow the general guidelines on relief passed down to them by the *zemskii nachal'nik* and the zemstvos. At the local level, however, some of the peasants, aided by certain members of the committee, sought to influence the drawing up of the relief rolls. At the meeting of November 27 it was revealed "that members of the committee were disclosing the discussions of the committee to persons in need, telling [them] exactly which member spoke against [giving aid] . . . to this or that needy persons. . . ."[63] Although it was not explicitly stated in the journal, it is clear that the disclosure of the views of those members who opposed loans subjected them to a form of community pressure and the possibility of unpleasant consequences. The committee therefore decided that in future its decisions would be taken in secret.[64]

With the beginning of winter, the demands of the *volost'* rose steadily, and the amount of grain given out by the committee increased sharply. But the sums available to the committee did not rise as fast as the need. Despite the careful rechecking of the lists and the discovery of a number of cases of cheating,[65] the committee was increasingly hard pressed. The relief handed down by the land captain and the district committee was not able to fill the gap. In desperation, Norman decided to take matters into his own hands, and in January he appealed directly to the Special Committee in St. Petersburg.

In his letter, dated January 15, 1892, Norman outlined the structure of his committee and gave a brief account of its operations. He pointed out that one of the main reasons for the plight of his *volost'* was the fact that the zemstvo had fixed the size of its monthly loans at twenty-five *funty* per "eater," excluding men of working age and children under two years. The way in which the zemstvo managed relief made it extremely difficult to meet the needs of the people. In the first place, the grain given out under zemstvo auspices was of poor quality, containing considerable admixtures of barley and chaff. Secondly, the exclusion of workers and children under two from the rolls was unrealistic. The men of the *volost'* had been unable to find employment, and children continued to eat grain without reference to zemstvo norms. As a result, the average "eater" in households receiving zemstvo loans got less than one-half *funt* of bread per day. The *volost'* committee had investigated the situation carefully and had concluded

> . . . that it is a rare family which can supplement the zemstvo loan. . . . And it is unusual [to see] a household among those receiving loans where wheat, meat, and other victuals can be found. By the sale of their meager . . . belongings and clothes, many persons can only cover their needs for salt and kerosene . . . and pay the cost of transporting flour from the *uezd* town to the *volost'*.[66]

Norman stated that while he was empowered to give out aid when zemstvo loans did not suffice, he was hampered by a lack of resources. As a result, he was forced to limit grants to those families where there were no workers, and to persons who were alone or sick. The consequences of this policy were tragic, and Norman complained that he was "often saddened to see many . . . good peasants who get weaker day by day due to lack of food."[67] He concluded his letter with an appeal for additional funds, stating that any extra money his committee received would be spent wisely.[68]

Norman's appeal for help got a sympathetic hearing from the Special Committee. On January 23, Pleve, in his capacity as manager of the

Committee's business, wrote to Count Bobrinskii in Tambov, calling his attention to the plight of Norman and his co-workers.[69] Bobrinskii responded quickly, and shortly thereafter he visited Norman in the village of Iambirnoe. There they apparently worked out measures to meet the needs of the *volost'*. Bobrinskii gathered materials on the work of Norman's committee and forwarded them to Pleve in the capital. On Pleve's original letter, Bobrinskii penned a brief, confident assertion in red ink: "Norman's *popechitel'stvo* is now completely provided for. . . ."[70]

We have no further information on the work of Norman and his colleagues. Our documents end with the local committee's journal for February 24, 1892. It is fairly safe to assume that the *popechitel'stvo's* financial troubles were ended, because no more appeals for aid are found among the correspondence relating to Tambov province. Certainly the problems of other local relief bodies were not solved so easily. But of the difficulties these committees faced, of their successes and failures, we know little, because almost no data are available. We can only hint at an answer to this problem when we make a final evaluation of relief operations as a whole. And it is to this question that we will address ourselves in the final chapter.

chapter eleven

CONCLUSIONS

On February 25, 1892 the Committee of Ministers, surveying the work of the administration in the struggle against the famine, expressed its satisfaction with the course of relief. "Never," the Committee declared, "neither in Russia nor in any other state, has the concern of the central government for helping the population ruined by crop failure been so great and achieved so much as at the present time."[1] The historian may not wish to take the ministers completely at their word, but our study of official efforts to mitigate the effects of the famine clearly shows that many of the myths about the crisis of 1891–92 need to be set aside. Certainly the government did not ignore the disaster; for as early as January 1891 it was taking steps to ease the situation in the Volga and black earth provinces. Nor did the regime attempt to suppress all news of the crisis. To be sure, state officials were anxious that reports of the famine be accurate and non-inflammatory, but this did not prevent extensive coverage of the situation in the Russian press.

The idea that the response of government personnel to the crisis was characterized by panic, bungling, and general incompetence must also be modified. Despite hesitations and mistakes, the government succeeded in mounting one of the largest relief campaigns in Russian history. At the height of the disaster, over 11 million people were receiving supplemental rations under official auspices.[2] Moreover, the regime did not limit itself solely to the distribution of food supplies; it attacked the problem of aiding the needy from many angles. Of course, not all state measures were effective, as the history of Annenkov's public works project clearly demonstrated. Still the range of government activity was remarkable, exceeding by far official efforts in previous famines.[3] Nor does a comparison of Russian relief in 1891–92 with British operations in Ireland and India put the Tsarist regime to shame.[4]

As for the much vaunted efforts of "society" on behalf of the needy, these, too, must be seen in new perspective. The tremendous work of the zemstvos in combatting the famine cannot be denied. But during 1891–92 the zemstvos were not acting as private agencies. Rather they were adjuncts to the state, fulfilling tasks assigned to them by law. Moreover, the zemstvos could have done nothing had not the government made available almost 150 million rubles to finance food and seed purchases. The cooperation of state officials at all stages of relief work was essential. This was especially true at the local level, where the proper distribution of supplies would have been extremely difficult without the assistance of the *zemskie nachal'niki*.

Purely private efforts seem small indeed beside the extensive relief work carried out under the government's aegis. The weakness of the measures taken by the Russian public was noted even by those who had no love for the regime of Alexander III. In an illegal proclamation issued during the crisis, N. K. Mikhailovskii gave a quite complete list of government actions and then commented: "But the reaction of 'society' to the famine has been sluggish (*vialym*)."[5] In the end, Mikhailovskii insisted that the people could do a better job than state officials; but this was an expression of faith rather than a realistic assessment of the situation.[6]

The size and scope of government relief measures are impressive; but when we attempt to assess their *effectiveness*, we are immediately faced with a difficult problem. Ideally, an evaluation of the success or failure of the food supply campaign of 1891–92 should be based on a thorough comparison between it and like operations in different times and places. This cannot be done, however, because few famines, either in Russia or in other countries, have been the subject of detailed examinations.[7] The paucity of information on famines generally, and particularly the absence of any overall study of past relief measures, means that there are few firm criteria for judgment which have been derived from previous experience. Nor can we rigidly apply the standards of modern relief operations to the events of 1891–92, given the advances in communications, transportation, medicine, and nutrition which have taken place since that time. Thus the historian must proceed cautiously, chastened by the realization that any evaluation he makes will be open to serious question.

In the absence of general criteria for judging relief operations, the best index of effectiveness would seem to be the mortality figures for the crisis period. But the use of demographic information is difficult because it is usually impossible to determine which deaths were famine-related and which were the results of other causes. In addition, the statistics on the death rates themselves are often extremely suspect. Consequently, many experts feel that attempts to arrive at firm conclusions regarding the effects of famine on mortality are likely to be fruitless.[8] Even when a particular famine has been the subject of extensive investigation, historians rarely attempt detailed analysis of its demographic impact.[9]

When we turn to the Russian famine of 1891–92, the reasons for scholarly caution become obvious at once. We possess fairly good data on mortality during the crisis, but there is considerable dispute as to their meaning and use. The question of the death rate is further clouded by the fact that very few cases of actual starvation were documented, and none were entered into official records.[10] The big killers in 1892 (the year which would show the immediate impact of the disaster) were, by all accounts cholera and typhus; yet the connection between these diseases and the famine is somewhat hazy.[11] In Russia, cholera and hunger were frequent traveling companions; but the disease had also appeared when there were no great agricultural difficulties.[12] Typhus was endemic to the Russian countryside, and so its presence cannot be blamed on a lack of food.[13]

There can be little doubt, however, that the number of those who died from both these diseases increased as a result of the famine. Malnutrition weakened many people, making them more susceptible to infection and less resistant to its ravages. More importantly, the movement of peasants in search of jobs and food helped spread sickness. Workers who crowded into provincial towns often contracted serious illness. When they returned home they would infect their families and neighbors. Wandering beggars, who were extremely common during the famine year, carried the typhus-bearing louse from village to village; they might also bring cholera.[14]

Because of the many factors which influenced the death rate in 1892, estimates of mortality vary extensively. The highest figure (and one which has gained considerable acceptance) lists about 650,000 dead as a consequence of the famine.[15] Yet this calculation is open to question. The estimate is for the nation as a whole, and it is extremely uncertain how many deaths outside the famine region can properly be attributed to the disaster. This is especially true given the coincidence of a massive cholera epidemic which claimed up to 300,000 lives in 1892 alone.[16] Thus for the purposes of accuracy and in order to assess better the value of relief operations, we should focus directly on the stricken provinces themselves. Even here the results are rough and tentative, but the margin for error is smaller.

According to information compiled by V. I. Pokrovskii,[17] the average death rate in the sixteen provinces of European Russia most severely affected by the famine, rose from 3.76 percent (the norm for the period 1881–90) to 4.81 percent in 1892. In absolute figures, the number of deaths in the famine-stricken *gubernii* during 1892 was about 406,000 above normal.[18] If the number of cholera deaths—103,364[19] for the area in question—is subtracted from abnormal mortality, the estimate can be reduced to around 303,000 deaths. Since a sizable portion of cholera mortality was undoubtedly famine-linked, however, this lower figure should not be accepted. An estimate that between 375,000 and 400,000 deaths occurred as a direct consequence of the disaster seems more reasonable.

The loss of over a third of a million people is appalling, and clearly indicates that the government's success in its battle with the famine was incomplete. Still, it is necessary to put these data on mortality in some kind of perspective. A decisive rise in the death rate is almost inevitable in any famine situation. Famine, as opposed to crop failure, is produced by a complex of socioeconomic forces, and reflects general rural poverty. Well before the crisis stage is reached, the population is living on the edge of hunger. Once a bad harvest occurs, consumption, already seriously low, drops sharply. Soon after, disease, if not actual starvation, begins to take its toll. In such conditions, not even the most massive relief program is likely to prevent an upturn in mortality. Given the seriousness of the crop failure of 1891 and the huge size of the afflicted region, the Russian government's ability to hold the overall rise in the death rate to between 25 and 30 percent[20] suggests that its performance, while not optimal, was at least acceptable.

Our favorable assessment of the Russian food supply campaign of 1891–92 is strengthened when we compare its results with those attained by British relief in India during the same period. This comparison is especially useful because British relief programs were generally admired even by those who opposed the English Raj.[21] Yet a cursory examination of the Indian Famine Commission reports for the 1890s presents a rather different picture. Even at their most successful, Indian officials could not prevent a rise in mortality of 20 percent in affected regions, and much higher increases were often noted.[22] During the famine of 1899–1900, which afflicted Central Provinces, Berar, Amjer, and parts of Bombay and

Punjab, death rates rose by over *300 percent* in some areas.[23] Moreover, although the commissioners judged relief to have been "excessive" in 1899–1900, state aid in India touched a far smaller percentage of the population of the famine tract than it did in Russia during 1891–92 (18 percent as opposed to about 30 percent).[24]

Beyond this, the experience of the two major famines which struck Russia in the twentieth century suggests that the *potential* for loss of life in 1891–92 was much greater than that which actually occurred. In 1921 a massive crop failure again blasted the Volga and black earth regions. The new Soviet government, just emerging from the trial of revolution, civil war, and foreign intervention, was unable to mount full-scale relief operations.[25] A major portion of the task of feeding the hungry was shouldered by the American Relief Administration led by Herbert Hoover. At the height of the crisis, the American agency was dispensing food to about 10 million persons,[26] a figure just slightly lower than the number obtaining state aid in 1892. Despite this, loss of life due to the famine was enormous. Reliable sources estimate that there were between 1 and 3 million victims of the disaster.[27] During the years 1932–33, another terrible famine ravaged the Ukraine, a region roughly comparable in size and population to the area stricken in 1891–92. No government aid was undertaken and, as a consequence, 5 million died.[28]

Thus the figures on mortality in 1891–92 when compared with those available for later "hungry years" seem to support the view that the efforts of the Imperial government were sufficient to limit sharply what could have been a truly disastrous rise in the death rate. The apparent absence of actual starvation should also be underlined as another indicator of the government's success, since in 1921–22 and 1932–33 deaths from hunger occurred on a large scale. Nor should the testimony of eyewitnesses and literature be ignored. Descriptions of the suffering which took place in 1891–92 are terrible and heart-rending, but they pale beside the scenes of human misery and degradation produced by the Russian famines of the 1920s and 1930s.[29]

The death rate alone, however, is not the only proper index by which to measure the Russian government's performance during the crisis. Although preventing loss of life is the main goal of any relief campaign, the struggle against famine also involves attempts to limit the economic and social consequences of the disaster. In 1891–92 state officials strove hard in this direction, taking a number of steps designed to avoid the ruin of the nation's agriculture and the collapse of the peasant economy. In these efforts the regime was considerably less successful than it was in holding the line against starvation. The public works program, intended to provide the destitute with employment, was a fiasco. The sale of horses to the needy was on far too small a scale to check the decline in the amount of animal power available to the villages. As a result of the famine, the number of horses and farm animals owned by the peasants fell rapidly. According to figures quoted by I. K. Sukhopliuev, as many as 2.5 million head of cattle may have been lost, and the number of horses per peasant household declined from 1.5 in 1891 to 1.2 in 1893.[30] The growth of peasant indebtedness was another indicator of the economic impact of the disaster. After the famine, the amount of money owed by the villagers to private persons and to the government rose sharply. Indeed, the decline of peasant well-being was so striking that high state officials quickly realized that it would be virtually impossible to collect the loans made to the needy during the famine crisis.[31]

Yet the government's economic policy was not a total failure. By means of an extensive seed loan program, the regime was able to prevent a precipitous reduction in the area under cultivation and so blocked the collapse of agriculture in the stricken region. Even here success was not complete, for the famine did produce a contraction in the size of sown fields. But the seed supplied through state and zemstvo auspices laid the basis for a quick recovery. A dramatic reversal of fortunes came in 1893. With the bumper crop of that year, the peasants of the famine zone began to get back on their feet.

Our survey of the impact of state aid programs in 1891–92 produces a surprisingly positive impression. Food supply operations were far from perfect, but they achieved the primary aims of any relief campaign. Government assistance averted the very real threat of mass starvation, held the death rate within acceptable limits, and prevented a total economic collapse in the stricken region. Admiration for official efforts increases, moreover, when we recall that they were undertaken in the face of serious institutional and political obstacles. From the outset, major defects in the state machine hampered the struggle against famine. Government information-gathering agencies were unable to develop quickly an accurate picture of the needs of the afflicted *gubernii*. At the center there was little cohesion between the work of the main ministries due to the absence of a cabinet capable of formulating policy and overseeing its execution. As a result, a comprehensive relief program was slow to jell. Even after plans had been drawn up, their implementation was hindered by the weakness of the chain of command which stretched from the capital into the countryside. Governors could and did defy ministers; *zemskie nachal'niki* frustrated governors. Hence central policy was often distorted by private wills. Beyond this, supplying the stricken area proved enormously difficult because of the inefficiency of the railroads and the haphazard character of zemstvo grain purchases. Finally, the lack of either state or zemstvo institutions at the *volost'* and village levels unquestionably made proper distribution of food to the needy extraordinarily hard.

In addition to its institutional deficiencies, the Russian government had to cope with a number of political difficulties in its struggle against the famine. The most serious stumbling block was the pernicious legacy created by the Tsarist regime's own policies during the 1880s. The counter-reforms had deliberately alienated a sizable portion of the educated public and had estranged many zemstvo workers. The onslaught of the famine caused the government to reverse its course. In order to carry out a broad relief program, the state had to turn toward "society," encouraging and supporting the work of the zemstvos and private citizens. State officials soon realized, however, that even as they stimulated private efforts, they would have to establish a degree of central coordination and control lest precious energy and resources be wasted. And these attempts to control matters created serious problems in themselves. A too-vigorous policy of government supervision and direction was likely to rankle, private initiative might atrophy, and relief work suffer. State officials had to move cautiously, attempting to establish and maintain a delicate balance between central domination and local autonomy.

By and large, the Russian government proved equal to the problems posed by its institutional weakness and the touchy political situation. While the regular machinery of state was often cumbersome and ineffective, government officials were able to jerry-build special agencies to bypass bottlenecks as they developed. Vendrikh's Temporary Administration for Transport was certainly the most visible and successful of these emergency creations, but other institutions designed to meet the crisis also made significant contributions. Of particular value were the provincial food supply conferences which helped achieve much-needed coordination between zemstvo and state workers. The Tsesarevich's Special Committee stimulated the development of private charitable efforts. On a smaller scale, Kabat's coordination of zemstvo grain purchases in the Caucasus must also be seen as an example of the state's ability to meet effectively the challenge of the famine.

In political terms, too, the regime responded adroitly to the crisis. By approaching the famine as primarily an administrative problem, and by giving the zemstvos a free hand at the outset, the government was able to prevent the politization of relief. Practical cooperation with the zemstvos was attained and the potential for partisan conflict was minimized. Although a number of disputes arose and bureaucrats were frequently accused of excessive meddling in the food supply campaign, official restraint was clearly in evidence. Indeed, a comparison of the policies adopted in Russia with those used by modern relief workers makes it possible to argue that in 1891–92 state officials erred on the side of too much local autonomy. Recent discussions of relief procedures have stressed the need for a single person to be given overall control of food supply operations. A famine "dictator" is particularly important when the population of several different administrative units is affected and regional officials engage in competition for available supplies.[32] If modern judgments are correct, a "dictator" was certainly in order during 1891–92. Such a proposal was, in fact, advanced by Governor Baranov of Nizhni-Novgorod. Yet Durnovo's decision to reject the plan was wise, given political considerations. An administrative dictatorship over relief could have precipitated a struggle with the zemstvos and private agencies. The efficiency which might have been gained as a consequence of better central direction could not have offset the losses which the resulting quarrels with representative of "society" and the zemstvos would have caused.

The Imperial government's ability to deal effectively with the famine in the face of its acknowledged political and institutional problems indicates that at the beginning of the 1890s the old regime had considerable reserves of strength. Its officials, while no doubt inefficient and venal by present standards, were capable of creative and imaginative response to a serious domestic crisis. Nor had the government so far alienated the public that it could not rally broad support for its activities. Despite the mood of distrust generated by the counterreforms, it was still possible to forge workable links between regular state officials, zemstvo personnel, the new *zemskie nachal'niki* and the representatives of peasant communes. Private citizens were also drawn into food supply operations at all levels. To be sure, many of those who joined the relief campaign did so out of love for the *narod*, harboring nothing but contempt for the regime. Still, others who struggled with the famine found it difficult to separate their humanitarian and patriotic motives.

In recent years much has been written about the viability of the Tsarist regime during the late nineteenth and early twentieth centuries. Nor is debate likely to end soon, given the powerful and convincing arguments which have been raised by both sides, and given the fact that the elements which determine "viability" have not been clearly defined.[33] But surely the ability of a state to mobilize its human and material resources to meet an immediate challenge is a token of its capacity to survive. In 1891–92 the Russian government accomplished this task. The story of the famine year suggests that the Tsarist regime was more resilient, its grip on life firmer, than its critics, past and present, have maintained.

And yet, the famine was the beginning of the end for Imperial Russia. From 1891 on, the Tsar's government faced a crescendo of criticism and opposition which would culminate first in the revolution of 1905 and then in the total collapse of 1917. Considering the creditable performance of the regime during the famine, this turn of events seems paradoxical and ironic. But the riddle of a process of decline starting with an apparent success is not difficult to solve. Famine does no one honor. Not even the biggest and most effective relief campaign can remove the stigma produced by hunger and misery. Indignation is inevitable; and when, as in Russia, the government makes little attempt to publicize its achievements,[34] such indignation is likely to be both strong and enduring.

For the Imperial government, moreover, the blow caused by the famine was particularly severe. The autocracy had always been justified because it had made Russia a powerful, modern nation. The disaster of 1891–92 gave the lie to that claim. The great states of Europe did not suffer famine; only backward, colonial lands like China, Ireland, and India starved. The occurrence of a major famine in Russia seemed to indicate that the Empire was falling still further behind the advanced and prosperous countries of the West. This revelation alarmed and agitated the public mind.

Who was to blame for the famine? Who was responsible for the humiliating backwardness which the crisis had exposed? To many, the answer seemed obvious: the government and its policies were at fault. Russia had famine because oppressive taxation was steadily ruining the peasants. Russia was backward because the regime stifled all sources of creativity in society. The experience of the West had shown that true progress was impossible without public participation in the life of the nation. If Russia were to avoid future famines and join the forward march of the European countries, significant changes would have to be accomplished.

Thus for many educated Russians, the famine impugned the basic economic, social, and political programs of the Imperial government. Yet in 1892–93 at least, it would be wrong to see the representatives of state and "society" facing each other across an unbridgable gulf of hostility. To be sure, small revolutionary groups existed which were excited by the famine and spoke of resuming the struggle against autocracy. The majority of Russians were by no means as adamant.

Public opinion is always difficult to gauge, but available information indicates that Rusia's mood on the morrow of the famine was one of positive anticipation. Recent history had shown that when severe crises shook the country, dramatic alterations in policy could occur. Might not the famine produce similar shifts? Such a hope was expressed at the very height of the relief campaign by the newspaper *Novosti*. It wrote:

> The famine is a great lesson. . . . Just as thirty years ago the Sevastopol campaign displayed the weak side of our [national] life and brought about its improvement, so the present disaster may result in our further edification and renewal.[35]

In the wake of the famine this kind of expectation seemed well founded. For surely the crisis had made even the most obtuse *chinovnik* aware of the plight of the peasant and of the need to improve his condition. Moreover, the policies adopted by the government during the food supply campaign seemed to augur well for improved relations between the state and "society." The regime had encouraged public initiative in many spheres and had developed good working relations with the zemstvos. To some, like A. I. Guchkov, the experiences of the "hungry year" suggested that state power could be enchanced by closer cooperation between the agencies of the government and the public. Indeed, this vision would underline much of Guchkov's later political activity. Others were neither as sanguine nor as conciliatory as the future Octobrist. Yet even among activist *zemtsy* and members of the "third element," there were hopes for better days. The zemstvos, after all, had "proved" themselves during the crisis. They had demonstrated both the willingness and the capacity to serve the country. Was it unreasonable to expect that in the years to come there would be greater opportunities to participate in the vital affairs of the nation?

The aspirations of "society" in immediate, practical terms were not grandiose; nor did they in any way threaten the security of the state. Basically, civic-minded Russians looked forward to the strengthening of the kind of cooperation between the government and the public which had developed during the famine. One minor incident serves to underline this fact. Soon after the crisis of 1891–92, the Ministry of Internal Affairs decided to embark on a thorough review of the existing food supply system. In order to have a clear picture of the situation, the MVD summoned provincial conferences composed of local officials, *zemtsy*, and other knowledgeable individuals to discuss a number of specific problems.[36] The views of the conference members varied widely, but on one point there was general agreement: in the future, institutional arrangements governing relief operations ought to link the zemstvos and the state in such a way as to facilitate their *joint* struggle with famine. There was a strong sense of mutual dependence. Few government officials claimed that the state alone could manage the task of aiding the needy; few *zemtsy* suggested that the local institutions of self-government could handle the job themselves.[37]

Nor was the desire for more cooperation between state and "society" limited to the members of the provincial conferences reviewing the system of famine relief. During the cholera epidemic of 1892–93, Russian doctors had been given support and considerable freedom of action by state officials. As the emergency passed, they voiced the hope that the government would assist in the expansion of zemstvo medicine and so make possible the eradication of the diseases which were endemic to the countryside.[38] Even to the Tsar's more politicized subjects, better relations with the government appeared both desirable and possible. Viewed against the background of the famine, the petitions of the Tver and other zemstvos asking that these institutions be able to "express their views on matters concerning them"[39] seem little more than pleas for the preservation of those ties between government and "society" which had been created during the crisis.[40]

The weakness of the state and the economy which the famine exposed, and the demands within society which the crisis generated, confronted the Russian government with a major challenge. But that challenge brought with it opportunity. If the regime could take steps to repair its insufficient institutions, ease the pressure on agriculture, and give the public improved access to the councils of government, the Empire would emerge from the trial of the famine strengthened and revitalized. The achievements of the food supply campaign might mark the start of a new era in which the hopes of the *Novosti* correspondent could be realized.

And for a brief moment, it appeared as if the state would move in a positive direction. In the midst of the crisis, talk of agricultural reform was in the air. High-placed government officials spoke of the need for radical changes in the agrarian structure which would liberate the peasant from the stifling control of the commune.[41] The possibility for change seemed further enhanced when, in 1893, A. S. Ermolov assumed control of the Ministry of State Properties with the mandate to convert that agency into a real Ministry of Agriculture. Ermolov had justly acquired the reputation of an expert on the economic problems of the countryside. His book, *Neurozhai i narodnoe bedstvie*, which he published anonymously in 1892, was the first major examination of the causes and impact of the famine. In his work, Ermolov pointed to communal land tenure as one of the factors which had led to the decline of the peasantry. He suggested that this system would have to change before any real betterment in the life of the agricultural population could be expected.

In the area of institutional improvements and in its dealings with "society," the government moved more timidly. But even here, the aftermath of the famine brought a few hopeful signs. Some of the proposed counterreforms were postponed or abandoned. State officials seemed willing to reopen the question of administrative reform and to invite the participation of the public. The discussion of the food supply system by provincial conferences composed of *zemtsy* as well as bureaucrats may appear a token concession, but its significance should not be ignored. As noted in chapter 2, the weakness of Russian famine relief operations was directly related to the general inadequacy of local administration, especially the absence of firm institutional links with the peasant world. Any meaningful improvement in the food supply system would undoubtedly lead to the creation of *volost'* or village units for handling relief. Moreover, if the wishes of the provincial conferences were adhered to, the units would embody cooperation between state and zemstvo personnel. Should such an arrangement prove workable in meeting the challenge posed by future crop failures, it might be expanded to other aspects of local government.

The small government gestures in the direction of reform and improved ties with "society" quickly ceased, however. No sooner had the regime regained its balance, than it resumed more familiar ways. Agricultural reform was shelved. Under the leadership of S. Iu. Witte, Vyshnegradskii's successor at the Ministry of Finance, Russia pursued a vigorous policy which emphasized industrial growth and fiscal stability. During the 1890s the Ministry of Agriculture was reduced to gathering information on rural conditions while the Ministry of Finance determined the direction of the state. The peasant was subject to increasingly burdensome exactions, and his general well-being declined further. In 1898 and 1901 famine returned. Ominous rumbles of discontent began to be heard in the countryside.

Attempts by elements within the government to accommodate public opinion also ended abruptly. The regime's hostility to local self-government was soon on full display. In 1893 zemstvo doctors were threatened by increased administrative control over rural medical programs.[42] At the same time, V. K. Pleve was given charge of the review of the food supply statute. Under his direction the opinions of the provincial committees regarding the restructuring of the relief machinery were, in the main, ignored. The draft law which emerged from the Ministry of Internal Affairs established firm state control over relief, and virtually excluded the zemstvos from food supply matters.[43]

As the hopes for expanded cooperation between state and "society" in local affairs were frustrated, so the larger aspirations of citizens for more participation in national affairs were denied. In 1895 the new Emperor, Nicholas II, denounced the modest expectations of zemstvo spokesmen as "senseless dreams," and vowed to preserve the autocracy as of old. During the famine, Nicholas' role as head of the Special Committee had made him a symbol of the government's willingness to cooperate with the public. Thus his rejection of the zemstvos' petitions seemed an especially sharp and cruel blow to hopes for meaningful change.

The refusal of state officials to embark on a new course in the wake of the famine requires some explanation. In part the rigidity of the government reflects a general unwillingness of hidebound bureaucrats to change. But there were other reasons, more subtle and complex. The continued emphasis on industrial growth during the "Witte era" was not simply a manifestation of the regime's lack of concern for the peasantry. It was the result of a conviction, held by the Minister of Finance and many others, that Russia could never become strong and wealthy unless she created a firm industrial base. Moreover, the champions of industry argued that prosperous factories and mines and expanding railroads would have a stimulating effect on the economy as a whole. Ultimately, the peasant, too, would be favorably affected; his standard of living would rise and the grip of rural poverty would be broken. Of course a program of resolute industrial expansion would entail sacrifice, but it was justified by the long-term benefits it would bring both in terms of state power and national well-being.[44]

The regime's resistance to exapanding and institutionalizing cooperation with the zemstvos and other organs of "society" was less rationally motivated. The close advisors of Alexander III and Nicholas II were convinced that to expand the role played by institutions of local self-government would ultimately be dangerous to the autocracy and the state. Ironically, the events of 1891–92, far from shaking the views of these men, had the effect of reinforcing them. For the conservative entourage which surrounded the throne, the activity of the zemstvos during the famine, and the participation of suspicious figures like Tolstoi and Korolenko in relief operations seemed unhealthy signs. Through the efforts of the public to aid the needy, the revolutionary virus could enter the countryside. Beyond this, many bureaucrats drew lessons from the famine year which were radically different from those derived by *zemtsy* and persons engaged in private charitable activity. A number of state officials who surveyed the results of the food supply campaign of 1891–92 were struck by the weakness of "society's" efforts to aid the destitute and by the incompetence of the zemstvo institutions. There was some justification for this vew. Private relief work was on a rather small scale, and the zemstvos did make many mistakes. Yet such arguments ignored the fact that the government, too, had erred, and that many of the weaknesses of private and zemstvo activity were the direct or indirect consequences of state policy. Political fear, however, clouded reason. The defects of the zemstvo institutions and the lack of initative on the part of the public were not seen as problems requiring solution. Instead they were used to justify the government's takeover of a number of important functions, including famine relief itself.[45]

Whatever its motives, the government's attempt to return Russia to the calm it had known during the *zatisha* of the 1880s was doomed to fail. Too many questions had been posed by the famine; too many aspirations had been raised by the regime's own programs for combatting the crisis. In the years that followed the disaster, intellectual circles were agitated by a great debate on Russia's future in which the meaning of the famine was a central question. These discussions, conducted mainly by scholars and confined to the pages of the "fat journals" and learned monographs, were not in themselves subversive. But for a public attuned to Aesopian language, these dry tomes carried a critical message which, indirectly at least, stimulated more active resistance. The government's rebuff to the modest hopes of zemstvo "constitutionalists" and liberal "society" also produced deep resentments. At first these discontents were voiced only by the boldest oppositionists. Yet, by the end of the decade the regime's continued intransigence and its attempts to expand bureaucratic control into areas heretofore dominated by the public were helping to convert resentment to rebellion. Finally, the government's determination to press the industrialization drive enraged populist intellectuals, agrarian interests, and the peasants. More important, however, the expansion of industry strengthened immeasurably a new social force. In the strikes of the later 1890s could be seen the red dawn of working-class revolt.

A new century found Russian life politicized. Every movement on the part of "society" seemed to produce governmental repression; state action generated further resistance. And as the rift between *vlast'* and *obshchestvo* widened, the positions of those on either side hardened. Symbolic of this growing alienation between the rulers and the ruled were the myths which sprang up concerning the famine of 1891–92. State officials and spokesmen for "society" both saw the event as a crucial turning point, but their interpretations of the meaning of the disaster were very different. For leading bureaucrats the famine marked the start of a new wave of sedition under the guise of relief.[46] For those in opposition, the famine was a clear sign of the government's incompetence, and proof that "society" could handle the needs of the nation better than the bureaucracy. Quickly forgotten by both sides was the true lesson of the hungry year: neither state nor "society" could function effectively without the other. Only genuine cooperation between the representatives of the government and the public would enable Russia to weather future crises.

APPENDIX

SOME RUSSIAN WEIGHTS AND MEASURES

1 *funt*	0.9022 lbs.
1 *pud**	36.11 lbs; 40 *funty*.
1 *chetvert*†	5.775 bushels.
1 *verst*	0.66 mile.
1 *desiatina*	2.7 acres.

*A Russian railroad boxcar holds approximately 610 *pudy*.

†A *chetvert* of wheat usually weighs 10 *pudy*; one of rye, 9 *pudy*; one of oats, 6 *pudy*.

APPENDIX TABLE 1. Harvest of 1891 in the Sixteen Famine Provinces as Compared with the Harvests of 1888, 1889, and 1890 (In *chetverty*; all cereal grains; potatoes excluded)

Province	*1891*	*1888*	*1889*	*1890*
Kazan	3,231,500	8,614,100	7,743,300	6,031,700
Kursk	6,499,600	10,687,100	6,682,900	11,023,100
Nizhni	4,104,200	6,061,900	5,547,300	4,192,300
Orel	6,164,500	7,849,600	7,194,100	9,311,700
Orenburg	2,793,000	5,727,700	13,199,700	4,483,900
Penza	3,636,900	8,235,100	6,993,500	4,548,000
Perm	7,253,500	8,400,100	10,513,900	7,660,300
Riazan	3,906,900	8,593,900	8,080,000	7,207,600
Samara	4,028,400	8,366,500	8,428,200	7,902,800
Sartov	4,807,700	10,176,900	9,544,500	8,388,100
Simbirsk	3,307,200	7,527,900	6,817,500	5,443,300
Tambov	6,353,500	16,087,700	9,351,800	14,286,900
Tula	5,346,700	8,688,100	7,696,200	7,877,600
Ufa	3,979,700	5,010,700	7,146,100	3,948,100
Viatka	9,362,100	12,772,400	14,167,400	12,355,400
Voronezh	2,799,300	13,745,100	6,617,200	14,912,400
Total	77,574,700	146,535,800	135,723,600	129,575,300

Source: Tsentral'nyi statisticheskii komitet, *Urozhai 1891 goda v 60 guberniiakh Evropeiskoi Rossii* (St. Petersburg, 1892).

APPENDIX TABLE 2. NUMBER OF PERSONS RECEIVING FOOD LOANS, 1891–1892

	1891						
Province	*July*	*August*	*September*	*October*	*November*	*December*	*January*
Archangel	—	5,545	8,526	27,388	32,996	44,003	54,611
Kazan	—	3,816	20	24,678	363,503	621,036	814,125
Kherson	—	—	13,390	4,311	23,629	37,802	54,789
Kursk	—	5,344	—	40,027	66,059	107,961	226,146
Nizhni	148,913	73,153	27,569	28,277	114,565	244,891	320,239
Olonets	—	40	—	—	—	—	—
Orel	—	—	—	—	2,122	59,500	223,089
Orenburg	—	—	9,790	197,143	356,065	483,319	484,766
Penza	248,659	23,253	5,362	104,758	164,861	432,213	568,714
Perm	—	2,359	59	40	40,757	133,561	197,362
Riazan	2,783	11,006	—	—	207,152	377,982	515,794
Samara	—	—	330,540	538,665	651,744	756,318	836,638
Saratov	—	1,318	15,838	172,336	378,658	521,712	690,107
Simbirsk	62,108	34,217	13,854	68,028	356,567	497,587	677,127
Tambov	—	—	—	3,177	84,211	363,449	577,360
Taurida	—	2,152	1,585	3,023	23,807	57,849	98,353
Tobol'sk	66,513	24,208	22,556	74,197	37,214	67,731	68,012
Tula	—	—	1,190	8,635	24,737	161,621	280,945
Ufa	—	—	—	389	3,197	48,902	161,940
Viatka	44,876	5,275	7,438	2,069	1,433	29,705	233,195
Voronezh	—	8,403	37,726	33,544	214,134	417,015	622,315
Total	573,852	200,089	495,443	1,330,685	3,147,411	5,464,157	7,705,627

Source: Statisticheskye dannye, pp. 42–43.

1892								
February	*March*	*April*	*May*	*June*	*July*	*August*	*Total*	*Average per Month*
64,441	69,650	85,149	85,995	84,100	73,843	31,531	667,778	51,368
920,333	1,006,374	1,023,651	1,088,869	1,110,846	659,293	2,329	7,638,873	587,606
62,459	32,116	9,288	2,432	—	—	—	240,216	26,691
297,554	442,175	418,822	402,707	342,370	24,374	—	2,373,539	215,776
387,371	540,779	644,398	658,493	662,548	310,627	—	4,161,823	320,140
—	5,113	11,794	19,772	20,724	27,760	13,406	98,609	14,087
324,218	450,662	497,208	443,710	391,949	48,969	—	2,141,427	271,270
491,734	498,564	467,356	464,738	419,539	320,354	—	4,193,368	381,215
712,850	815,891	844,803	814,517	804,947	543,489	—	6,084,317	468,024
243,485	335,474	350,320	383,161	341,756	272,421	7,953	2,308,708	177,593
608,354	688,336	701,663	648,129	624,955	24,239	—	4,410,393	400,945
907,097	979,331	1,007,810	1,027,311	953,206	85,754	—	8,074,414	734,038
850,285	938,427	926,115	795,705	610,886	129,723	—	6,031,410	502,618
760,205	837,594	887,278	864,189	843,748	636,931	—	6,539,433	503,033
780,514	873,919	922,098	982,933	1,025,446	472,825	6,448	6,092,380	553,853
145,716	178,800	108,115	54,279	27,708	15,111	7,957	724,455	55,727
186,625	313,574	338,106	332,814	314,852	270,238	67,103	2,183,743	155,982
379,933	462,028	461,995	443,788	449,142	320,245	—	2,994,259	272,205
297,413	360,048	377,426	406,947	307,748	1,013	392	1,965,415	178,674
391,914	693,453	782,219	891,768	888,361	655,361	—	4,627,067	355,928
856,269	997,545	985,914	929,815	916,658	114,438	8,963	6,142,739	472,518
9,668,770	11,519,853	11,851,828	11,742,072	11,141,489	5,070,008	146,082	79,994,366	5,713,890

APPENDIX TABLE 3. DEATH RATES IN THE SIXTEEN PROVINCES OF EUROPEAN RUSSIA MOST SERIOUSLY AFFECTED BY THE FAMINE OF 1891–92

Province	*Deaths per 100 Population, 1892*	*Deaths per 100 Population, 1881–1890*	*Percent of Increase in Death Rate, 1892*
Kazan	4.51	3.32	36
Kursk	3.84	3.58	7
Nizhni	4.35	4.18	4
Orel	4.10	3.83	7
Orenburg	6.08	4.33	40
Penza	4.98	3.85	30
Perm	4.54	4.45	2
Riazan	4.06	3.40	19
Samara	6.38	4.08	56
Saratov	5.91	3.81	55
Simbirsk	4.74	3.52	37
Tambov	4.38	3.38	29
Tula	4.64	3.84	21
Ufa	4.70	3.16	49
Viatka	4.30	3.96	8
Voronezh	5.41	3.63	49
Average	4.81	3.76	28

Source: V. I. Pokrovskii, "Vliianie kolebanii urozhaia i khlebnykh tsen na estestvennoe dvizhenie naseleniia."

APPENDIX TABLE 4. Mortality in the Sixteen Provinces of European Russia Most Seriously Affected by the Famine of 1891–92

Province	*Total Mortality,* 1892	*Average Mortality,* 1888–90, 1893–94	*Increased Mortality,* 1892
Kazan	102,498	75,301[a]	27,197
Kursk	97,024	84,072[a]	12,952
Nizhni	69,315	65,634	3,681
Orel	88,604	78,716	9,888
Orenburg	86,152	56,110	30,042
Penza	80,603	62,346[a]	18,257
Perm	129,637	117,368	12,269
Riazan	79,956	64,740	15,216
Samara	175,453	104,859[a]	70,594
Saratov	146,516	92,507	54,009
Simbirsk	79,662	59,611[a]	20,051
Tambov	127,258	104,863	22,395
Tula	70,585	61,187	9,398
Ufa	99,041	64,240	34,801
Viatka	133,061	117,589	15,472
Voronezh	152,121	101,700	50,421
Total	1,717,486	1,310,843	406,643

[a] Mortality figured on an average of four years, 1888–90 and 1894

Source: V. I. Pokrovskii, "Vliianie kolebanii urozhaia i khlebnikh tsen na estestvennoe dvizhenie naseleniia."

NOTES

1. THE FAMINE AND ITS CAUSES

1. Tsentral'nyi gosudarstvennyi arkhiv Oktiabrskoi revoliutsii (hereafter cited: TsGAOR), *fond* Aleksandra III-ogo (No. 677), *delo* 741, "Pis'ma gr. Vorontsova-Dashkova imperatoru Aleksandru III-emu (1866–1894)," pp. 129–30.

2. See the proposal of the Minister of Internal Affairs to the Committee of Ministers dated December 26, 1891, "O priniatii nekotorykh mer po narodnomu prodovol'stviiu," and related materials in [Komitet Ministrov], *Prodovol'stvennoe delo* (n.p. [SPb.], n.d. [1891–92]), I, 169–79, and especially the chart on p. 174.

3. This description of weather conditions is drawn primarily from data compiled by the Department of Agriculture of the Ministry of State Properties. See Department zemeledeliia i sel'skoi promyshlennosti Ministerstva gosudarstvennykh imushchestv, *1891 god v sel'skokhoziaistvennom otnoshenii po otvetam, poluchennym ot khoziaev*, I (SPb., 1891), i–ii. Further discussion of the meteorologic causes of the crop failure can be found in "Besedy v I otdelenii Obshchestva po voprosam o prichinakh neurozhaia 1891 goda i merakh protiv povtoreniia podobnykh neurozhaev v budushchem," *Trudy Imperatorskogo Vol'nogo Ekonomicheskogo Obshchestva* (SPb., 1892), I, 70–76. See also [A. S. Ermolov], *Neurozhai i narodnoe bedstvie* (SPb., 1892), pp. 3–15.

4. *1891 god*, II (1891), ii.

5. The norms are based on the period 1883–87. See: [Ermolov], *Neurozhai i narodnoe bedstvie*, p. 16. Ermolov used data presented by the Department of Agriculture (*1891 god*) and the Central Statistical Committee (Tsentral'nyi statisticheskii komitet Ministerstva vnutrennikh del, *Urozhai 1891 goda v 60 guberniiakh Evropeiskoi Rossii* [SPb., 1892]). Ermolov's book contains the best available analysis of the harvest of 1891.

6. [Ermolov], *Neurozhai i narodnoe bedstvie*, p. 19. As compared with the 1883–87 norm, Voronezh, −75 percent; Kazan, −67 percent; Tambov, −65 percent; Simbirsk, −64 percent; Penza, Riazan, and Tula, −55 to −50 percent; Nizhni-Novgorod and Samara, −45 to −40 percent; Saratov, −34 percent; Kursk, −29 percent; Orel, −18 percent; Viatka, −15 percent; Ufa, −3 percent; and Perm, +4.8 percent. See also Table 1.

7. *Ibid.*, p. 26.

8. *Ibid.*, p. 22. In a report on conditions in Tambov province, A. B. Mikhailov, a *revizor* for the Department of Direct Taxes (*Departament okladnykh sborov*), noted this phenomenon. He wrote that "alongside fields in excellent condition, you can see lands where, besides the goosefoot, only a single, barren ear has sprouted. The differences in this regard are visible

not only over the territory of a *volost'*, but even within the boundaries of the property of the smallest commune." Mikhailov's report to D. F. Kobeko, Director of the Department, is dated July 28, 1891. Tsentral'nyi gosudarstvennyi istoricheskii arkhiv SSSR [hereafter cited: TsGIA], f. Khoziaistvenogo departamenta MVD (No. 1287), *opis'* 4, d. 2132, "O ssude Tambovskomu gubernskomu zemstvu," p. 68.

9. [Ermolov], *Neurozhai i narodnoe bedstvie*, p. 23. For a cartographic representation of this, see the maps of the harvest at the end of *Urozhai 1891 goda*. (The entire volume is without pagination.)

10. According to figures published by the Department of Agriculture, the total harvest of food grains from the black soil areas was 52,432,600 *chetverty* below normal. The bulk of this deficit, 48,527,500 *chetverty*, was assigned to thirteen provinces: Kazan, Kursk, Nizhni-Novgorod, Orel, Orenburg, Penza, Riazan, Samara, Saratov, Simbirsk, Tambov, Tula, and Voronezh. See *1891 god*, vol. III, pt. 2 (1892), pp. 238–39.

11. *Ibid.*, pp. 144–45.

12. *Ibid.*, II (1891), 112–15. There are no detailed statistics available as to the precise size of the harvest in the Caucasus. See also [Ermolov] *Neurozhai i narodnoe bedstvie*, p. 28.

13. This was the case in India during the last half century of British rule. Between 1908 and 1943 there were no famines despite numerous crop failures. This was due to the adoption of effective administrative and relief measures. See Henry Knight, *Food Administration in India, 1939–1943* (Stanford, 1954), p. 68. Greater detail on Indian famines can be found in B. M. Bhatia, *Famines in India: A Study in Some Aspects of the Economic History of India, 1860–1945* (Bombay, 1963).

14. This was a factor in the Soviet famine of the 1930s. For a survey of the evidence concerning this event, see the article by Dana G. Dalrymple, "The Soviet Famine of 1932–1934," *Soviet Studies*, XV (January, 1964), 250–84.

15. [Ermolov], *Neurozhai i narodnoe bedstvie*, p. 17. The harvest of 1880 was 251,574,000 *chetverty*, that of 1885 was 247,209,000. Ermolov estimates that in 1891 232,500,000 *chetverty* were harvested. His figure is based on the average of data presented by the Department of Agriculture and the Central Statistical Committee. The figures given by the Central Statistical Committee were lower than those of the Department of Agriculture.

16. Learned discussions of the emancipation and its consequences abound. The most convenient general survey of the problem is that of P. A. Zaionchkovskii, *Otmena krepostnogo prava v Rossii* (3rd ed., rev.; Moscow, 1968). Other useful sources include Lazar Volin, *A Century of Russian Agriculture: From Alexander II to Khrushchev* (Cambridge, Mass., 1970), pp. 40–76; Alexander Gerschenkron, "Russia: Agrarian Policies and Industrialization," in *Continuity in History and Other Essays* (Cambridge, Mass., 1968), pp. 153–206; and, of course, Geroid T. Robinson, *Rural Russia under the Old Regime* (New York, 1932).

17. The impact of the commune is surveyed in Volin, *Russian Agriculture*, pp. 77–93, and in Francis M. Watters, "The Peasant and the Village Commune," *The Peasant in Nineteenth Century Russia*, W. S. Vucinich, ed., (Stanford, Calif., 1968), pp. 133–57. Also Gerschenkron, "Russia: Agrarian Policies," pp. 185–98.

18. Gerschenkron, "Russia: Agrarian Policies," pp. 194–96.

19. Francis M. Watters, "Land Tenure and Financial Burdens of the Russian Peasant," (unpublished Ph.D. dissertation, University of California, Berkeley, 1966), p. 195. For a

detailed discussion of the world agricultural crisis and its impact on Russia, see N.A. Egiazarova, *Agrarnyi krizis kontsa XIX veka v Rossii* (Moscow, 1959).

20. A general survey of Vyshnegradskii's financial program is provided by T. H. Von Laue, *Sergei Witte and the Industrialization of Russia* (New York, 1963), pp. 23–32. For information on Vyshnegradskii's taxation policy, see P. Kh. Shvanebakh, *Nashe podatnoe delo* (SPb., 1903), pp. 11–15.

21. P. A. Golubev wrote: "It is obvious to all [that] there are mass sales of peasant grain because they are forced under the influence of the collection of taxes. . . . Right after the harvest, the gathering of taxes begins first with a simple reminder, then with legal methods of compulsion, and finally even with the auctioning off of the peasant's property" ("Podat' i narodnoe khoziaistvo," *Russkaia mysl'* [July, 1893], p. 17). It should be noted, however, that the collection of taxes in the fall was not motivated solely by a desire to squeeze the peasants when they were fat. According to the law, taxes were to be gathered twice a year, once in the spring and again in the fall. But since most peasants were without means in the spring, they were allowed to postpone payments until autumn.

22. Shvanebakh, *Nashe podatnoe delo*, pp. 11–15. Also A. P. Pogrebinskii, *Ocherki istorii finansov dorevoliutsionnoi Rossii* (Moscow, 1954), pp. 85–86, and S. A. Pokrovskii, *Vneshniaia torgovlia i vneshniaia torgovaia politika Rossii* (Moscow, 1947), pp. 317–18.

23. P. Kh. Shvanebakh was one of the most eloquent critics of Vyshnegradskii. In his study of Russian currency reform, Shvanebakh charged that the Minister of Finance was so diverted by his passion for the accumulation of gold that he "failed to take the pulse of the country, did not notice its weakening and the threatening symptoms of atrophy, did not see, or did not want to see, that the brilliant results of his administration were purchased at the price of overexertion. Let us agree that the crop failure of 1891 was an 'accidental' phenomenon, but this 'accident' played the role of an accidental cold infecting a weakened subject: a strong organism throws it off with little difficulty, [but if] the organism [is] already exhausted, the accidental cold leads to a serious and prolonged illness." *Denezhnoe preobrazovanie i narodnoe khoziaistvo* (SPb., 1901), p. 28.

24. Leopold H. Haimson, *The Russian Marxists and the Origins of Bolshevism* (Cambridge, Mass., 1955), p. 49.

25. In her study of Russian financial policy, Olga Crisp suggests that despite pressure from the treasury, the peasants during the Vyshnegradskii era were holding their own. She implies that the idea that the Treasury was sucking the country dry is extreme. "Russian Financial Policy and the Gold Standard at the End of the Nineteenth Century," *Economic History Review*, VI (2nd ser.) (December, 1953), 164–65. A preliminary survey by the author of the present work suggests that in the period 1886–90 reserves of cash and grain put aside by the peasants under terms of the *ustav narodnogo prodovol'stviia* were increasing on the whole, and that the percentage of these reserves out on loan was declining. A slight improvement was shown in about half the provinces affected by the crop failure of 1891. But the size of reserves in the Volga and black earth region generally remained small.

26. Toward the end of his tenure as Minister of Finance, S. Iu. Witte argued along just these lines. He justified heavy extractions from the peasantry because they made possible state relief in times of famine. "Where," Witte asked rhetorically, "are we to find the sums to aid the population [in the event of crop failure] if we conduct the economy [of the state] in such a manner so as not to have savings for a rainy day?" Vsepoddanneishii doklad

Ministra finansov o gosudarstvennoi rospisi dokhodov i raskhodov na 1901 god," *Vestnik finansov, promyshennosti i torgovli*, January 7, 1901, p. 6; cited in Shvanebakh, *Nashe podatnoe delo*, pp. 21–22. In the wake of the famine of 1891, the anonymous author of the column "Sobytiia i novosti," *Severnyi vestnik* (May, 1892), p. 103, pointed out that relief for the hungry population was made possible, in part, by the existence of government reserves of cash.

27. A. I. Skvortsov, *Ekonomicheskie etiudy*, Vol. I: *Ekonomicheskie prichiny golodovok v Rossii i mery k ikh ustraneniiu* (SPb., 1894), p. 22. Skvortsov estimated that in the black earth provinces alone, there were 1 million such households containing about 5.8 million persons.

28. L. N. Maress, "Pishcha narodnykh mass v Rossii," *Russkaia mysl'* (October, 1893), pp. 56–58.

29. Dr. Petrov's statement quoted in F. K. Stefanovskii, *Materialy dlia izucheniia svoistv "golodnogo" khleba* (Kazan, 1893), pp. 213–14. (Italics in the original.)

30. TsGIA. f. Dep. obshchikh del, op. 223, 1891, d. 201, "Vsepoddanneishii otchet Nachal'nika Samarskoi gubernii za 1891 god," pp. 3–4.

31. Sokolovskii is quoted in Nizhegorodskaia gubernskaia uprava, Statisticheskoe otdelenie, *Urozhai 1891 goda v Nizhegorodskoi gubernii* (N. Novgorod, 1891), pp. 106–7. Sokolovskii's observations are confirmed by other sources. In his study of the causes of the famine, L. Vesin noted that in the provinces affected by the crop failure the ratio of meadow to plowed fields on peasant property was considerably smaller than that on nonpeasant lands. "Neurozhai v Rossii i ikh glavnye prichiny," *Severnyi vestnik* (February, 1892), pp. 63–64. He also stated that there had been as much as a 40-percent decline in forests in some of the areas hit by the famine (*ibid.*, pp. 53–54). For further detail on the expansion of peasant cultivation to the detriment of pasture land, see the article by S. Lazarovich, "Krest'ianskaia tesnota i zasukhi poslednikh let v Novorossiiskom krae," *Severnyi vestnik* (May, 1893), pp. 17–19.

32. Vesin, "Neurozhai v Rossii," pp. 63–64. Also, Lazar Volin, "The Russian Peasant: From Emancipation to Kolkhoz," *The Transformation of Russian Society*, Cyril E. Black, ed. (Cambridge, Mass., 1960), p. 298.

33. L. N. Voronov, "Ekonomicheskoe obozrenie," *Russkoe obozrenie* (September, 1891), pp. 392–93. The provinces noted by Voronov were Voronezh, Viatka, Kazan, Nizhni-Novgorod, Orenburg, Penza, Riazan, Samara, Saratov, Simbirsk, Tambov, Tula, and Ufa.

34. In the years immediately preceding the famine, all the affected provinces, with the exception of Tula, experienced at least one year when the grain harvest fell below the normal for the period 1883–87. The provinces of Kazan, Nizhni-Novgorod, Samara, Simbirsk, and Viatka had below-normal harvests three years in succession. For data, see: *1888 god*, vol. III, pt. 1 (1889), pp. 174–75, 180–81; *1889 god*, vol. III (1890), pp. 155–56, 162–63; *1890 god*, vol. III, pt. 1 (1892), pp. 130–31, 135. (The harvest of 1890 is compared only with that of 1889.)

35. P. L. Korf, "Poezdka v neurozhainye mestnosti Kurskoi gubernii," *Trudy IVEO* (1892), II, 110.

36. A plant of the genus *Chenopodium*, often found in the same fields with regular food grains. For details on the plant and its use in Russia, see "Lebeda," *Novyi entsiklopedicheskii slovar'*, XXIV (191?), 166–67.

37. The operation of grain speculators was a major cause of government concern during the famine crisis. Local officials were often very critical of unscrupulous grain merchants, and sometimes held them to blame for food supply difficulties in their provinces. The head of the Tula *zhandarmskoe upravlenie* reported to the Department of Police that "local grain would have been sufficient to feed the population if it had not been bought up in the beginning by the *kulaks.*" Report dated October 14, 1891 and marked "*sovershenno sekretno.*" TsGIA, f. Khoz., dep. op. 4, d. 2116, "O ssude Tul'skomu gubernskomu zemstvu," p. 114.

38. The following discussion of conditions in the famine-stricken areas of Russia is based on a large number of personal accounts and public documents. Only where a particular incident is referred to will the source will be indicated.

39. This process of verifying need was repeated as many as six times in some areas. It produced considerable discontent among the population. For details, see the chapters on relief work in the provinces.

40. Often used by peasants as a source of fuel.

41. In July the Economic Department of the Ministry of the Interior dispatched a circular to the governors to which was appended information on the use of cheaper grains as substitutes for rye. Circular dated July 11, No. 4833, *Tambovskie gubernskie vedomosti*, No. 82, *chast' ofitsial'naia*, August 1, 1891, p. 1.

42. Information on "famine bread" is drawn from the following sources: Stefanovskii, *Materialy*, pp. 86–87, 203, 210–25; F. Erisman, "Pitanie golodaiushchikh," *Russkaia mysl'* (April, 1892), pp. 145–46; I. K. Sukhopliuev, "Neurozhai i massovye zabolevaniia golodaiushchego naseleniia," *Russkaia mysl'* (March, 1906), p. 43; Sukhopliuev, "Posledstvie neurozhaev v Rossii," *Russkaia mysl'* (June, 1906), p. 151.

43. The Department of Agriculture reported: "In the present year, as the result of the complete failure of crops in almost the entire black soil area of European Russia, field labor was everywhere extraordinarily cheap, since the supply of labor significantly exceeded the demand" (*1891 god*, vol. III, pt. 3 [1892], p. 69).

44. TsGAOR, f. Departamenta politsii, 3-oe deloproizvodstvo (102), 1893, d. 152, *chast'* 35, "Politicheskii obzor Moskovskoi gubernii za 1893 god," pp. 2–5, 17. Police officials noted a curtailment of demand for manufactured goods which led to a cutback in factory production. "The crop failure of 1891 had an unfortunate effect on the activities of factories and shops. Some stopped work altogether, others cut back on the number of workers or on the length of the working day" (*ibid.*, p. 17).

45. Iurii Stepanovich Nechaev-Mal'tsev, sent to Kazan province as a special representative for the Tsesarevich's Committee on Famine Relief, noted that peasants seeking work in the provincial capital found "three conditions favoring the development of typhus—need, idleness . . . [and] filth. . . . The number of victims afflicted by the disease grew with each day." The roads leading away from Kazan became highways of contagion. Nechaev-Mal'tsev stated that "the largest number of sick persons were to be found in villages either lying directly along the main roads or very close to them." TsGAOR, f. Nikolaia II-go (601), op. 1, d. 821, "Raport upolnomochennogo Osobogo Komiteta po Kazanskoi gubernii . . . O pomoshchi naseleniiu vidu neurozhaia," p. 10.

46. E. Shmurlo, "Nuzhda v Cheliabinskom uezde," *Severnyi vestnik* (June, 1892), 29, quotes a letter to the effect that a peasant mother attempted the slaughter of her two children aged four and six. When asked to explain her crime, she replied, " 'It's all the same, they would have died of hunger; now they are angels and will pray for me. . . .' "

47. The governor of Simbirsk reported: "In the spring, when it appeared that the winter crops were almost [completely] destroyed, and the state of the weather left few hopes for the harvest of spring grains, . . . there developed primarily among the peasant of Ardatovskii and Korunskii *uezdy* an urge to migrate; and there existed the popular notion that [this] migration would be accomplished at state expense. At the time of sowing the spring fields, the migration movement took on enormous proportions. Without any authorization, [these would-be] migrants sold their property and cattle, leased their allotments and absolutely refused to sow the spring fields. In order to explain to the peasants that the rumors concerning migration were groundless, and to convince them to remain calm and to continue their regular work in the fields, I took all necessary measures, both personally and through the marshals of the nobility, the *zemskie nachal'niki*, the police and the permanent members of the provincial council (*prisutstvie*). By the measure adopted, [we] succeeded in terminating the disturbance among the peasantry, and in inducing them to sow their allotment lands. Among the measures I adopted in the migration affair was . . . the order to the effect that the spring seed would be given out to the needy at once, without hindrance, avoiding delays and superfluous formalities." TsGIA, f. Dep. obshchikh del, op. 223, 1891, d. 160, Vsepoddanneishii otchet Nachal'nika Simbirskoi gubernii za 1891 god," pp. 36–37. See also, N. A. Vokach, "Pereselencheskoe delo," *Russkaia mysl'* (August, 1892), pp. 65–66. Vokach notes that migration to Siberia was especially heavy from famine provinces. L. F. Skliarov, *Pereselenie i zemleustroistovo v Sibiri v gody Stolypinskoi agrarnoi reformy* (Leningrad, 1962), pp. 69–70, has information on unauthorized peasant migrations. Also, Donald W. Treadgold, *The Great Siberian Migration* (Princeton, 1957).

2. RUSSIA'S SYSTEM OF FAMINE RELIEF

1. The Chinese approach to famine relief is discussed at length in Kuang-Chuan Hsiao, *Rural China, Imperial Control in the Nineteenth Century* (Seattle, 1960), pp. 144–83. A useful picture of the Chinese relief system in operation can be found in the work by Paul Richard Bohr, *Famine in China and the Missionary: Timothy Richard as Relief Administrator and Advocate of National Reform, 1876–1884* (Cambridge, Mass., 1972), pp. 25–82.

2. Bhatia, *Famines in India*, p. 324.

3. For a discussion of the techniques used in India today, see Alan Berg, "Famine Contained: Notes and Lessons from the Bihar Experience," in *Famine: A Symposium Dealing with Nutrition and Relief Operations in Times of Disaster*, ed. G. Blix, Y. Hofvander, and B. Vahlquist (Uppsala, 1971), pp. 113–29. Also useful are Wendy and Allan Scarfe, *Tiger on a Rein: Report on the Bihar Famine* (London, 1969), and Musafir Singh, *People Can Avert Famine* (New Delhi, 1970).

4. Before Peter, a number of Russian rulers, most notably Boris Godunov, had undertaken attempts to alleviate the effects of famine. But these efforts had been a kind of royal charity. Only with Peter did relief become a *state* enterprise.

5. *Polnoe sobranie zakonov Rossiiskoi imperii* (hereafter cited PSZ), 1st ed., Nos. 4420, 4430.

6. *Ibid.*, No. 4168.

7. *Ibid.*, No. 4272.

8. *Ibid.*, No. 4193.

9. *Ibid.*, No. 4634.

10. Eighteenth-century legislation on food supply and famine relief is enormous. It is admirably systematized and discussed in the article by F. I. Leontovich, "Golodovki v Rossii do kontsa proshlogo veka," *Severnyi vestnik* (March, 1892), pp. 46–76; (April, 1892), pp. 33–63; (May, 1892), pp. 41–60. See also A. V. Romanovich-Slavatinskii, "Goloda v Rossii i mery pravitel'stva protiv nikh," *Izvestiia Kievskogo universiteta*, XXXII (1892), 27–68, and E. E. Kartavtsev, "Nashe zakonodatel'stvo o narodnom prodovol'stvii: Istoricheskii ocherk," *Vestnik Evropy* (January, 1892), pp. 628–72.

11. The problems of administering relief under the system developed during the eighteenth century are capably presented and analyzed by P. A. Shafranov, "Neurozhai khlebov v Rossii i prodovol'stvie naseleniia v 20-kh godakh nastoiashchego stoletiia," *Russkoe bogatstvo* (May, 1898), pp. 82–115; (June, 1898), pp. 114–37; (July, 1898), pp. 119–54. Shafranov's monograph is one of the few studies of Russian famines based on archival documents.

12. PSZ, 1st ed., No. 19000.

13. Kartavtsev, "Nashe zakonodatel'stvo," pp. 659–62.

14. PSZ, 2nd ed., No. 7253; and Kartavtsev, pp. 663–64.

15. S. Frederick Starr, *Decentralization and Self-Government in Russia, 1830–1870* (Princeton, 1972), especially pp. 3–50.

16. *Ustav o obespechenii narodnogo prodovol'stviia* in *Svod zakonov Rossiiskoi imperii*, XIII (St. Petersburg, 1892), secs. 10, 11, 12. In our outline of the postreform food supply system we will refer to the statute in the *Svod zakonov* because it is more systematic and convenient than the law in the PSZ. The discussion will refer to those aspects of the law which pertained to rural areas where zemstvo institutions existed. Supervision and administration of famine relief in urban areas was the business of the city governments and the local police. In provinces without zemstvos, state officials were in control. *Gubernii* like Arkhangel'sk and Astrakhan and the whole of Siberia, which had peculiar food supply problems, were covered by special statutes.

17. *Ibid.*, sec. 38.

18. *Ibid.*, secs. 39, 40.

19. *Ibid.*, secs. 15, 48, 50, 55, 56, 58, 60. These capital funds were formed from money raised under the terms of the law of July 5, 1834 which had established a 10-kopek-per-year assessment on the peasants until the sum of 1 ruble 60 kopeks for each "soul" had been accumulated. Of the sums in the hands of state authorities in 1864, when the problem of famine relief was turned over to the zemstvos, 48 kopeks per "soul" went to form the provincial capital; the remainder became the central fund.

20. *Ibid.*, secs. 46, 49, 50, 52.

21. *Ibid.*, secs. 45, 46.

22. *Ibid.*, sec. 20.

23. *Ibid.*, sec. 70.

24. *Ibid.*, sec. 75.

25. *Ibid.*, sec. 88.

26. *Ibid.*, secs. 88, 89.

27. *Ibid.*, sec. 79.

28. *Ibid.*, sec. 81.

29. *Ibid.*, secs. 90, 91.

30. *Ibid.*, secs. 92–95.

31. *Ibid.*, secs. 102, 103.

32. *Ibid.*, secs. 99, 110.

33. *Ibid.*, sec. 111.

34. I. P. Belokonskii, "Zemstvo i narodnoe prodovol'stvie," *Severnyi vestnik* (March, 1892), p. 22.

35. For a more complete discussion of the weaknesses of the reformed food supply system, see my article "Russia's System of Food Supply Relief on the Eve of the Famine of 1891–92," *Agricultural History*, XLV (October, 1971), 259–69.

36. Just before the famine of 1891, none of the affected provinces had more than 45 percent of their required grain reserves on hand for disbursal to the needy. The majority had much less. For a graphic representation of this situation, see *Prodovol'stvennoe delo*, III, 126–27.

37. Until 1891, loans from the central fund were, for the most part, quite small. With few exceptions, grants to the provinces rarely exceeded 1 million rubles. Despite these limitations, however, arrears had already accumulated to the sum of 5,876,667 rubles as of January 1, 1891. A detailed list of all loans from the central fund can be found *ibid.*, I, 3–11.

38. For a discussion of this weakness in the zemstvo structure, see A. D. Gradovskii, "Vsesoslovnaia melkaia edinitsa," *Sobranie sochenenii* (9 vols.; St. Petersburg, 1899–1904), VIII, 572–73.

39. On the segregation of the peasants in the postreform period, see Peter Czap, Jr., "Peasant Class Courts and Peasant Customary Justice in Russia 1861–1912," *Journal of Social History*, I (Winter, 1967), 149–78.

40. One of the most unjust features of the food supply law was that while relief loans could be made only to individuals, the peasant commune as a whole was obligated to pay back the grant. This arrangement tended to penalize the hard-working, self-sufficient peasants and to reward the shiftless.

41. A. A. Kizevetter, *Mestnoe samoupravlenie v Rossii, IX–XIX st. Istoricheskii ocherk* (Moscow, 1910), pp. 144–45.

42. The weakness of the Committee of Ministers will be discussed in greater detail in chapter 5.

43. The views of leading state officials on the zemstvo question are outlined by L. G. Zakharova, *Zemskaia konterreforma 1890 g.* (Moscow, 1968), pp. 47–71.

44. Distrust of the zemstvos at the local level was heightened by the fact that during the 1870s and 1880s the power of the nobility in the *uezd* assemblies declined while the number of peasant representatives grew steadily (*ibid.*, pp. 13–27). Thus the creation of a *melkaia zemskaia edinitsa* would not only strengthen the zemstvos as institutions, it would have also enhanced the *political* power of the peasantry.

45. For a discussion of the origins of the Kakhanov commission, see P. A. Zaionchkovskii, *Krizis samoderzhaviia na rubezhe 1870–1880 godov* (Moscow, 1964), pp. 430–34.

46. P. A. Zaionchkovskii, *Rossiiskoe samoderzhavie v kontse XIX stoletiia* (Moscow, 1970), pp. 219–26.

47. *Ibid.*, pp. 226–32.

48. Zaionchkovskii provides a lucid discussion of the counterreform legislation (*ibid.*, pp. 366–411). For greater detail on the zemstvo law of 1890, see Zakharova *Zemskaia konterreforma*, especially pp. 139–50.

49. The sacrifice of administrative rationality to the class interests of the nobility is most clearly illustrated by the law of the *zemskie nachal'niki.* In deference to the antibureaucratic feelings of the *dvorianstvo*, the land captains were not really integrated into the state machine. They were chosen, first of all, from lists of candidates drawn up by the *uezd* assemblies of the nobility. Once installed in office, the *zemskie nachal'niki* were able to operate quite independently, supervised immediately by the *uezd* marshals of the nobility and at greater distance by the governors and provincial councils. Even the powerful governors were not able to discipline the land captains freely. Since the *zemskie nachal'niki* were royal officials, they could not be removed without ministerial sanction. Thus the law of July 12, 1889 did not create an effective chain of command in the countryside. The independence of the land captains would have many undesirable administrative side effects. During the famine of 1891–92, the freedom of the *zemskie nachal'niki* would, on at least one occasion, threaten to disrupt the proper management of relief. See chapter 10.

50. This fact was pointed out to me by Nancy Frieden, who is currently completing a most interesting doctoral dissertation on the medical intelligentsia of the 1890s.

51. The powers of the land captains with regard to food supply were rather vague. See *Ustav narodnogo prodovol'stviia*, sec. 25.

52. By 1891, however, the new zemstvo law had not been implemented in the provinces affected by the famine.

3. THE CRISIS BEGINS

1. In October, 1891, *Russkie vedomosti* charged that the nation had been completely unprepared to meet the famine crisis (October 27, 1891, p. 1). Similarly, most of the available memoirs and diaries give the impression that the government took no measures to deal with the food supply problem until well into the summer. State Secretary Polovtsov's diary does not indicate that before he left the country in July he was seriously concerned about the state of the crops or the nation's grain reserves. He did not mention the crisis until he returned from abroad in October (*Dnevnik Gosudarstvennogo Sekretaria A. A. Polovtsova*, P. A. Zaionchkovskii, ed. [Moscow, 1966], II, 382–83). Aleksandra Viktorovna Bogdanovich, through whose *salon* passed a large portion of the St. Petersburg élite, did not note the appearance of famine until the end of August (*Tri poslednikh samoderzhtsa, Dnevnik A. V. Bogdanovich* [Moscow-Leningrad, 1924], p. 140). General A. A. Kireev, who was extremely well informed on the activities of the government, does not refer to the crisis until August 21 (*Dnevnik A. A. Kireeva, 1887–1894*, Otdel rukopisei Gosudarstvennoi Ordena Lenina Biblioteki SSSR imeni V. I. Lenina, [hereafter cited: GBL], f. Kireevikh-Novikovikh (No. 126), k. 11, p. 238).

2. For information on loans from the central food supply capital fund during 1890, see *Prodovol'stvennoe delo*, I, 3–11.

3. Witte to D. F. Kobeko, January 23, 1891, No. 600, TsGIA, f. Ministerstva finansov, Departament zheleznodorozhnykh del (No. 268), op. 4, d. 1279, "O l'gotakh v zheleznodorozhnykh tarifakh na prevozki khlebnykh gruzov v mestnosti postradavshie ot neurozhaia," pp. 1–2.

4. Kobeko to Witte, January 24, 1891, No. 599, *ibid.*, p. 50.

5. Vyshnegradskii to Durnovo, January 23, 1891, No. 610, *ibid.*, p. 3.

6. Durnovo to Vyshnegradskii, January 27, 1891, No. 538, *ibid.*, p. 4.

7. *Ibid.*

8. *Ibid.*, pp. 11–12.

9. *Ibid.*, p. 12.

10. Witte to P. N. Cheremisinov (Director of Affairs for the General Conference of the Representatives of Russian Railroads), February 9, 1891, No. 1114, *ibid.*, pp. 29–32.

11. A. N. Kulomzin to Durnovo, January 26, 1891, *Prodovol'stvennoe delo*, I, 1.

12. Durnovo to the Committee of Ministers, April 25, 1891, No. 2813, *ibid.*, pp. 2–11.

13. Kulomzin to Durnovo, May 27, 1891, No. 1203, *ibid.*, p. 12.

14. *Ibid.*

15. The Economic Department of the MVD sent out a circular to the provincial governors requesting information on the condition of the local granaries and food supply capital in mid-June (circular dated June 15, 1891, No. 4165, TsGIA, f. Khoz. dep., op. 46, d. 2922, "Tsirkuliary za 1891 god," p. 7), but officials at the center were apparently slow to systematize the data they received. Durnovo did not present detailed reports on the state of food and cash reserves until late 1891 and early 1892. Much of the information gathered by the MVD was later published in *Urozhai 1891 goda.*

16. *1891 god*, I (1891), 1–87.

17. *Russkie vedomosti*, April 7, 1891, p. 2.

18. *Ibid.*, May 29, 1891, p. 1.

19. *Ibid.*, June 18, 1891, p. 1.

20. Ermolov, *Nashi neurozhai, i prodovol' stvennyi vopros* (SPb., 1909), I, 100.

21. *Ibid.*

22. *Ibid.* Ermolov's account of his clash with Vyshnegradskii is not supported by the testimony of any other observers. Nor was I able to uncover the report he claims to have submitted to the Minister of Finance in the Leningrad State Archives. It may be, then, that the story is apocryphal. But Ermolov's own character lends credence to this tale. Ermolov was, by all accounts, a modest, unambitious, and honest man. It seems unlikely that he would have fabricated a legend out of whole cloth.

23. V. P. Rokasovskii to A. G. Vishniakov, June 7, 1891, No. 2385, TsGIA, f. Khoz. dep., op. 4, d. 2132, "O ssude Tambovskomu gubernskomu zemstvu," pp. 1–2.

24. Vishniakov to Rokasovskii, June 15, 1891, No. 5096, *ibid.*, pp. 3–4.

25. Durnovo to Vyshnegradskii, June 19, 1891, No. 4254, TsGIA, f. Min. finansov, Dep.

zheleznodorozhnykh del, op. 4, d. 1279, "O l'gotakh v zheleznodorozhnykh tarifakh," p. 136.

26. On June 17, Witte sent a series of dispatches to local trade committees (*birzhevye komitety*) in Nizhni-Novgorod, Kazan, Odessa, Riga, Reval, Rostov-na-Donu, Moscow, Elets, Warsaw, Taganrog, and other commercial centers. Witte asked the committees to tell him what kinds of grain were available in their localities and in what quantities. He also wished to know if these grains were moving onto the internal market and, if so, how much. The same day Witte also requested the directors of the *kazennye palaty* (local agencies of the Ministry of Finance) in Samara, Simbirsk, Kazan, Viatka, Ufa, Orenburg, and Perm to provide information on local stores of grain, regional prices, and the amounts of grain being shipped into their areas from other provinces. On June 18 Witte proposed to Vishniakov that they share information on local conditions, Witte's dispatches to the trade committees, and *kazennye palaty*, *ibid.*, pp. 78–81. Proposal to Vishniakov, *ibid.*, pp. 176–77.

27. Vyshnegradskii to Durnovo, June 25, 1891, No. 5286, *ibid.*, pp. 146–51. At the old rates it cost 4.17 kopeks to ship one *pud* of grain 100 *versty*; under the new tariff, it cost only 1 kopek. Similarly, to transport one *pud* of grain 900 *versty*, which used to cost 20.25 kopeks, would now cost only 9 kopeks. The greatest reduction of shipping rates under the new arrangements applied to short hauls. This was probably designed to encourage the movement of grain within the regions affected by the crop failure. This was important, because, as we noted above, even within the blighted provinces there were areas which had had relatively good harvests. The new rates could assist in bringing about a more even distribution of the grain within these *gubernii*.

28. Vsepoddanneishii doklad Ministra Finansov, June 27, 1891, *ibid.*, pp. 182–87.

29. Zinov'ev's report to Durnovo is found in TsGIA, f. Khoz. dep., op. 4, d. 2116, "O ssude Tul'skomu gubernskomu zemstvu," pp. 1–3. A summary of the situation in Tula and Zinov'ev's requests can be found in a document which Durnovo presented to the Committee of Ministers. See Zapiska Ministra vnutrennikh del, Departament khoziaistvennyi, June 20, 1891, No. 109 in *Prodovol'stvennoe delo*, I, 13–14. (Hereafter, all such documents will be cited according to the following formula: Zapiska MVD, date, number of the document, followed by its location in *Prodovol'stvennoe delo*.) For Goriainov's proposals, see Zapiska MVD, June 20, 1891, No. 113, *ibid.*, pp. 17–19. Baranov's telegram is noted in Vypiska iz zhurnala Komiteta Ministrov, June 25, 1891, *ibid.*, p. 20.

30. Report of the Governor of Tula, June 15, 1891, TsGIA, f. Khoz. dep. op. 4, d. 2116, "O ssude Tul'skomu gubernskomu zemstvu," p. 1.

31. *Ibid.*, pp. 1–2.

32. *Ibid.*, p. 2.

33. *Ibid.*, p. 3.

34. Zapiska MVD, June 20, 1891, No. 113, *Prodovol'stvennoe delo*, I, 17.

35. *Ibid.*, pp. 17–18.

36. *Ibid.*, p. 18–19. The Economic Department was apparently willing to grant the Penza zemstvo only 900,000 rubles. Durnovo, however, raised the size of the loan to 1 million, exactly the sum recommended by Goriainov.

37. At this time the MVD estimated that it had only 7,245,456 rubles to meet the food supply needs of the country (Zapiska MVD, June 20, 1891, No. 109, *ibid.*, p. 13).

38. To counteract the alleged tendency of the zemstvos to request more than they really needed, the MVD would, on occasion, assign money to the province, but make only a portion of it directly available to the zemstvo. The other part of the money would remain in the hands of the Ministry until it was clear that the zemstvos actually required it. The initial request of the Governor of Tula was handled in this manner. Although the 500,000 rubles he asked for was assigned to the account of the province, only 300,000 were made immediately available to the zemstvo. The remaining 200,000 rubles were kept under the control of the MVD. A telegram from Durnovo to Zinov'ev, dated June 27, informed the governor of this condition, and warned him that he was to see that the zemstvos observed the greatest economy in the use of these sums. TsGIA, f. Khoz. dep., op. 4, d. 2116, "O ssude Tul'skomu gubernskomu zemstvu," p. 11.

39. Zapiska MVD, June 20, 1891, No. 113, *Prodovol'stvennoe delo*, I, 18.

40. When Governor Baranov tried to limit the role of the zemstvos in relief work, Durnovo rejected his scheme and expressed confidence in the zemstvos. The minister's views were stated in a confidential letter to Baranov dated July 1, 1891, No. 4579, TsGIA, f. Khoz. dep., op. 4, d. 2112, "O ssude Nizhegorodskomu gubernskomu zemstvu," p. 71. Baranov's attempts to bring relief operations under his control will be discussed in chapter 9.

41. See p. 22.

42. Vypiska iz zhurnala Komiteta Ministrov, June 25, 1891, *Prodovol'stvennoe delo*, I, 20–21.

43. Zapiska MVD, June 20, 1891, No. 113, *ibid.*, p. 19.

44. Vypiska iz zhurnala Komiteta Ministrov, June 25, 1891, *ibid.*, pp. 20–21.

4. SETTING THE PATTERN FOR RELIEF

1. For a more detailed discussion of the limitations on the power of the Committee of Ministers, see chapter 5.

2. Zapiska MVD, October 3, 1891, No. 134. *Prodovol'stvennoe delo*, I, 23. In the course of the summer the following grants were made: Crimea, 100,000 rubles; Kazan, 3,000,000; Kursk, 200,000; Nizhni-Novgorod, 2,800,000; Olonetsk, 150,000; Orel, 200,000; Orenburg, 1,000,000; Penza, 3,000,000; Perm, 1,000,000; Riazan, 900,000; Samara, 3,400,000; Saratov, 2,500,000; Simbirsk, 5,000,000; Tambov, 2,300,000; Tobolsk, 1,211,500; Tula, 58,000; Ufa, 1,300,000; Viatka, 764,000. These sums include the grants made to Penza, Nizhni-Novgorod, and Tula discussed in chapter 3.

3. TsGAOR, f. Pleve, op. 1, d. 80, "Vsepoddanneishii doklad Ministra vnutrennikh del o merakh priniatykh po okazaniiu pomoshchi raionam postradavshim ot neurozhaia," p. 13.

4. Loans from the treasury were granted on 12 and 19 July and 1 and 29 August. Zapiska MVD, October 3, 1891, No. 134, *Prodovol'stvennoe delo*, I, 25–26.

5. In an article carried in *Grazhdanin* (November 28, 1891, p. 4), the condition of the Economic Department was described as follows: "It is common knowledge that . . . [the Economic] Department, instead of being seen for what it is, the most important Department of the Ministry, has, from time immemorial, acquired the legendary reputation as something despised and neglected. In all probability as the result of this the [Economic] Department has lacked (also from time immemorial) that without which it is difficult to imagine the practical activity of the Department—*living people*." (Italics in original.)

6. I tried to obtain the files relating to Vishniakov's revision at the Central State Historical Archives in Leningrad but was not successful. The papers may have been lost or hopelessly scattered among various *dela*.

7. According to Korolenko, Vishniakov "taught . . . the lessons of moderation and supplied the Governors with the corresponding circulars." V. G. Korolenko, "Tretii element (Pamiati N. F. Annenskogo)," *Sobranie sochinenii*, VIII, 267. During his tour Vishniakov constantly reminded local officials that during past famines relief grants from the central government rarely exceeded 2 or 3 million rubles per province. He also stressed the small size of the sums at the disposal of the MVD. See L. V. Dashkevich, *Nashe Ministerstvo vnutrennikh del* (Berlin, 1895), pp. 39–40. Also useful is the account of Vishniakov's visit to Saratov on July 26, 1891, published in *Russkie vedomosti*, August 2, 1891, p. 2.

8. A. B. Mikhailov, an agent of the Department of Direct Taxes of the Ministry of Finance, describes the methods Vishniakov used to intimidate the Tambov zemstvo. Upon arriving in Tambov, Vishniakov called a conference to discuss the needs of the province and invited Mikhailov and the local tax inspectors to participate. The reports of the tax inspectors, which apparently implied that zemstvo estimates were excessive, produced a strong impression at the meeting. As a result "the representatives of the zemstvo, after a brief struggle, surrendered and recognized that, for the time being, their further requests for loans [would be] superfluous." Mikhailov to Kobeko, July 28, 1891, TsGIA, f. Khoz. dep., op. 4, d. 2132, "O ssude Tambovskomu gubernskomu zemstvu," p. 75.

9. Governor Baranov of Nizhni-Novgorod spoke of Vishniakov's "open criticism of my actions" during the latter's visit to Nizhni. Baranov had been among the first of the provincial governors to request help from the center. At the time of Vishniakov's tour, Baranov was supporting the zemstvo's request for additional funds. Baranov to Durnovo, July 17, 1891, No. 3397, TsGIA, f. Khoz. dep., op. 4, d. 2112, "O ssude Nizhegorodskomu gubernskomu zemstvu," p. 156.

10. Vishniakov to Durnovo, telegram dated July 17, 1891, *ibid.*, p. 150.

11. The origin and function of the food supply conferences will be discussed pp. 50–51.

12. The initial request of the *uezd* zemstvos had been for a total of 13 million rubles. The provincial zemstvo had already reduced this to 8 million. Baranov to Durnovo, telegram dated July 5, 1891, TsGIA f. Khoz. dep., op. 4, d. 2112, "O ssude Nizhegorodskomu gubernskomu zemstvu," p. 78.

13. In addition to the 1 million rubles granted at the end of June, another million had been given to the zemstvo on July 10. Durnovo to Baranov, telegram dated July 10, 1891, *ibid.*, p. 82.

14. Vishniakov to Durnovo, telegram dated July 17, 1891, *ibid.*, p. 152. Vishniakov's skeptical views concerning the accuracy of the Nizhni-Novgorod zemstvo's estimates were supported by A. B. Mikhailov. Like Vishniakov, Mikhailov felt that the zemstvos and Governor Baranov overestimated the danger. He stated that the data upon which the provincial requests were based had been gathered much too hastily to be accepted at face value. Mikhailov to Kobeko, July 12, 1891, *ibid.*, pp. 229–38.

15. According to Kulomzin, Vishniakov stated that the harvest had failed, but there was no famine. See Zaionchkovskii, *Rossiiskoe samoderzhavie*, p. 184.

16. Durnovo referred to Vishniakov's report in a letter to the governor of Tambov. The Minister stated that upon reading the report, "it was impossible not to be convinced that

the situation [with regard to] food supply in certain areas was really rather serious." Durnovo to Rokasovskii, August 19, 1891, No. 5992, TsGIA, f. Khoz. dep., op. 4., d. 2132, "O ssude Tambovskomu gubernskomu zemstvu," p. 78.

17. Zapiska MVD, October 3, 1891, No. 134, *Prodovol'stvennoe delo*, I, 22.

18. The Governor's views were presented in a report to Durnovo dated July 10, 1891. TsGIA, f. Khoz. dep., op. 4, d. 2132, "O ssude Tambovskomu gubernskomu zemstvu," p. 13. The MVD's award to the zemstvo is found, *ibid.*, p. 44.

19. Vorontsov-Dashkov to Durnovo, telegram dated July 22, 1891, *ibid.*, p. 49.

20. Request of the MVD to the Ministry of Finance, July 23, 1891, No. 5116, *ibid.*, p. 48.

21. Durnovo to Vorontsov-Dashkov, telegram dated July 23, 1891, *ibid.*, p. 53.

22. Durnovo to Rokasovskii, telegram dated July 23, 1891, *ibid.*, p. 52.

23. On July 15 the marshal of the Tambov nobility wired the Ministry warning that the crops in the province had failed. His message concluded with the flat statement: "There will be famine. . . ." Four days later, however, the marshal wired in a more optimistic vein, stating that rain had come and that the spring grains were reviving, *ibid.*, pp. 5–6. The MVD received a number of such optimistic notices from other provinces.

24. See chapter 9.

25. Apparently, these guidelines were issued separately to each governor. No general circular was sent out, or if it was, it is not preserved among the documents I saw in the Central State Archives in Leningrad. The five basic points listed above are drawn from two ministerial proposals. Both documents are virtually identical in content. Proposal of the MVD to Baranov, July 11, 1891, No. 4852, TsGIA, f. Khoz. dep., op. 4, d. 2112, "O ssude Nizhegorodskomu gubernskomu zemstvu," pp. 140–42; Proposal of the MVD to Zinov'ev, July 26, 1891, TsGIA, f. Khoz. dep., op. 4, d. 2116, "O ssude Tul'skomu gubernskomu zemstvu," pp. 69–70.

26. See for example the article by D. F. Samarin, "Est' li v Rossii golod ili net?" *Moskovskie vedomosti*, November 17, 1891, pp. 2–3.

27. By no means all zemstvos excluded children from the rolls. This does seem to have been the case in Kazan, although this ruling was later modified. The neglect of children appears very callous from a modern perspective. But one should bear in mind that the special and complex dietary needs of the very young were not recognized until well into the twentieth century. W. R. Aykroyd, "Definition of Different Degrees of Starvation," in *Famine: A Symposium*, pp. 20–21.

28. During the summer of 1891, the Ministry of Internal Affairs changed its guidelines and stated that every person "of working or nonworking age" was eligible for loans. Zemstvo and government personnel were urged, however, to examine the material conditions of all who requested aid so as not to give out unnecessary loans. Zapiska MVD, October 3, 1891, No. 134, *Prodovol'stvennoe delo*, I, 24.

29. According to G. B. Masefield: "If practically the whole of the energy requirements has to be supplied by a cereal, a daily allowance of some 700 grams of grain per adult has to be envisaged; *but in practice, a grain allowance of approximately 300 grams per day as a supplement to other available foods has been much more commonly used in famine relief*" (italics are mine). *Food and Nutrition Procedures in Times of Disaster* (Rome, 1967), p. 43. The Russian relief norm in 1891–92 was around 400 grams per day.

30. During the period from January to June 1892, the average food loan in the famine zone exceeded the 30-*funt* limit. Ministerstvo vnutrennikh del Tsentral'nyi statisticheskii komitet, *Statisticheskie dannye po vydache ssud na obsemenie i prodovol'stvie naseleniiu postradavshemu ot neurozhaia v 1891–1892 gg.*, *Vremennik tsentral'nogo statisticheskogo komiteta*, No. 28 (SPb., 1894), p. 63. Hereafter this source will be cited: *Statisticheskie dannye*.

31. Baranov's original suggestion was for a committee which would exercise a "general supervision of the use of the loans . . . given to the zemstvo." The Governor envisioned a body composed of some *zemskie nachal'niki*, grain merchants, and police *ispravaniki* (Baranov to Durnovo, June 24, 1891, No. 2906, TsGIA, f. Khoz. dep., op. 4, d. 2112, "O ssude Nizhegorodskomu zemstvu," p. 57). Durnovo, however, felt that the powers of the special committee should be wider and suggested that "its obligations should not [only] include supervision of the use of loans by the zemstvo . . . but [also] cooperation with it" in the task of relief (Durnovo to Baranov, telegram dated June 28, 1891, *ibid.*, p. 60).

32. As in the case of the guidelines for zemstvo loans, it is not clear whether a single ministerial circular was issued or whether instructions were issued to the governors on an individual basis. If one special circular was issued, I did not find a copy of it.

33. The Kazan governor was ordered to establish the Conference in July, but this body may not have met until October. The first journal of the Kazan Food Supply Conference to appear among the documents relating to relief in that province is dated October 19. TsGIA, f. Khoz. dep., op. 4, d. 2125, "O ssude Kazanskomu gubernskomu zemstvu," pp. 45–50. The first mention of such a conference in Tula is found in a report sent by the Governor to the MVD in September. Zinov'ev to Durnovo, September 27, 1891, No. 3450, TsGIA, f. Khoz. dep., op. 4, d. 2116, "O ssude Tul'skomu gubernskomu zemstvu," pp. 97–100. The Conference met on September 18.

34. Circular of the Economic Department, August 21, 1891, No. 5971, TsGIA, f. Khoz. dep., op. 46, d. 2922, "Tsirkuliary za 1891 god," p. 19.

35. Circulars of the Economic Department, July 11, 1891, No. 5454, and September 20, 1891, No. 7118, *ibid.*, pp. 15 and 30.

36. Circular of the Economic Department, September 12, 1891, No. 6856, *ibid.*, p. 27.

37. Circular of the Economic Department, September 25, 1891, No. 7323, *ibid.*, p. 32. Apparently some zemstvo *upravy* were giving out the certificates which would allow shipment of grain at special rates without proper verification by whom and for what purpose they were to be used. The circular noted that "these certificates (*svidetel'stva*) are becoming items of trade and are transferred from hand to hand." The MVD recommended that the zemstvos institute tighter controls and more accurate record-keeping.

38. Circular of the Economic Department, September 27, 1891, No. 7366, *ibid.*, p. 33.

39. Circular of the Zemskii Otdel, August 1, 1891, No. 30, TsGIA, f. Dep. obshchikh del, op. 238, d. 78, "Tsirkuliary za 1891 god," p. 31.

40. *Ibid.*

41. *Ibid.*, pp. 32–33.

42. Circular of the Economic Department, September 1, 1891, No. 6395, published in *Pravitel'stvennyi vestnik*, September 3, 1891, p. 1.

43. *Ibid.*, pp. 1–2. In a later circular, the governors were ordered to keep the Ministry

informed on a regular basis as to the collection of contributions for the relief of victims of the crop failure. Circular of the Economic Department, September 5, 1891, No. 6519, TsGIA, f. Khoz. dep., op. 46, d. 2922, "Tsirkuliary za 1891 god," p. 24.

44. In July the governor of Tula noted that local charity had virtually collapsed as a result of excessive demand. In some areas whole villages had turned to charitable relief. Zinov'ev to the Ministry of Internal Affairs, July 20, 1891, TsGIA, f. Khoz., dep., op. 4, d. 2116, "O ssude Tul'skomu gubernskomu zemstvu," p. 67.

45. A. A. Kornilov, *Sem' mesiatsev sredi golodaiushchikh krest'ian* (Moscow, 1893), p. 4.

46. This comment is S. Iu. Witte's *Vospominaniia* (3 vols.; Moscow, 1960), I, 303, but others shared this view. See P. A. Zaionchkovskii, *Rossiiskoe samoderzhavie*, pp. 151–52.

47. When he was selected to fill the place of the late Dmitri Tolstoi, Durnovo was appalled. He told the Emperor he was not competent to hold the post. A. V. Bogdanovich, *Tri poslednikh samoderzhtsa. Dnevnik A. V. Bogdanovich* (Moscow-Leningrad, 1924), p. 95.

48. A clear illustration of the tendency of governors to resist ministerial orders is supplied in Zaionchkovskii, *Rossiiskoe samoderzhavie*, p. 183.

49. This outline of events is based on a report which Anis'in sent to Durnovo on August 17, 1891. The Ministry did not dispute the facts. TsGIA, f. Khoz. dep., op. 4, d. 2122, "O ssude po Viatskomu gubernskomu zemstvu," pp. 90–92.

50. *Ibid.*

51. A circular of the Viatka governor ordered police "to be on the alert (*zorko sledit'*) not to permit grain [to pass] beyond the borders of the province," *ibid.*, p. 147.

52. In a report to the *uezd* assembly, the Tsarevokokshaiskii *uezd uprava* noted "that plainclothesmen from Iaranskii and Urzhumskii *uezdy* are turning up at our bazaars to spy on their own peasants so as not to permit any grain [from Viatka] to be sold to us. Several of these agents have been detained by our local police authorities." Report of the *uprava* dated October 24, 1891, TsGIA, f. Khoz. dep., op. 4, d. 2125 "O ssude Kazanskomu gubernskomu zemstvu," p. 99.

53. In a report to D. F. Kobeko, the head of the Viatka *Kazennaia palata*, Vinogradov, noted that Viatka ordinarily sold grain to other provinces even though Viatka itself was not self sufficient. Report dated September 21, 1891, TsGIA f. Khoz. dep., op. 4, d. 2122, "O ssude po Viatskomu gubernskomu zemstvu," pp. 244–48.

54. Durnovo to Anis'in, August 27, 1891, No. 6245, *ibid.*, p. 97.

55. Telegram from Poltaratskii to Durnovo, *ibid.*, pp. 105–6.

56. Durnovo to Anis'in, telegram dated September 7, 1891, *ibid.*, p. 107.

57. Anis'in to MVD, telegram dated September 8, 1891, *ibid.*, p. 108.

58. MVD to Anis'in, telegram dated September 10, 1891, *ibid.*, p. 109.

59. Durnovo to Anis'in, September 19, 1891, No. 7081, *ibid.*, p. 130.

60. Telegrams from Poltaratskii to the Ministry dated September 25 and 27, 1891, *ibid.*, pp. 152–53; 160–61.

61. Anis'in to Durnovo, telegram dated September 29, 1891, *ibid.*, p. 174.

62. Durnovo to Anis'in, October 11, 1891, No. 7796, *ibid.*, pp. 203–4.

63. The complaint was presented by Kazan's Vice-Governor A. P. Engel'gardt on November 29, 1891, No. 6080, TsGIA, f. Khoz. dep., op. 4, d. 2125, "O ssude Kazanskomu gubernskomu zemstvu," pp. 97–98.

64. MVD to Poltaratskii, December 14, 1891, No. 10682, *ibid.*, p. 113.

65. The Committee of Ministers' pressure on Durnovo and the latter's response are discussed in chapter 5.

66. The *ukaz* of July 28, 1891 forbade the export of rye and rye products from ports on the Baltic and Black Seas and the Sea of Azov and also the transport of said grains across the western land frontiers of the Empire (PSZ, 3rd ed., No. 7939). On August 29 a supplemental regulation prohibited the export of wheat from the Transcaspian *oblast'* into Persia. *Sobranie uzakonenii i rasporiazhenii pravitel'stva 1891 g.* pt. 2, No. 950. The ban on rye exports extended to the ports of Archangel province on September 1 (*ibid.*, No. 975). On October 16 the export restrictions were extended to all grains except wheat (PSZ, 3rd ed., No. 8010), and finally, wheat, too, was placed on the forbidden list (*ibid.*, No. 8037, November 3, 1891).

67. *Vestnik finansov promyshlennosti i torgovli* (St. Petersburg), July 14, 1891, pp. 72–74.

68. *Ibid.*, August 4, 1891, p. 277.

69. On June 22 V. N. Lamsdorf noted in his diary: "The Minister of Finance is very concerned: should he stop the export of grain or ease its return to Russia? The general crop failure, dangers of a political character, etc." *Dnevnik 1891–92* (Moscow-Leningrad, 1934), p. 148.

70. On the new tariffs, see chapter 3.

71. Vsepoddanneishii doklad Ministra finansov, July 12, 1891, TsGIA, f. Min. finansov, Dep. zheleznodorozhnykh del, op. 4, d. 1279, "O l'gotakh v zheleznodorozhnykh tarifakh," p. 235.

72. *Vestnik finansov*, August 4, 1891, p. 274.

73. *Ibid.*, p. 276.

74. V. A. Zolotov, *Khlebnyi eksport Rossii cherez porty chernogo i azovskogo morei v 60-90-e gody XIX veka* (Rostov-na-Donu, 1966), p. 165.

75. O. Margulies, *Yidishe Folksmasn in Kamf kegn zeire Unterdriker (Etiudn)* (Moscow, 1940), pp. 92–97. I wish to express my thanks to Dr. Z. Y. Gitelman for calling my attention to this valuable Yiddish language source, and for translating the relevant passage.

76. Zolotov, *Khlebnyi eksport*, p. 165.

77. Ermolov, *Nashi neurozhai*, I, 104–5.

78. Zolotov, *Khlebnyi eksport*, pp. 163–64.

79. Unfortunately, much of this discussion of the reasons for the export ban is little more than educated conjecture. Time did not permit me to pursue this problem on the basis of archival documents.

80. One student of the problem insists the ban on export was a panic measure taken on the basis of inadequate information. "The prohibition on [grain] exports was taken in the dark and spread panic that we would not have sufficient bread to feed the country until the new harvest. This opinion existed only among the agents of the government and our intelligentsia. . . ." The grain merchants of the country knew better. After the food supply

crisis was over, there remained sizable stores of grain unsold and undelivered. Dashkevich, *Nashe Ministerstvo*, pp. 34–35.

81. When the government announced a ban on the export of all grains except wheat, there was a crisis on the money market and panic in trading circles. See *Russkie vedomosti*, October 26, 1891, p. 1.

82. This inference was drawn by the liberal press. *Ibid.*, August 2, 1891, p. 1.

5. THE CRISIS DEEPENS

1. Information on area and population of famine stricken *gubernii* is drawn from N. S. Petlin, *Opyt opisanniia gubernii i oblastei Rossii* (2 vols.; SPb., 1893).

2. For a map showing the relationship of railroad lines to the areas affected by the crop failure of 1891 see p. 80.

3. *Vestnik finansov*, September 29, 1891, pp. 836–37.

4. Edward Ames, "A Century of Russian Railroad Construction, 1837–1936," *American Slavic and East European Review*, VI (December, 1947), 64–65.

5. *Russkie vedomosti*, October 28, 1891, p. 1.

6. See chapter 4.

7. The food supply law, under whose provisions zemstvo loans were granted, covered only peasants who were members of village communes.

8. See notes 43 and 44 for chapter 1.

9. The slowness with which private charity developed in 1891 was due in part to apprehension inspired by the governmental regulations concerning private relief which had been issued on September 1, 1891. This distrust was largely based on a misinterpretation of the MVD's regulations. Even the liberal *Russkie vedomosti* admitted that the rules did not set up any legal barriers to the development of private charity (November 10, 1891, p. 1).

10. Polovtsov, *Dnevnik*, II, 383.

11. TsGIA, f. Filippovikh (No. 728), op. 1, d. 1, "Dnevnik Tertiia Ivanovicha Filippova za 1892 g.," p. 20.

12. Polovtsov states that grain purchased in Tomsk, and intended for the provisioning of workers at a factory in Bogoslovskii *okrug* was stopped in transit through Tobolsk province because of an order from the MVD blocking grain exports from Tobolsk province. Polovtsov intervened, and Durnovo sent out a special order permitting the passage of the shipment (*Dnevnik*, II, 389).

13. Bogdanovich, *Tri poslednikh samoderzhtsa*, p. 149.

14. Quoted in *Russkie vedomosti*, September 24, 1891, p. 1.

15. According to A. A. Kireev, Durnovo himself complained bitterly that " 'the public . . . does not know what we are doing and how much [aid] we are giving out' " (Kireev to Petrovskii, August 5, 1891, GBL, f. Petrovskogo, k. 1, d. 64, "Pis'ma Kireeva k Petrovskomu," p. 1).

16. The use of the word *golod* to describe the situation in 1891 was questioned even outside government circles and not only by reactionaries. For some people, the word *golod* could

be employed only when the population had been reduced practically to cannibalism. Korolenko noted that many educated persons came to Nizhni-Novgorod province and traveled about, but they failed to find *golod*, although they must have encountered misery and hunger on every hand. V. G. Korolenko, *V golodnyi god* in *Sobranie Sochenenii* (Moscow, 1955), IX, 101–2.

17. This rumor was false. Lamsdorf, *Dnevnik, 1891–92*, p. 207.

18. Bogdanovich, *Tri poslednikh samoderzhtsa*, p. 144. The official in question was A. A. Abaza.

19. *Ibid.*, pp. 144–45.

20. *Ibid.*, p. 142.

21. Kireev estimated that 33 million persons were among the starving (letter to Petrovskii, October 22, 1891, k. 1, d. 64, "Pis'ma Kireeva k Petrovskomu," p. 1). Page citations in this correspondence refer to the pagination of individual letters.

22. On August 21 Kireev entered in his diary that his nephew, A. I. Novikov, a *zemskii nachal'nik* in Tambov, had written that "babies are dying like flies, *their mothers have no milk*" (italics in original). *Dnevnik A. A. Kireeva*, GBL, f. Kireevikh-Novikovikh, k. 11, p. 238.

23. Bogdanovich, *Tri poslednikh samoderzhtsa*, p. 144.

24. *Ibid.*, p. 142. Bogdanovich later noted that this rumor had proved groundless.

25. The *dela* in the archives of the Economic Department of the Ministry of Internal Affairs contain many directives calling on individual governors to explain, confirm, or deny stories that appeared in the press concerning events in their provinces. The use of newspaper accounts by the MVD is clearly illustrated by papers relating to relief in Kazan. In October the Ministry asked for information concerning an alleged case of death from starvation. In this instance the Governor responded that the person in question had died as a result of untreated illness not lack of food. Poltaratskii to MVD, October 9, 1891, TsGIA, f. Khoz. dep., op. 4, d. 2125, "O ssude Kazanskomu gubernskomu zemstvu," pp. 2–3. Later the MVD sent out a series of telegrams asking the Governor's comments on reports that had appeared in the press concerning serious difficulties with local relief operations. The Ministry's telegrams are dated November 9, 14, and 20 (*ibid.*, pp. 51, 58, 60).

26. This ministerial order was dated October 20, 1891. See Zaionchkovskii, *Rossiiskoe samoderzhavie*, p. 186.

27. On November 19, 1891 the MVD issued a second warning to *Russkie vedomosti*. Since this warning followed closely the appearance of "*Strashnyi vopros*" on November 6, it is reasonable to suppose that the two acts were connected. Yet one should remember that the stated reason for the warning was the publication of some misinformation concerning the state of the nation's grain supply. By warning *Russkie vedomosti* about this rather than Tolstoi's article, the Ministry seems to have been engaging in a form of "crypto-communication." It was trying to indicate that it was prepared to permit the press to discuss the famine with relative freedom provided it continued to serve as a vehicle of accurate information about conditions.

28. Durnovo's account of his activities between July and October is contained in the following document: Zapiska MVD, October 3, 1891, No. 134, *Prodovol'stvennoe delo*, I, 22–25.

29. A good survey of the powers and limitations of the Committee of Ministers is to be found in Gradovskii's *Nachala russkogo gosudarstvennogo prava* in *Sobranie sochinenii, VIII, 241–53*. See also G. V. Vernadskii, *Ocherk istorii prava russkogo gosudarstva XVIII–XIX vv.* (*Period imperii*) (Prague, 1924), pp. 73–76.

30. The efforts of the Committee of Ministers in regard to food supply are surveyed in the various volumes of S. M. Seredonin, *Istoricheskii obzor deiatel'nosti Komiteta Ministrov* (5 vols.; SPb., 1902–1904). Of special value are the documents which pertain to the Committee's activities during the reign of Nicholas I (Vol. II, pt. 1, pp. 293–366).

31. Zaionchkovskii, *Rossiiskoe samoderzhavie*, pp. 98–99. This larger role resulted from the government's desire to avoid sending certain legislative projects to the more liberal State Council.

32. Vypiska iz zhurnala Komiteta Ministrov, October 8, 1891, *Prodovol'stvennoe delo*, I, 26. The next day Durnovo was able to be more specific about the sums he intended to request from the treasury. He stated that he and Vyshnegradskii would ask for a supplemental grant of 32 million rubles. Zapiska MVD, October 9, 1891, No. 142, *ibid.*, p. 33.

33. Sostavlennaia Kantseliarieiu Komiteta Ministrov spravka k zapiskam MVD Nos. 182, 184, 186, 188, *ibid.*, pp. 72–73.

34. This problem was discussed at the session of October 22. For a convenient summary of the debates in the Committee of Ministers between January and December 1891 see Spravka iz polozhenii Komiteta Ministrov sostoiavshikhsia pri rassmotrenii v tekushchem godu predstavlenii Ministra vnutrennikh del po prodovol'stvennym delam, *ibid.*, pp. 134–42.

35. *Ibid.*, p. 135.

36. *Ibid.*

37. *Ibid.*, pp. 135–36.

38. *Ibid.*

39. *Ibid.*, p. 136.

40. *Ibid.*, p. 137.

41. *Ibid.*, p. 138.

42. *Ibid.*

43. The text of the Imperial Rescript can be found in *Vestnik Evropy* (December, 1891), p. 881.

44. V. E. Maksimov, *Ocherki po istorii obshchestvennykh rabot v Rossii* (SPb., 1905), pp. 117–18.

45. A. A. fon Vendrikh, *Otchet po upravaleniiu perevozkami po zheleznym dorogam v mestnosti postradavshie ot neurozhaia* (*dekabr' 1891 g.—mart 1892 g.*) (SPb., 1896), pp. 9–10.

46. Because the transportation crisis was of such importance in the government's struggle against the famine, it will be treated in a separate chapter.

47. Zapiska Ministra Finansov, December 8, 1891, *Prodovol'stvennoe delo*, I, 115–20.

48. Zapiska MVD, December 17, 1891, No. 247, *ibid.*, III, 100–2.

49. Zapiska MVD, December 27, 1891, No. 260, *ibid.*, pp. 103–5.

50. The most important of these reports were Zapiska MVD, December 13, 1891, No. 242, *ibid.*, I, 129–33 and Zapiska MVD, December 20, 1891, No. 253, *ibid.*, pp. 158–60.

51. Zapiska MVD, December 26, 1891, No. 259, *ibid.*, pp. 169–72.

52. *Ibid.*, p. 169. Durnovo stated that the population of the affected provinces needed about 9,027,000 *pudy* of food per month, or about 40,397,000 *pudy* between December 15 and May 1, 1892. Local resources could account for 14,534,000 *pudy*. Thus 25,863,000 *pudy* of food grain had to be obtained outside the affected region. 6,825,000 *chetverty* of seed were also required, but only 839,000 *chetverty* were on hand in the stricken *gubernii*. Some 6 million *chetverty* of seed (about 30 million *pudy*) had to be delivered. Durnovo reminded his colleagues that shipments designed to cover the needs of the population in the period between December and May had to arrive by the first of March in order to avoid the transport difficulties caused by the *rasputitsa*.

53. *Ibid.*, p. 170.

54. *Ibid.*, p. 171.

55. *Ibid.*

56. *Ibid.*, p. 171–72. Durnovo asked that he be empowered to take such actions in all the famine-stricken provinces and also in Astrakhan and Kharkov *gubernii* and Akmolinsk *oblast'*.

57. *Ibid.*, p. 171.

58. Zapiska MVD, December 13, 1891, No. 242, *ibid.*, pp. 131.

59. Zapiska MVD, December 26, 1891, No. 259, *ibid.*, p. 171.

60. Durnovo did not state what difficulties caused him to abandon the plan. On December 13, he stated that he would take the matter up with the State Council, but Polovtsov, the State Secretary, does not mention the question having been discussed. Most probably, Durnovo encountered opposition from other ministers who may have felt that the institutional and administrative problems involved in such a scheme would make it unworkable. The original idea for centralized management of the grain trade seems to have come from I. I. Kabat, an MVD official. For further details on Kabat's proposal, see chapter 6.

61. Zapiska MVD, December 26, 1891, No. 259, *Prodovol'stvennoe delo*, I, 171.

62. Vypiska iz zhurnala Komiteta Ministrov, December 31, 1891, *ibid.*, pp. 197–98.

63. Polovtsov, *Dnevnik*, II, 405.

6. THE RAILROAD CRISIS

1. *Vestnik finansov*, December 1, 1891, pp. 548–49.

2. *Ibid.*, September 8, 1891, pp. 634–35, and August 4, 1891, p. 277.

3. *Ibid.*, September 1, 1891, pp. 561–62.

4. *Ibid.*, August 4, 1891, p. 278.

5. *Ibid.*, October 6, 1891, pp. 2–3. See also A. Izmailov, *Zheleznye dorogi v neurozhai 1891 goda* (SPb., 1895), p. 15.

6. Edward Ames, "A Century of Russian Railroad Construction, 1837–1936." *American Slavic and East European Review*, VI (December, 1947), 64–65.

7. Many of the men who held the post of Minister of Transportation had dubious credentials. V. A. Bobrinskii, Minister from 1869 to 1871, was a sugar magnate. K. N. Pos'et, who held office from 1874 to 1888, was an admiral. His successor, G. E. Pauker, was an army general and military engineer.

8. Giubbenet had been Assistant Minister of Transportation from 1880 to 1885.

9. Witte, *Vospominaniia*, I, 253; S. M. Propper, *Was nicht in die Zeitung kam: Erinnerungen der Chef redakturs der "Birschewyja Wedomosti"* (Frankfort-am-Main, 1929), pp. 159–60.

10. State Secretary A. A. Polovtsov stated that Giubbenet was "not a stupid person, but lacked all education [and was] without any outstanding abilities. . . ." Concerning Giubbenet's appointment as Minister of Transportation, Polovtsov lamented: "This was an extremely unfortunate choice. It lowers the intellectual level of the government . . . [and] introduces into the higher administrative circles an undesirable element [characterized by] narrow views and servility." Polovtsov, *Dnevnik*, II, 182–83.

11. *Grazhdanin*, October 28, 1891, p. 1. During the famine, some of the most perceptive analyses of the problems of the Russian railroads appeared on the pages of this newspaper.

12. This absence of unity had long plagued the Russian railroads. In 1878 a Council for Railway Affairs (*Sovet po zheleznodorozhnym delam*) had been established in the hopes of pulling things together. But the Council was never accepted as a unifying agency. Its large and diverse membership made the Council cumbersome and inefficient. See J. N. Westwood, *A History of Russian Railways* (London, 1964), p. 82. And Gradovskii, *Nachala russkogo gosudarstvennogo prava*, pt. 2, in *Sobranie Sochinenii*, VIII, 492–93.

13. Witte, *Vospominaniia*, I, 205–6, and T. H. Von Laue, *Sergei Witte*, p. 65.

14. Izmailov, *Zheleznye dorogi*, pp. 21–22. The author argues that state officials should have been able to foresee the difficulties which were developing, especially after the growth of traffic on the southwestern railroads during the second half of August.

15. *Ibid.*, pp. 22–23.

16. *Ibid.*, pp. 12–14.

17. A. A. fon Vendrikh, *Otchet po upravleniiu perevozkami po zheleznym dorogam v mestnosti postradavshie ot neurozhaia (dekabr' 1891 g.—mart 1892 g.)* (SPb., 1896), p. 171. Vendrikh's account of the railroad crisis will be used extensively in this chapter because it is the only source which provides a detailed account of the work of the railways during the famine. The fact that Vendrikh was a participant in the events described in the report may make some of his statements open to question; but in general, I find Vendrikh's *Otchet* quite truthful. His statements concerning the quantity of grain shipped into the famine region conform to data found in *Prodovol'stvennoe delo*. Vendrikh's account of the many difficulties he faced may be somewhat exaggerated, but the works of Witte and Izmailov (both critical of Vendrikh) tend to support his statements generally.

18. Izmailov, *Zheleznye dorogi*, pp. 27–28.

19. *Ibid.*, p. 28. Also see Spravka iz polozhenii Komiteta Ministrov, sostoiavshikhsia pri rassmotrenii v tekushchem godu predstavlenii Ministra vnutrennikh del po prodovol'stvennym delam, *Prodovol'stvennoe delo*, I, 137.

20. Izmailov, *Zheleznye dorogi*, p. 28. See also the Circular of the MPS, Department of Railways, October 29, 1891, No. 14,227, *Pravitel'stvennyi vestnik*, October 31, 1891, pp. 1–2.

21. Izmailov, *Zheleznye dorogi*, p. 28.

22. Vendrikh, *Otchet*, pp. 171–72.

23. Kabat's report is entitled "Zapiska o perevozke zemskikh prodovol'stvennykh i semiannykh gruzov po zheleznym dorogam i o merakh k uporiadochneniiu etogo dela." Although it is not clear to whom the report was addressed, it was probably intended for Durnovo or Pleve. The date November 27, 1891 is written in pencil on the report. TsGAOR, f. Pleve, op. 1, d. 70, "Instruktsiia volostnym prodovol'stvennym komitetam, zapiski i pis'ma raznykh lits Pleve i drugim litsam," pp. 13–19.

24. *Ibid.*, p. 15.

25. *Ibid.*, pp. 17–19.

26. Circular of the Economic Department of the MVD, November 30, 1891, No. 9489, TsGIA, f. Khoz. dep., op. 46, d. 2922, "Tsirkuliary za 1891 god," p. 45.

27. Vendrikh, *Otchet*, pp. 9–10.

28. *Grazhdanin*, November 1, 1891, p. 3, and November 2, 1892.

29. On November 13, 1891, *Grazhdanin* carried a front page story on Vendrikh which discussed his long experience in railway affairs. The article summarized a paper which Vendrikh had read to the Railroad Section of the Imperial Russian Technical Society. Meshcherskii's enthusiasm for Vendrikh was well founded. Vendrikh was expert in both the theoretical and the practical side of railroad work. He had managed traffic on one of the Baltic railways and had served as a senior railroad inspector in the MPS. Vendrikh also taught specialized courses on the exploitation of railroads during wartime at the Nicholas Engineering Academy and had written a number of scholarly articles on railroad affairs. For more information about Vendrikh, see the article on him in N. I. Afanas'ev, *Sovremenniki*: *Albom biografii* (2 vols.; SPb., 1909–10), II, 66–69.

30. Giubbenet claimed that Vendrikh had been foisted upon him at Meshcherskii's suggestion. Polovtsov, *Dnevnik*, II, 415.

31. Vendrikh, *Otchet*, p. 171.

32. When the telegram was sent and to whom it was addressed, is not clear. Vyshnegradskii read it to the Committee of Ministers on December 10, 1891. Vypiska iz zhurnala Komiteta Ministrov, December 10, 1891, *Prodovol'stvennoe delo*, I, 126.

33. Vendrikh notes that while the backlog of grain on the Vladikavhaz declined in November by about 1.2 million *pudy*, the volume of grain awaiting shipment on other railways had risen significantly. *Otchet*, pp. 8–9.

34. Vendrikh, *Otchet*, p. 16; Izmailov, *Zheleznye dorogi*, pp. 32–33.

35. Vendrikh, *Otchet*, pp. 17–20.

36. *Ibid.*, pp. 20–22.

37. *Ibid.*, pp. 23–24.

38. *Ibid.*, pp. 30–32.

39. *Ibid.*, pp. 32–33.

40. At one point, Vendrikh was informed that almost all grain was headed for the Syzran-Viaz'ma line. His own investigations, however, revealed that almost 800 carloads of grain were intended for delivery by other railroads (*ibid.*, pp. 47–48).

41. *Ibid.*, pp. 48–51.

42. Namely, the Vladikavkaz, the Voronezh, and the Kursk-Kharkov and Azov lines.

43. Vendrikh, *Otchet*, pp. 52–53.

44. *Ibid.*, pp. 51–53.

45. *Ibid.*, pp. 52–53.

46. Izmailov, *Zheleznye dorogi*, pp. 33–34.

47. Vendrikh, *Otchet*, pp. 12–16.

48. *Ibid.*, pp. 171–72.

49. Svodnaia spravka o kolichestve khlebnykh gruzov, dostavlennykh v postradavshie ot neurozhaia gubernii zheleznym dorogam s 1 Sentiabria 1891 g. po 1 Maia 1892 g., *Prodovol'stvennoe delo*, III, 137.

50. This was noted in a report of the Minister of Transportation to the Committee of Ministers (Zapiska MPS, January 5, 1892, No. 97, *ibid.*, II, 12).

51. Izmailov, *Zheleznye dorogi*, pp. 33–34.

52. Vendrikh, *Otchet*, p. 63.

53. *Ibid.*, p. 59.

54. *Ibid.*, p. 61.

55. On the mentality of railroad technical people, see Witte, *Vospominaniia*, I, 87 and *passim*. There is a good discussion of this problem in an article which appeared on the pages of *Birzhevye Vedomosti* entitled "Politika protivodeistviia i ee grustnye posledstviia" (January 22, 1892, p. 1). Also useful is the article "Nuzhna-li korporatsiia puteitsev?" published in *Grazhdanin*, January 29, 1892, pp. 1–2.

56. Izmailov, *Zheleznye dorogi*, p. 16. The author notes the exhaustion of railroad workers during the famine crisis. The Special Administration tried to ease the situation by hiring additional personnel and by bringing in other workers from different railways. But these new people were often inexperienced, and thus the main burden continued to fall on the regular workers.

57. Witte, *Vospominaniia*, I, 254–55.

58. Izmailov argues that the rapidity with which the new railroad schedules were introduced proves that conflict between Vendrikh and regular railway personnel was minimal. *Zheleznye dorogi*, p. 37.

59. Vendrikh, *Otchet*, pp. 95–97.

60. Izmailov, *Zheleznye dorogi*, pp. 19–20.

61. Vendrikh, *Otchet*, pp. 112–15.

62. *Ibid.*, p. 139.

63. *Ibid.*, pp. 112–15.

64. *Ibid.*, pp. 100–1, 106–7.

65. *Ibid.*, pp. 105–6; Izmailov, *Zheleznye dorogi*, pp. 44–45.

66. Vendrikh, *Otchet*, pp. 102–3.

67. *Ibid.*

68. Izmailov, *Zheleznye dorogi*, pp. 44–45.

69. Some of the attacks on Vendrikh were reported in *Grazhdanin*, December 12, 1891, p. 2, and December 28, 1891, p. 3. See also Witte, *Vospominaniia*, I, 255.

70. Vypiska iz zhurnala Komiteta Ministrov, January 7, 1892, *Prodovol'stvennoe delo*, II, 14–15.

71. Polovtsov, *Dnevnik*, II, 409.

72. Witte, *Vospominaniia*, I, 255.

73. The plot against Giubbenet was a topic of considerable interest in St. Petersburg society. One of the visitors to the salon of Alexandra Bogdanovich felt that Vendrikh was being manipulated by Vyshnegradskii and Witte in order to embarrass Giubbenet and so prepare a ministerial portfolio for Witte. Bogdanovich, *Tri poslednikh samoderzhtsa*, p. 152. Meshcherskii kept the problem of the railroads before the public and the Emperor by running regular attacks on the leadership and staff of the MPS on the pages of *Grazhdanin*.

74. The index to volume II of *Prodovol'stvennoe delo* states that the Committee of Ministers created the conference on January 14. The extract from the Committee's journal on this point is missing from the collection, however.

75. *Grazhdanin*, January 16, 1892, p. 3.

76. *Ibid.*, January 26, 1892, p. 3.

77. *Ibid.*, January 18, 1892, p. 2 and *Birzhevye Vedomosti*, January 19, 1892, p. 2.

78. Polovtsov, *Dnevnik*, II, 420; Lamsdorf, *Dnevnik 1891–92*, p. 273.

79. Polovtsov gives primary credit to Vyshnegradskii (*Dnevnik*, II, 421). Meshcherskii may not have directly influenced the Tsar in this matter, although it is very likely that he did. In any case, Meshcherskii was obviously pleased with Witte's appointment. See *Grazhdanin*, February 16, 1892, p. 2, and February 18, 1892, p. 3.

80. Polovtsov, *Dnevnik*, II, 427.

81. *Ibid.*, 421; Witte, *Vospominaniia*, I, 255.

82. Lamsdorf attests to the closeness of the tie between Vendrikh and the Tsar. According to Lamsdorf, Vendrikh himself recounted a revealing conversation he had had with the Emperor. Vendrikh stated that when he told the Tsar of the obstacles created by the resistance of railroad personnel to his orders, the Emperor listened and exclaimed: " 'Yes, all those railway men [*puteitsy*] are pigs!' " *Dnevnik 1891–92*, p. 302. At the end of February capital newspapers reported that the Tsar had sent Vendrikh birthday greetings and had praised him for his outstanding services (*ibid.*, p. 303).

83. Polovtsov, *Dnevnik*, II, 427.

84. In the order terminating Vendrikh's special powers (Prikaz po Ministerstvu Putei Soobshchenii, April 18, 1892, No. 3), Witte stated that on February 24, 1892 "His Majesty was pleased to permit me to dispatch Colonel fon Vendrikh for [the purpose] of directing, on the spot, the transportation of grain and other shipments *according to my orders and under my control*" (italics mine). *Pravitel'stvennyi vestnik*, April 21, 1892, p. 1).

85. Witte, *Vospominaniia*, I, 258.

86. The amount of grain delivered increased from 17,681,812 to 18,085,229 *pudy*. Svodnaia spravka o kolichestve khlebnykh gruzov, dostavlennykh v postradavshie ot neurozhaia gubernii . . . , *Prodovol'stvennoe delo*, III, 137.

87. *Ibid.*

88. Vypiska iz zhurnala Komiteta Ministrov, February 11, 1892, *ibid.*, II, 99–100.

89. Vypiska iz zhurnala Komiteta Ministrov, February 25, 1892, *ibid.*, p. 132.

90. *Ibid.*

91. *Ibid.*, p. 133.

92. Witte, *Vospominaniia*, I, 258–59.

93. Prikaz po Ministerstvu Putei Soobshcheniia, April 18, 1892, No. 3, *Pravitel'stvennyi vestnik*, April 21, 1892, p. 1.

94. Witte, *Vospominaniia*, I, 254–55.

95. Izmailov, *Zheleznye dorogi*, pp. 49–52.

7. THE SPECIAL COMMITTEE ON FAMINE RELIEF

1. A typical expression of this point of view can be found in the recent work by Allan K. Wildman, *The Making of a Workers' Revolution: Russian Social Democracy, 1891–1903* (Chicago, 1967). Wildman states that the government of the Russian Empire lacked the financial resources needed to tide the peasants over until the next harvest, and was forced to call on "society" to fill the gap. With regard to the Imperial decree which established the Special Committee, Wildman writes: "Despite its qualms, the government bowed to the inevitable, and an imperial rescript of November 17, 1891 (o.s.), called upon the public to form voluntary organizations and rush aid to the afflicted regions" (p. 5). Compare Wildman's interpretation of the Imperial rescript with the text of the document.

2. Rossiiskoe obshchestvo Krasnogo kresta, *Obzor deiatel'nosti Rossiiskogo obshchestva Krasnogo kresta v 1891 i 1892 godakh po okazaniiu pomoshchi naseleniiu postradavshemu ot neurozhaia, i po bor'be s kholernoi epidemiei* (SPb., 1893), pp. 2–7.

3. *Ibid.*, 5–6.

4. The uneven development of local charitable institutions was noted in the reports of almost all the representatives of the Special Committee.

5. Thus, V. G. Zemskii [V. I. Charnoluskii and G. A. Fal'bork] wrote: "Our 'society' pharisaically donating . . . one percent of its income to the famine victims and giving concerts and theatricals for the same purpose, at the same time exudes from its midst a horde of persons who, in order to exploit the people, make use of [this] the most terrible moment of our era." "Vnutrenniaia khronika," *Russkoe bogatstvo* (November, 1891), p. 175.

6. Although many accounts of the famine year mention the harrassment of private relief workers, most authors state that they personally did not encounter official obstructionism. V. A. Obolenskii states that he did not meet with any interference from government personnel, even when he violated the law in the course of his relief work. *Ocherki minuvshego* (Belgrade, 1931), pp. 230–31.

7. Letter dated August 27, 1891, TsGAOR, f. Aleksandra III-go, d. 741, "Pis'ma gr. Vorontsova-Dashkova imperatoru Aleksandru III-emu," p. 137.

8. Seredonin et al., *Istoricheskii obzor deiatel'nosti Komiteta Ministrov*, III, 242.

9. Durnovo stated that the letter in question was dated October 16, 1891. TsGAOR, f. Pleve, op. 1, d. 73, "Vsepoddanneishii doklad Ministra vnutrennikh del ob uchrezhdenii osobogo komiteta dlia ob'edineniia i rukovodstva chastnoi blagotvoritel'nostiu v polzu neurozhainykh mestnostei," p. 1.

10. In an entry in his diary dated October 28, 1891, A. A. Kireev wrote that rumor had it that such a committee would be set up under the direction of the heir to the throne. A conversation with Pleve confirmed this rumor in Kireev's mind. *Dnevnik Kireeva*, GBL, f Kireevikh-Novikovikh, k. 11, p. 245.

11. The rescript is reprinted in *Vestnik Evropy* (December, 1891), p. 881.

12. Polozhenie ob Osobom Komitete dlia pomoshchi nuzhdaiushchimsia v mestnostiakh postignutykh neurozhaem, TsGAOR, f. Nikolaia II-go, op. 1, d. 812, "Reskripty Aleksandra III v.k. Nikolaiu Aleksandrovichu. . . . Prilozheno polozhenie ob osobom komitete," p. 4.

13. *Ibid.*, pp. 3–4.

14. *Russkie vedomosti*, November 26, 1891, p. 2.

15. TsGIA, f. Vol'nogo Ekonomicheskogo Obshchestva (No. 91), op. 2, d. 955, "Ob uchrezhdenii pri Soveta Obshchestva vremennogo biuro dlia izucheniia voprosa o neurozhae 1891 goda," pp. 16–17.

16. Zvegintsev to the Secretary of the VEO, December 13, 1891, *ibid.*, pp. 31–32.

17. In any case, the Society decided to base its research primarily on information gathered from newspapers and journals (Zhurnal Soveta VEO, December 2, 1891, *ibid.*, p. 22).

18. *Dnevnik Kireeva*, GBL, f. Kireevikh-Novikovikh, k. 11, pp. 247–48. Kennan had been permitted to investigate the conditions of political exiles in Siberia because the government believed he was favorably disposed to the Tsarist regime. When Kennan's book appeared, it contained a blistering indictment of policies of the Russian government. Naturally enough, the MVD was not eager to have other foreigners poking about in other embarrassing areas.

19. *Ibid.*, pp. 248–49.

20. Letter from E. W. Brooks to A. A. Kireev, December 4/16, 1891, GBL, f. Kireevikh-Novikovikh, k. 22, d. 1b.

21. *Dnevnik Kireeva*, GBL f. Kireevikh-Novikovikh, k. 11, p. 253.

22. Richenda Scott, *Quakers in Russia* (London, 1964), pp. 130–37.

23. This description of Nicholas' conduct is based on the recollections of D. N. Liubimov who, as a young official, helped to compile the Committee's journals. "Russkaia smuta nachala deviatisotykh godov 1902–1906: Po vospominaniiam, lichnym zapiskam i dokumentam" (unpublished manuscript, Archive of Russian and East European History and Culture, Columbia University), pp. 83–84. According to Liubimov, Nicholas remembered fondly his work during the famine. Years later, when the Emperor had occasion to recall the activities of the Committee, he remarked with pride: "Those were good days . . ." (*ibid.*, p. 81).

24. What appear to be the agendas of the meetings of the Special Committee are preserved in the personal archive of Nicholas II (TsGAOR, f. Nikolaia II-go, op. 1, d. 814, "Materialy o deiatel'nosti Osobogo Komiteta," pp. 4–88).

25. Zhurnal Osobogo Komiteta, November 29, 1891, TsGIA, f. Osobogo Komiteta, d. 2, pp. 1–7. The committees in Moscow and St. Petersburg were excepted from these provisions, although they were subordinate to the overall authority of the Special Committee.

26. *Ibid.*, pp. 7–13. Note that this union did not include the many strictly private relief groups. Only the affiliates of the governors' and bishops' committees and the Red Cross were required to join the new provincial committees. Private individuals and groups could ally with the provincial organs of the Special Committee if they so chose; they would then be eligible to receive funds from the Committee.

27. *Ibid.*, pp. 14–15.

28. *Ibid.*, pp. 15–16.

29. *Ibid.*, pp. 17–19.

30. Zhurnal Osobogo Komiteta, December 13, 1891, *ibid.*, pp. 57–58.

31. Zhurnal Osobogo Komiteta, January 29, 1892, *ibid.*, pp. 169–71, 198–99.

32. Bobrinskii's report is dated March 14, 1892, TsGIA, f. Osobogo Komiteta, d. 100, "Perepiska po Tambovskoi gubernii," p. 135. Bobrinskii's emphasis on the role of the nobility and its elected officials in the relief campaign is perhaps excessive. Bobrinskii was, after all, a stout defender of the nobility's rights and privileges, and he might have been inclined to exaggerate the services of this class during the crisis.

33. TsGAOR, f. Nikolaia II-go op. 1, d. 821, "Raport upolnomochenogo Osobogo Komiteta po Kazanskoi gubernii," p. 2.

34. *Ibid.*, p. 3. Some of the most important provisions governing the operations of the provincial committee were: (1) all relief was to be given out without regard to class or religion (especially important as Kazan had a large non-Christian population); (2) the committee was to avoid restricting the work of individuals engaged in charitable work on a private basis; (3) the committee was responsible for publishing a monthly report of its activities in the newspapers.

35. *Ibid.*, p. 4.

36. Although there were well-documented cases of abuse of authority by *zemskie nachal'niki*, these seem to have been the exception rather than the rule. Almost all reports from the provinces contain high praise for their work. The activities of the land captains in the administration of local relief will be discussed in greater detail in chapter 10.

37. Zhurnal Osobogo Komiteta, December 13, 1891, TsGIA, f. Osobogo Komiteta, d. 2, pp. 50–52.

38. Zhurnal Osobogo Komiteta, January 3, 1892, *ibid.*, pp. 112–14.

39. Vendrikh, *Otchet*, pp. 39–40. Vendrikh's order giving preference to shipments made by the Special Committee did not interfere with the movement of zemstvo grain. The Committee's loads were not so large as to constitute a hindrance to zemstvo shipments.

40. Zhurnal Osobogo Komiteta, December 27, 1891, TsGIA, f. Osobogo Komiteta, d. 2, pp. 99–100.

41. Zhurnal Osobogo Komiteta, January 3, 1892, *ibid.*, pp. 110–12.

42. Zhurnal Osobogo Komiteta, February 19, 1892, *ibid.*, d. 3, pp. 55–57.

43. Zhurnal Osobogo Komiteta, March 11, 1892, *ibid.*, pp. 122–25.

44. By the end of 1892, horses had been given out in the following provinces: Viatka, 3680 head; Kazan, 6030; Orenburg, 18,000; Orel, 502; Penza, 5004; Perm 3550; Riazan, 2822; Samara, 6348; Saratov, 5624; Simbirsk, 5288; Tambov, 2000. Vedomost' assignovanii Osobogo Komiteta na blagotvoritel'nuiu pomoshch' naseleniiu 17 gubernii naibolee postradavshikh ot neurozhaia, TsGAOR, f. Nikolaia II-go, op 1, d. 814, "Materialy o deiatel'nosti Osobogo Komiteta," p. 86.

45. Richard A. Pierce, *Russian Central Asia, 1867–1917* (Berkeley and Los Angeles, 1960), p. 159.

46. Zhurnal Osobogo Komiteta, December 18, 1891, TsGIA, f. Osobogo Komiteta, d. 2, pp. 69–72.

47. Zhurnal Osobogo Komiteta, December 20, 1891, *ibid.*, pp. 81–82.

48. S. A. Davydova, *Zapiski o zhenskikh rabotakh v Voronezhskoi i Nizhegorodskoi guberniiakh* (SPb., 1894), pp. 1–2.

49. *Ibid.*, pp. 5, 44, 106. The works were restricted to Voronezh and Nizhni-Novgorod. The plan to set up *kustar'* works in Kazan was abandoned due largely to difficulties in travel caused by the onset of the *rasputitsa* in the spring of 1892 (*ibid.*, pp. 3–4).

50. Zhurnal Osobogo Komiteta, August 14, 1892, TsGIA, f. Osobogo Komiteta, d. 5, pp. 41–42.

51. Zhurnal Osobogo Komiteta, December 20, 1891, *ibid.*, d. 2, p. 85.

52. Zhurnaly Osobogo Komiteta, February 28, March 24, April 28, May 13, 1892, *ibid.*, d. 3, pp. 79–81, 181; d. 4, pp. 87–88, 106–7.

53. Accounts of American aid during 1891–92 are provided by G. S. Queen, "American Relief in the Russian Famine of 1891–92," *Russian Review*, XIV (1955), 140–50, and Merle Curti, *American Philanthropy Abroad: A History* (New Brunswick, N.J., 1963), pp. 99–119. For an example of the good impression the Russians made on a representative of American charity, see Francis B. Reeves, *Russia Then and Now, 1892–1917* (New York, 1917).

54. I have no final account of the sums received by the Committee. These approximate figures come from the Journal of the Committee (Zhurnal Osobogo Komiteta, December 30, 1892, TsGIA, f. Osobogo Komiteta, d. 5, pp. 74–76), and Ermolov, *Nashi neurozhai*, I, 114–15.

55. The most complete figures on the disbursal of Committee funds is found in Vedomost' assignovanii Osobogo Komiteta . . . , TsGAOR, f. Nikolaia II-go, op. 1, d. 814, "Materialy o deiatel'nosti Osobogo Komiteta," p. 86. These figures cover expenditures of the Committee up to the end of December of 1892 and correspond to the data given in the Journal of December 30, 1892.

56. One of the most notable politically suspect persons to participate in relief work under the auspices of the Committee was V. G. Korolenko. His participation caused some concern in police circles, but Korolenko was defended by the governor of Nizhni-Novgorod.

57. This view was expressed by V. A. Maklakov, *Vlast' i obshchestvennost' na zakate staroi Rossii* (*Vospominaniia*) [Paris, 1936], pp. 128–29.

8. PUBLIC WORKS

1. The best survey of the development of public works in Russia is the work by V. E. Maksimov, *Ocherki po istorii obshchestvennykh rabot v Rossii* (SPb., 1905).

2. Seredonin, *et al.*, *Istoricheskii obzor deiatel'nosti Komiteta Ministrov*, Vol. II, pt. 1, p. 264.

3. Vsepoddanneishii doklad Ministra vnutrennikh del, November 18, 1891, TsGIA, f. Kantseliarii Ministra vnutrennikh del (No. 1282), op. 2, d. 201, "Ob organizatsii obshchestvennykh rabot v guberniiakh postradavshikh ot neutrozhaia," p. 14.

4. *Ibid.*, p. 15.

5. The telegrams sent out by the MVD are not preserved. The responses of the governors, dated November 5, 1891, are found *ibid.*, pp. 1–5.

6. Vsepoddanneishii doklad Ministra vnutrennikh del, November 18, 1891, *ibid.*, p. 16.

7. *Ibid.*

8. *Ibid.*

9. *Ibid.*, p. 17.

10. *Ibid.*, p. 18.

11. *Ibid.*

12. Durnovo to Vyshnegradskii and Abaza, November 19, 1891, *ibid.*, pp. 19–20.

13. Report of the Conference of Abaza, Durnovo, and Vyshnegradskii, November 22, 1891, *ibid.*, p. 38.

14. *Ibid.*, p. 39.

15. *Ibid.*, p. 40.

16. *Ibid.*, pp. 40–42.

17. Telegrams dated November 23, 1891, *ibid.*, pp. 24–30.

18. Durnovo to Annenkov, November 26, 1891, *ibid.*, p. 34.

19. Vsepoddanneishii doklad Ministria vnutrennikh del, November 28, 1891, *ibid.*, p. 43.

20. *Ibid.*, p. 44.

21. *Ibid.*, pp. 44–45.

22. Agenda for the conference on the establishment of public works, *ibid.*, pp. 168–69.

23. Zhurnal soveshchaniia ob ustroistve obshchestvennykh rabot v mestnostiakh, postignutykh neurozhaem sostoiavshegosia 2–5 dekabria pod predsedatel'stvom Ministra vnutrennikh del, *ibid.*, p. 184.

24. *Ibid.*, pp. 184–85.

25. *Ibid.*, pp. 185–90.

26. The conference tried beforehand to examine the question of how many workers might be employed by the project. Its deliberations were fruitless, however, because, with the exception of the representatives of Nizhni-Novgorod province, none of the delegates could present accurate estimates as to the number of peasants who might seek work. Seeing that this line of discussion was useless, Annenkov moved that the conference pass on to the next order of business (*ibid.*, p. 190).

27. *Ibid.*, pp. 190–95.

28. *Ibid.*, pp. 195–96.

29. Instruktsiia zavedyvaiushchemu obshchestvennymi rabotami, TsGIA, f. Kants. MVD, op. 2, d. 202, "O rassmotrenii v Osobom Soveshchanii voprosa ob assignovanii sredstv na obshchestvennye raboty v guberniiakh, postradavshikh ot neurozhaia," pp. 9–10.

30. Vsepoddanneishii doklad Ministra vnutrennikh del, December 12, 1891, TsGIA f. Kants. MVD, op. 2, d. 201, "Ob organizatsii obshchestvennykh rabot," p. 225.

31. Zhurnal Vysochaishe uchrezhdennogo Osobogo Soveshchaniia ob obshchestvennykh rabotakh v mestnostiakh postradavshikh ot neurozhaia [hereafter cited Zhurnal Osobogo Soveshchaniia], Session of December 18, 1891, TsGIA, f. Osobogo Soveshchaniia ob obshchestvennykh rabotakh (No. 1225), d. 1, p. 3. (This is the only *delo* in the *fond.*) See also Maksimov, *Ocherki*, p. 118.

32. Zhurnal Osobogo Soveshchaniia, December 18, 1891, TsGIA, f. Osob. Soveshchaniia, d. 1, pp. 4–6.

33. *Ibid.*, pp. 6–12.

34. *Ibid.*, p. 16.

35. *Ibid.*, pp. 16–17.

36. Zhurnal Osobogo Soveshchaniia, February 9, 1891, *ibid.*, pp. 53–61. Three types of elevators were considered, small ones near railroad stations for the storage of local grain, and larger ones along railroad lines which could hold grain brought from various local storage houses. In this second type of elevator, the grain could be cleaned and sorted according to type. The third kind of elevator would be large ones constructed at the ports to hold grain designed for export. Vyshnegradskii proposed that several of the various types of elevators be built along one railway to test the feasibility of a nationwide system. The Conference rejected the idea, preferring to give more general coverage to the famine area.

37. Zhurnal Osobogo Soveshchaniia, January 21, 1892, *ibid.*, p. 35.

38. By February, 8, 250,600 rubles of the original grant of 10 million rubles had been assigned to finance various works (Zhurnal Osobogo Soveshchaniia, February 9, 1892, *ibid.*, p. 62), and by April, 9.6 million rubles had been allocated (Maksimov, *Ocherki*, p. 119). Both these sums do not include the monies intended for forestry operations.

39. Ministrerstvo vnutrennikh del, *Obshchii otchet po obshchestvennym rabotam proizvedennym soglasno vysochaishemu poveleniiu ot 28 noiabria 1891 g., v guberniiakh postradavshikh ot neurozhaia* (SPb., 1895), p. 1. Also Maksimov, *Ocherki*, p. 120.

40. Maksimov, *Ocherki*, p. 120.

41. *Russkie vedomosti*, October 13, 1892, p. 2. Also Maksimov, *Ocherki*, p. 150.

42. Maksimov does not provide total figures for the number of workers employed, but he implies that the number was not large. These rough figures are drawn from *Russkie vedomosti*, October 13, 1892, p. 2.

43. Maksimov, *Ocherki*, p. 148.

44. *Ibid.*, p. 135.

45. *Ibid.*, p. 136–37.

46. *Ibid.*, pp. 140–41, 148.

47. *Ibid.*, pp. 124–32.

9. RELIEF IN THE PROVINCES: THE WORK OF GUBERNIIA INSTITUTIONS

1. The main sources for the next two chapters are documents found in the Central State Archives in Leningrad, especially the *fond* of the Economic Department of the MVD and the published records of the provincial zemstvos. These materials are supplemented by documents from other archives (most importantly Korolenko's personal *fond*), the press, and various published sources.

2. See chapter 2. Also A. D. Gradovskii, *Nachala russkogo gosudarstvennogo prava*, pt. III: *Organy mestnogo upravleniia* in *Sobranie Sochenenii*, Vol. IX (SPb., 1904), pp. 249–50.

3. See pp. 44–46.

4. In most provinces the vice-governors were almost invisible during the famine crisis. The exception to this rule was Kazan, where Vice-Governor A. P. Engel'gardt proved more able than Governor Poltaratskii and assumed many burdens during relief operations. On the weakness of the *guberniia pravlenie* as an institution, see the article by V. Gessen, "Gubernator, kak organ nadzora," *Severnyi vestnik* (January 1898), 199.

5. The great difference between the personalities of the various governors may in part reflect the somewhat haphazard way in which these officials were selected. The law did not prescribe any particular set of qualifications for the office, and gubernatorial posts were filled with men of widely differing backgrounds. Many governors were drawn from the military, and their outlook and attitudes often made them unfit for civil service. In the case of our three provinces, however, inexperience in the field of civilian work cannot account for the differing levels of performance. Baranov and Rokasovskii both had military training, but also had served extensively in the field of provincial administration. Poltaratskii had worked in the Ministry of Internal Affairs and had been governor of Arkhangel'sk and Ufa provinces before taking up his post in Kazan. Baranov's career will be discussed in detail below. Rokasovskii's service record can be found: TsGIA, f. Dep. obshchikh del, op. 45, d. 158–1881, "O naznachenii . . . Barona Rokasovskogo Ekaterinoslavskim vitse-gubernatorom i Tambovskim gubernatorom." For background on Poltaratskii see the article on him in N. I. Afanas'ev, *Sovremeniki: Albom biografii* (SPb., 1909), I, 226.

6. The province had experienced bad harvest for the two preceding years (see note 34 of chapter 1), and in December of 1890 the Kazan zemstvo requested and received 200,000 rubles from the Imperial capital fund to aid the needy. Weather conditions in the spring of 1891 were poor and should have given warning of an impending disaster. These conclusions are found in a report by N. A. Troinitskii, Director of the Central Statistical Committee of the MVD, which was presented to Durnovo on June 26, 1892, No. 484. TsGIA, f. Khoz, dep., op. 4, d. 2178, "Po khodataistvu Kazanskogo zemstva, o naznachenii pravitel'stvennye ssudy na prodovol'stvie i obsemenenie polei, po sluchaiiu neurozhaia," pp. 198–99.

7. *Ibid.* Troinitskii implies that the zemstvo did nothing until ordered to do so by the MVD. Actually his criticism is too harsh. According to the *doklad* presented by the Kazan provincial zemstvo *uprava* to a meeting of the assembly on July 4, 1891, the *uprava* had begun to gather information on the state of the harvest, the condition of local grain reserves, and the needs of the village communes in May. Kazanskoe gubernskoe zemskoe sobranie, *Postanovleniia XXXIV ekstrennogo Kazanskogo gubernskogo zemskogo sobraniia 4–5 iiulia 1891 goda* (Kazan, 1891); the *doklad* of the *uprava* is in an appendix, p. 25.

8. Kazanskoe gubernskoe zemskoe sobranie, *Postanovleniia XXXIV ekstrennogo sobraniia*,

appendix, pp. 40–44. The *uezdy* requested 2,399,545 rubles for seed; the provincial *uprava* felt that only 1,070,000 rubles were needed.

9. *Ibid.*, pp. 16–20.

10. The statement of Governor Poltaratskii which accompanied the initial zemstvo request has not been preserved in the Leningrad archives. Documents relating to food supply operations in Kazan start with October 1891. From the contents of other documents, however, we can surmise what Poltaratskii said. In a report to the Committee of Ministers, Durnovo stated that the data upon which the Kazan zemstvo had based its requests had been "gathered with great speed," and required "reliable, on-the-spot verification." Zapiska MVD, October 16, 1891, No. 154, *Prodovol'stvennoe delo*, I, 39–40. This criticism of zemstvo estimates was probably based on information supplied by the Governor.

11. Kazanskaia gubernskaia zemskaia uprava, *Otchet o deistviiakh Kazanskoi gubernskoi zemskoi upravy s 1-go sentiabria 1890 po 1-e sentiabria 1891 goda* (Kazan, 1891), pt. III, pp. 44–45.

12. Zapiska MVD, October 16, 1891, No. 154, *Prodovol'stvennoe delo*, I, 39–40.

13. Troinitskii to Durnovo, June 26, 1892, No. 484, TsGIA, f. Khoz. dep., op. 4, d. 2178, "Po khodataistvu Kazanskogo zemstva," pp. 202–3.

14. *Ibid.*, p. 200.

15. Poltaratskii's reply to the MVD's questions is dated October 14, 1891, No. 4964, TsGIA, f. Khoz. dep., op. 4, d. 2125, "O ssude Kazanskomu gubernskomu zemstvu," pp. 4–6.

16. MVD's questions were apparently sent out on October 30. Governor's reply is dated November 17, 1891, No. 5708, *ibid.*, pp. 71–74.

17. Departament politsii to Poltaratskii, October 31, 1891, No. A 4449/870, TsGAOR, f. Dep. politsii 3-oe deloproizvodstvo, 1891, d. 899, "Svedeniia po Kazanskoi gubernii," p. 1.

18. On the question of deaths from starvation: P. N. Durnovo to Poltaratskii, November 30, 1891, No. 4952/994, *ibid.*, p. 5; on demoralization of the peasantry: P. N. Durnovo to Poltaratskii, December 3, 1891, No. 4974/995, *ibid.*, p. 7.

19. Poltaratskii replied to the questions from the Department of Police in documents dated November 10 (*ibid.*, p. 2), November 13 (*ibid.*, pp. 3–4), and in two separate dispatches dated December 14, 1891, Nos. 6459 and 6460 (*ibid.*, pp. 10, 11–14). The Governor's replies to the MVD are cited in notes 15 and 16 above.

20. The report of events which appeared in *Volzhskii vestnik* (January 5, 1892, p. 2), implied that the would-be assassin, a certain Kachurikhin, acted alone and without political intent. (His alleged motive was a desire to call attention to himself.) Others, however, felt the affair was part of a conspiracy designed to produce a popular uprising. In a letter dated January 13, 1892, Iu. S. Nechaev-Mal'tsev, the Special Committee's representative in Kazan wrote: "The attempt [on the life of the Governor] showed that persons have been sent to Kazan to provoke peasant disorders. But the people have remained completely calm. Several confederates [of the would-be assassin] have been arrested. . . . I also received a letter, probably from one of the conspirators, in which [the author] explained the reasons which caused them to resort to violence. I have turned [the letter] over to the gendarmes." This letter was apparently sent by Nechaev-Mal'tsev to his sister, who in turn copied the

relevant passages and passed them on to Pobedonostsev. TsGAOR, f. Pleve, op. 1, d. 76. "Pis'mo Nechaevoi, A. S. Pobedonostsevu, K. P. s vyderzhkami iz pis'ma Nechaeva, Iu. S. Nechaevoi (?) o polozhenii naseleniia Kazanskoi gubernii v sviazi s neurozhaem," p. 1).

21. Report of Troinitskii to Durnovo, January 28, 1892, No. 166, TsGIA, f. Khoz. dep., op. 4, d. 2125, "O ssude Kazanskomu gubernskomu zemstvu," p. 247.

22. *Ibid.*

23. Troinitskii to MVD, reports dated February 25, 1892, No. 270, and February 26, 1892, No. 272, *ibid.*, pp. 300 and 303. Here Troinitskii overestimated the power a governor could wield in the matter of local relief. As we shall see below, it was extremely difficult for a governor, no matter how energetic, to achieve a really unified relief policy at the local level.

24. Troinitskii to MVD, February 26, 1892, No. 272, *ibid.*, p. 304.

25. Governor Poltaratskii's report on his tour is dated April 9, 1892, No. 2328, TsGIA, f. Khoz. dep., op. 4, d. 2178, "Po khodataistvu Kazanskogo zemstva," pp. 1–33. Appended to the actual report are the journals of the conferences of local relief workers which were held during the Governor's visit. The Governor's concern for the amount of relief being given out was prompted by the fact that in March more than a million persons, over half the population of the province, had received zemstvo food loans (*Statisticheskie dannye*, pp. 42–43).

26. Troinitskii to Durnovo, June 26, 1892, No. 484, TsGIA, f. Khoz. dep., op. 4, d. 2178, "Po khodataistvu Kazanskogo zemstva," pp. 202–3.

27. TsGAOR, f. Nikolaia II-go, op. 1, d. 821, "Raport upolnomochenogo Osobogo Komiteta po Kazanskoi gubernii," pp. 6, 16–17.

28. Report of Poltaratskii to Durnovo, July 12, 1892, TsGIA, f. Osobogo Komiteta, d. 154, "Po otchetam lits komandirovannykh Osobym Komitetom," pp. 95–96. Poltaratskii's defense of the loan policy of the zemstvo seems to be correct, at least as far as the amount of food given out per "eater" is concerned. Between October and December 1891, zemstvo food loans averaged about half a *pud* (twenty *funty*) per "eater." The number of persons receiving zemstvo loans in Kazan during October was slightly smaller than the number in most stricken provinces. By November, however, this situation had changed, and Kazan gave out more zemstvo food loans than any other province with the exception of Samara and Saratov (*Statisticheskie dannye*, pp. 42–43, 46–47, 66–67).

29. Baranov to Bashkirov, Blinov, and Bugrov, letters dated June 6, 1891, Nos. 2561, 2562, 2563, TsGIA, f. Khoz. dep., op. 4, d. 2112, "O ssude Nizhegorodskomu gubernskomu zemstvu," pp. 27–28.

30. Telegrams dated June 6, 1891 to the Marshals of the Nobility of Makarevskii, Kniagininskii, and Lukoianovskii *uezdy* and the *zemskii nachal'nik* of the fourth district of Arzamasskii uezd (*ibid.*, p. 29). At the same time, Baranov dispatched a letter to P. P. Zubov, Marshal of the Nobility in Vasil'skii *uezd*, putting him in charge of the distribution of grain to the needy in his *uezd* (*ibid.*, pp. 30–31).

31. Baranov to Bazhenov, letter, June 6, 1891, *ibid.*, pp. 32–33.

32. The date of this circular is not clear; it was probably issued in the first week of June (*ibid.*, pp. 34–35).

33. Baranov to I. K. Shirshev, Chairman of the Nizhni-Novgorod Merchants' Committee,

letter, June 14, 1892, *ibid.*, pp. 49–50. In the letter, Baranov praised the public spirited efforts of Bugrov, Bashkirov, and Blinov. The Governor noted, however, that there were others who sought to take advantage of the difficult situation in order to make large profits. "Several days ago," Baranov wrote, "a certain merchant S., who was buying a large quantity of rye flour on the Nizhni-Novgorod market, passed himself off as an agent of the zemstvo commissioned to purchase grain for the hungry . . . , in order to gain concessions with regard to price. Finding well-intentioned people who believed him, and who were willing to lower prices [to help] a good cause, Mr. S. [then turned around] and sold the grain he purchased on the same market, realizing a huge profit" (*ibid.*, p. 49).

34. Nizhegorodskaia gubernskaia zemskaia uprava, *Otchet Nizhegorodskoi gubernskoi zemskoi upravy po prodovol'stvennoi operatsii 1891–92 gg.* (N. Novgorod, 1893), pp. 4–5; and Baranov's opening speech to the provincial assembly (Nizhegorodskoe gubernskoe zemskoe sobranie, *XXVI ocherednoe Nizhegorodskoe gubernskoe zemskoe sobranie 3–7 dekabria 1890 goda i chrezvychainye sobraniia sozvyvavshiesia v 1891 godu* (N. Novgorod, 1891), pt. III, pp. 10–11).

35. *Statisticheskye dannye*, p. 42.

36. See chapter 3.

37. Baranov to MVD, June 25, 1891, No. 2952, TsGIA, f. Khoz. dep., op. 4, d. 2112, "O ssude Nizhegorodskomu gubernskomu zemstvu," p. 64.

38. *Ibid.*

39. Baranov to Durnovo, telegram dated June 28, 1891, *ibid.*, p. 72.

40. See note 31 of chapter 4.

41. Durnovo to Baranov, confidential letter, July 1, 1891, TsGIA, f. Khoz. dep., op. 4, d. 2112, "O ssude Nizhegorodskomu gubernskomu zemstvu," p. 71.

42. Nizhegorodskoe gubernskoe zemskoe sobranie, *XXVI ocherednoe sobranie* . . . , pt. III, pp. 10–11, and Nizhegorodskaia gubernskaia zemskaia uprava, *Otchet po prodovol'stvennoi operatsii*, p. 5.

43. Proposal of the *uprava* is found: Nizhegorodskoe gubernskoe zemskoe sobranie, *XXVI ocherednoe sobranie* . . . , pt. III, p. 33. Debate on the question *ibid.*, pp. 11–13.

44. Nizhegorodskaia gubernskaia zemskaia uprava, *Otchet po prodovol'stvennoi operatsii*, p. 6.

45. *Ibid.*, pp. 6–7.

46. Baranov to MVD, July 5, 1891, No. 3144, TsGIA, f. Khoz. dep. op. 4, d. 2112, "O ssude Nizhegorodskomu gubernskomu zemstvu," pp. 85–86.

47. *Ibid.*, pp. 84–85. Baranov proposed to have the MVD grant 2,378,000 rubles at once, and then to give an additional 2,851,000 on September 15. Another 2 million rubles would be made available on February 1, 1892.

48. On July 10 the MVD assigned an additional 1 million rubles to the account of the Nizhni-Novgorod zemstvo (MVD to Baranov, telegram dated July 10, 1891, *ibid.*, p. 82). But in a letter to the Governor, the Economic Department stated it could not see its way clear to increase the grant beyond the 2 million rubles already given (letter from the Economic Department to Baranov, July 11, 1891, No. 4852, *ibid.*, p. 141).

49. Apparently, Baranov wished 1 million rubles more than Vishniakov was willing to grant to the province. According to Baranov, Vishniakov criticized the Governor's stand on famine relief. Baranov to Durnovo, July 17, 1891, No. 3397, *ibid.*, pp. 155–60.

50. Nizhegorodskoe gubernskoe zemskoe sobranie, *XXVI ocherednoe sobranie*, pt. III, pp. 77–78.

51. The zemstvo stuck by its demand for 8,229,000 rubles and requested that the government grant 3.8 million for immediate grain purchase (*ibid.*, pp. 83, 101–2). Baranov felt that these requests were exaggerated, but he admitted that the hopes for the harvest of spring grains had not been realized. Baranov to MVD, August 8, 1891, No. 210, TsGIA, f. Khoz. dep., op. 4, d. 2112, "O ssude Nizhegorodskomu gubernskomu zemstvu," p. 185. In the course of the summer, the Governor was able to convince the Ministry to grant an additional 800,000 rubles.

52. Baranov to Durnovo, letter dated September 28, 1891, GBL, f. V. G. Korolenko (No. 135), razdel III, k. 1, d. 26, "Materialy po golodu 1891–1892 gg.," p. 3.

53. *Ibid.*

54. *Ibid.*, p. 4. Baranov charged that the Marshals' role as chairmen of the *uezd upravy* had made them completely dependent on the zemstvos. According to Baranov, even the new institution of the *zemskie nachal'niki* was dominated by the zemstvos. Because most of the land captains were inexperienced, they turned to the Marshals for advice, and the latter encouraged them to go along with the zemstvos.

55. Baranov wrote that although according to the law the governor was the personal representative of the Emperor, the Great Reforms and subsequent rulings of the Senate "have turned . . . [the governor] into something altogether pathetic. To him remains only one responsibility; he retains [the power] to supervise, to observe, . . . to give advice to all, [which is], however, not binding on anyone etc. The role of the ideal governor is [to make] speeches without content, to chair eternally a myriad of committees, councils, and commissions, and to sign papers which he cannot read because of their sheer quantity. . . ." (*ibid.*, p. 5).

56. *Ibid.*, pp. 6–7. On restricting the power of the zemstvo, Baranov wrote: "The removal of the zemstvo from the first rank [in the struggle against famine] would be possible, first of all, because Russia is not a republic. . . . Secondly, [it] would be a logical and judicially sound act since, at the present time, the zemstvo is distinguishing itself if not by fraudulent, [then] at least by negligent bankruptcy, which does not inspire confidence in the wisdom of its use and control of the capital entrusted to it by the government."

57. *Ibid.*, pp. 7–8.

58. Unfortunately the documents held in the *fond* of the Economic Department of the MVD are not complete and do not preserve any reply that may have come from the Ministry.

59. In a subsequent letter, Baranov noted that the MVD had not approved his plan for a "dictatorship of the administration" (*diktatura vlasti*) in the famine region. Baranov to Durnovo, November 14, 1891, No. 538, GBL, f. Korolenko, raz. III, k. 1, d. 26, "Materialy po golodu," p. 4 (every letter in this *delo* has its own pagination).

60. In a letter to Durnovo dated November 5, 1891, Baranov informed the Minister that he was reactivating his own food supply commission and implied that the action had been encouraged by "certain signs of your [Durnovo's] approval." TsGIA, f. Kants. MVD, op. 2, d. 201, "Ob organizatsii obshchestvennykh rabot," p. 7.

61. Korolenko noted that while the new organization bore the formal title "Nizhni-Novgorod provincial food supply commission," the MVD continued to refer to the body in all its official communications as "The food supply conference of the Nizhni-Novgorod governor." This may imply that the Ministry did not fully recognize Baranov's action (*V golodnyi god*, pp. 184–85). But whether it approved or not, there was little the MVD could do about the situation. As we noted above, the power of the Ministry to compel governors to adopt a certain line of action was limited.

62. This incident is discussed in greater detail in chapter 10.

63. Baranov stressed the need for speed and decisiveness in the struggle against the famine in a speech to the Nizhni-Novgorod food supply commission: "In ordinary times . . . inattention to duty can still be tolerated because the immediate consequences are . . . not dangerous. But at the present time, when the price of grain rises day by day and hour by hour, waste of time is criminal. We are locked in a struggle with a most terrible and merciless enemy, an enemy we can neither escape nor avoid. We must either destroy him or ruin our . . . cause." *Zhurnal sobraniia Nizhegorodskoi gubernskoi prodovol'stvennoi kommissii* (hereafter cited: ZhNPK), November 10, 1891, p. 1.

64. It is all the more significant that Baranov did not use charges of political disloyalty against the zemstvos because the police authorities in Nizhni-Novgorod looked upon zemstvo circles with misgivings. A police report on conditions in the province during 1887 stated that "the provincial zemstvo continues to include among its personnel not only individuals who have previously been under political investigation, but also those who . . . have shown that they are capable of using . . . [zemstvo] service as a means of achieving their antigovernmental aims." TsGAOR, f. Dep. politsii, 3-oe deloproizvodstvo, 1888, d. 89, ch. 51, "Politicheskii obzor Nizhegorodskoi gubernii," p. 5. Two years later police reports noted that untrustworthy persons continued to occupy high posts in the zemstvo. The police considered N. F. Annenskii, the head of the *uprava*'s statistical bureau, to be a particular threat. The report described him as "a person enjoying enormous authority in the Nizhni-Novgorod provincial zemstvo *uprava* and who, at the same time, is very untrustworthy and dangerous." TsGAOR, f. Dep. politsii 3-oe deloproizvodstvo, 1890, d. 47, ch. 25, "Politicheskii obzor Nizhegorodskoi gubernii," p. 9.

Baranov, however, was unaffected by the views of the police. During the famine crisis, he permitted V. G. Korolenko and other suspicious characters to take an active part in relief work. When he was questioned about this by Durnovo, Baranov stood firm, stating that the persons in question were honorably fulfilling the tasks he had assigned them. "Whether they have been guilty in the past," Baranov wrote, "I do not know; are they defenders of the existing order, I do not think so; but their present actions deserve complete respect and, I may add, trust." TsGAOR, f. Dep. politsii, 3-oe deloproizvodstvo, 1892, d. 369, "Svedeniia po Nizhegorodskoi gubernii," p. 10. See also F. Pokrovskii, "V. G. Korolenko pod nadzorom politsii (1876–1903). K sorokaletiiu literaturnoi deiatel'nosti," *Byloe*, No. 13 (July, 1918), pp. 10–11.

65. Korolenko, "Tretii element," p. 267.

66. TsGIA, f. Dep. obshchikh del, op. 45, d. 182–1880 g., "O naznachenii chisliashchegosia po polevoi peshnei artillerii polkovnika Baranova . . . ," pp. 271–74. (This *delo* is Baranov's service record.)

67. P. A. Zaionchkovskii, *Krizis samoderzhaviia na rubezhe 1870–1880 godov* (Moscow, 1964), p. 304. According to his service record, Baranov was tired "on charges of having submitted unjustified complaints and [for having] insulted his superiors and [other] officials."

At the trial he was found guilty of having "submitted official papers containing expressions [which were] inappropriate and did not conform to the rules of military discipline." He was forced to leave the Navy, "but in consideration of his wartime service," his dismissal was to be regarded as "retirement." TsGIA, f. Dep. obshchikh del, op. 45, d. 182–1880 g., "O naznachenii . . . Baranova," p. 281.

68. One of Baranov's chief backers at this time was Pobedonostsev, a fact which may explain why his dismissal from the Naval service was of so little detriment to his career. Zaionchkovskii, *Krizis samoderzaviia*, p. 305.

69. Korolenko claims that Baranov was playing a double game, posing as a liberal in public while being a conservative at heart, because he felt that the entire system was on the verge of collapse ("Tretii element," pp. 267–68). This view is extreme. Baranov's reports and other communications to the Ministry do not give the impression that he feared a revolution or a change of regime. It would seem, rather, that Baranov felt that by taking strong, decisive action in the field of public welfare, the government could strengthen its position and even use politically suspect elements to its advantage.

70. Dashkevich, who was highly critical of the MVD's role in the famine crisis, praised Baranov and noted that his actions did not win him the favor of the Ministry. "The Nizhni-Novgorod governor," Dashkevich wrote, "stands out from among [the other governors]. He is an active man, without fear of criticism and publicity, [who] displays the rare capacity to admit his own mistakes. He has succeeded in taking all matters into his own hands as the Ministry demanded, but he seems to enjoy less support on the part of the Ministry than do [the other governors]." *Nashe Ministerstvo*, pp. 54–55.

71. In 1897 Baranov was chosen a senator. He died in 1901. *Novyi entsiklopedicheskii slovar'*, V, 163.

72. TsGIA, f. Dep. obshchikh del, op. 223, 1892, d. 232, "Vsepoddanneishii otchet Tambovskogo gubernatora za 1892 god," p. 14.

73. In Tambov, Nizhni-Novgorod, and Kazan, the process of collecting figures was done during the month of June. Both the Kazan and the Tambov zemstvos stated that they ordered the collection of data on the needs of the population to begin at the end of May. Tambovskoe gubernskoe zemskoe sobranie, *Zhurnal chrezvychainogo . . . sobraniia 3-go iiulia 1891 goda* (Tambov, 1891), pp. 1–3; and Kazanskoe gubernskoe zemskoe sobranie, *Postanovleniia XXXIV ekstrennogo . . . sobraniia 4–5 iiulia 1891 goda* (Kazan, 1891), appendix, p. 25.

74. In Tambov only two *uezdy* presented figures for both seed and food needs. The rest only requested seed but did not state how much food would be required. See Tambovskoe gubernskoe zemskoe sobranie, *Zhurnal chrezvychainogo . . . sobraniia 3-go iiulia 1891 goda*, pp. 3–6.

75. In Nizhni-Novgorod, the assembly reduced the requests of the *uezdy* from 13 million rubles to about 8 million. Baranov to MVD, telegram dated July 5, 1891, TsGIA, f. Khoz. dep., op. 4, d. 2112, "O ssude Nizhegorodskomu gubernskomu zemstvu," p. 78. In Tambov, too, the initial requests of the *uezdy* for money for seed purchases were reduced by the *uprava*. The assembly restored some of the cuts. *Zhurnal chrezvychainogo . . . sobraniia 4-go iiulia 1891 goda*, pp. 1–7. The exception to the rule was Kazan. There the *uezdy* requested 2.8 million rubles for seed and food, but the *uprava* reduced the estimate to 2.3 million rubles. The assembly rejected the *uprava*'s views and decided to ask for 5 million rubles. *Postanovleniia XXXIV ekstrennogo . . . sobraniia*, pp. 3–4, 16–20.

76. Of the three provinces we are considering, the Nizhni-Novgorod and Kazan zemstvos met again in August and September, respectively. The Tambov zemstvo did not meet again until its regular session in December. This was possible because Tambov possessed considerable reserves of grain, and the province could get along without extensive loans from the center until the new year.

77. Compare, for example, the article in the conservative journal *Russkoe obozrenie* attacking the zemstvo estimates ("Sovremennaia letopis'," *Russkoe obozrenie* [December, 1891], p. 853) with the views of the more liberal *Russkaia mysl'* ("Vnutrennee obozrenie," *Russkaia mysl'* [February, 1892], pp. 855–56).

78. The Nizhni-Novgorod zemstvo fixed the needs of the population at 8.2 million rubles to finance the purchase of seed and food. It received 6.6 million rubles which, on the whole, seemed to suffice. These sums enabled the zemstvo to feed an average of 320,000 persons per month (in the spring the number being fed was two times the average) at a rate of slightly more than thirty *funty* a month. After relief operations in Nizhni-Novgorod were over, a small surplus of grain remained on hand. *Statisticheskie dannye*, pp. 22–23, 42–43, 62–63. The Tambov zemstvo estimated the food needs of the stricken population at 6,441,466 *pudy* and it purchased 6,050,235 *pudy*. In the end, the zemstvo gave out loans totaling only 5,360,000 *pudy*, an error between estimates and actual loans of about 16.8 percent. Tambovskaia gubernskaia zemskaia uprava, *Otchet . . . po prodovol'stvennoi operatsii 1891–1892 gg.* (Tambov, 1892), III, 27, 77.

79. In September the Kazan provincial assembly fixed the needs of the province in terms of food and seed at 8 million rubles worth. In the end, however, it spent over 10 million rubles on these items. *Postanovleniia XXXV ekstrennogo . . . sobraniia 19–21 sentiabria 1891 goda* (Kazan, 1891), pp. 25–29; *Otchet o deistviiakh Kazanskoi gubernskoi zemskoi upravy s 1-go sentiabria 1891 po 1-e sentiabria 1892 goda* (Kazan, 1892), pp. 22–23.

80. *Statisticheskie dannye*, p. 22.

81. *Ibid.*

82. The Nizhni-Novgorod provincial zemstvo gathered information on the harvest of 1891 from three sources: *volost'* statistics, reports from correspondents, and the findings of a special statistical expedition which toured the most hard-hit *uezdy*. Once it had brought together all this information, the statistical bureau of the provincial *uprava* drew up supplemental tables which showed what the average rye harvest and the average sowing of spring grains had been in the years before the famine. On the basis of these data, all *volosti* in the province were divided into two big groups: those where the output-seed ratio for rye had exceeded 2 ("*sam*" 2) and those where it had not. Those *volosti* where the output-seed ratio was less than 2, were divided into three subgroups on the basis of the amount of spring seed sown in the *volost'*: (1) below average, (2) average, (3) above average. Each of these three groups were again divided into two subgroups on the basis of the size of the rye harvest in the volost': (a) output-seed ratio below 1, (b) output-seed ratio above 1. Aside from these groupings, another category (group 4) was established. Here the rye harvest exceeded "*sam*" 2, but was lower than average. This system of classification enabled the zemstvo to rank all *volosti* on the basis of need, with group 1a (combining a below average sowing of spring seed with a rye harvest below "*sam*" 1) at the bottom and group 4 at the top. ZhNPK, October 17, 1891, pp. 2–3. This number of the journal was not available in printed form; I used a handwritten copy found in Korolenko's archive (GBL, f. Korolenko, raz. I, k. 26, d. 1490, "Zhurnaly . . . prodovol'stvennoi komissii"). All these data were combined with lists of needy families drawn up by the *uezd upravy*, and other information on the population

and the consumption habits of the peasants. This information enabled the zemstvo to estimate the amount of food and seed each *volost'* would need to get through until the next harvest.

83. Thus, in September the Kazan zemstvo estimated the cost of grain needed to feed the population at about 1 ruble 25 kopeks per *pud* (*Postanovleniia XXXV ekstrennogo . . . sobraniia*, pp. 25–29). At that time the going price for rye in the province was about 1 ruble 20 kopeks per *pud* (Zapiska Ministra Finansov, February 6, 1892, No. 737, *Prodovol'stvennoe delo*, II, 96–97). By the end of the year, the price of rye had risen to 1 ruble 44 kopeks per *pud* (*ibid.*). In the end, the Kazan zemstvo bought rye at an average cost of 1 ruble 37 kopeks per *pud* (*Otchet o deistviiakh Kazanskoi . . . upravy 1891–1892*, pp. 40–41).

84. *Statisticheskie dannye*, p. 89.

85. See chapter 4.

86. See pp. 51, 83.

87. *Volzhskii vestnik*, February 1, 1892.

88. The Nizhni-Novgorod zemstvo worked through the agricultural society in Poltava in order to obtain considerable quantities of grain. It also had help from persons in other provinces. *Otchet . . . upravy po prodovol'stvennoi operatsii*, p. 44.

89. This problem was noted in Nizhni-Novgorod province as early as November 1891 (ZhNPK, November 10, 1891, pp. 2–4).

90. The government records dealing with the management of the food supply crisis contain few criticisms of the zemstvos on this score.

91. "Vnutrennee obozrenie," *Russkaia mysl'* (February, 1892), p. 190.

92. The question of the quality of the grain bought by the Nizhni-Novgorod zemstvo was raised in the provincial food supply commission after it had been discovered that some impure grain had been given out to peasants. A special subcommission was set up to investigate the quality of all grain brought in from outside the province. The subcommission found that much of the grain purchased in the Caucasus contained a high percentage of impurities, but it noted that this was normal for grain obtained in that area. On the whole, the subcommission found that the grain purchased by the Nizhni-Novgorod zemstvo was fit for consumption. In those cases where impurities were discovered, the subcommission stated that the grain could be cleaned by the peasants themselves without the use of any special equipment. *Otchet . . . upravy po prodovol'stvennoi operatsii*, pp. 45–46, 85–90.

93. *Statisticheskie dannye*, pp. 94–95.

94. Zvegintsev to Durnovo, November 14, 1891, TsGIA, f. Khoz. dep., op. 4, d. 2126, "O ssude Samarskomu gubernskomu zemstvu," pp. 7–8.

95. Vsepoddanneishii doklad Ministra vnutrennikh del, November 18, 1891, *ibid.*, pp. 30–31.

96. See Table 2.

97. See Table 3.

98. On the origins and structure of the food supply conferences, refer to chapter 4.

99. Korolenko's major works on the famine are: *V golodnyi god*, "Tretii element," and "Nekotorye osobennosti organizatsii prodovol'stvennogo delo v Nizhegorodskom krae," *Russkaia mysl'* (July, 1893), pp. 59–73.

100. The attack on zemstvo statistics occurred at the meeting of December 15. It was charged that the zemstvo statisticians did not really investigate the situation seriously, but simply made a rapid tour of the needy areas. As a result, zemstvo figures were only "theoretical data" (*kabinetnye svedeniia*) which bore little relation to reality. ZhNPK, December 15, 1891, p. 8. As head of the statistical bureau, N. F. Annenskii undertook the defense of his estimates and succeeded in demonstrating their rational bais. The confrontation between Annenskii and his critics is masterfully described by Korolenko in his article "Tretii element," pp. 270–83.

10. RELIEF IN THE PROVINCES: THE WORK OF LOCAL INSTITUTIONS

1. The diversity in the management of local relief is brought out in a report submitted by Governor Poltaratskii of Kazan. In his account of his tour of the famine-stricken areas of the province, the Governor noted that in different *uezdy* the responsibility for granting loans was assumed by different institutions. Thus, in Cheborkarskii *uezd* the zemstvo was in complete control and made loans without reference to the *zemskie nachal'niki*, while in Spasskii *uezd* the opposite system prevailed. There the zemstvos took almost no part in the work of relief. Poltaratskii to MVD, April 9, 1892, No. 2328 and related materials, TsGIA, f. Khoz. dep., op. 4, d. 2178, "Po khodataistvu Kazanskogo zemstva," pp. 15–16.

2. According to the food supply law, a *prigovor* was required before loans could be given out to a member of a commune. This declaration obligated the *mir* as a whole to pay back the debt (see chapter 2). Since many communes objected to this collective obligation, there was resistance to this procedure. In some cases, the communes were unwilling to declare any of their members to be needy. To counter this tendency, the government decided to permit loans to be granted solely on the basis of need without the commune formally assuming the obligation to repay. Sazanov, *Obzor deiatel'nosti zemstv po narodnomu prodovol'stviiu*, II, 473–74.

3. In his reminiscences of his work during the famine, L. L. Tolstoi insisted that the method of personal inspection used by the zemstvos and *zemskie nachal'niki* was a poor one because it aroused distrust and resentment among the peasantry. He argued that it was better simply to accept the information gathered by peasant officials. L. L. Tolstoi, *V golodnye goda* (Moscow, 1900), pp. 122–23. The resentment caused by repeated inspections of the peasants receiving aid was called to the attention of the governor of Kazan during his tour of the province in March 1892. Poltaratskii to MVD, April 9, 1892, No. 2328 and related materials, TsGIA, f. Khoz. dep., op. 4, d. 2178, "Po khodataistvo Kazanskogo zemstvo," p. 19.

4. This practice is universally documented. See for example the statement by the liberal *Vestnik Evropy*: "Iz obshchestvennoi khroniki," *Vestnik Evropy* (November, 1891), p. 420.

5. *Nizhegorodskie gubernskie vedomosti, chast' neofitsial'naia*, November 27, 1891, p. 4.

6. Zapiska MVD, October 3, 1891, No. 134, *Prodovol'stvennoe delo*, I, 24.

7. A. I. Novikov, who, as a *zemskii nachal'nik* in Kozlovskii *uezd* of Tambov province, was actively engaged in both private and governmental relief efforts, was not impressed with the charitable character of Russians generally. He stated that despite the great stirring in Russian "society" as a result of the famine of 1891, the actual figures on the amount of money raised for the benefit of the needy do not indicate any great generosity. *Zapiski zemskogo nachal'nika* (SPb., 1899), pp. 175–80.

8. K. K. Arsen'ev, "Iz nedavnei poezdki v Tambovskuiu guberniiu: Vpechatleniia i zametki," *Vestnik Evropy* (February, 1892), p. 847. (Italics in original.)

9. During his tour of Kazan province, Governor Poltaratskii often encouraged the *zemskie nachal'niki* and others in charge of relief to keep the size of loans as small as possible. He was concerned lest the population be burdened with a huge debt which it would find difficult to repay. Poltaratskii to MVD, April 9, 1892, No. 2328 and related documents, TsGIA f. Khoz. dep., op. 4, d. 2178, "Po khodataistvu Kazanskogo zemstva," pp. 8, 15–16.

10. *Ibid.*, p. 12.

11. *Statisticheskie dannye*, pp. 22, 42, 63.

12. *Ibid.*, p. 43.

13. *Ibid.*, p. 63. In Kazan, Nizhni-Novgorod, and Tambov, this trend to increased sizes of food loans applied. The average size of loans granted in Kazan rose from 0.68 *pudy* per "eater" in January to 0.73 *pudy* in March to 0.75 in May (*ibid.*, p. 67). In Nizhni-Novgorod, loans were below the norm until March when they jumped sharply (from 0.65 *pudy* to 0.83 *pudy*). Loans remained above the MVD's norms through June (*ibid.*, p. 69). In Tambov, food loans which averaged 0.70 *pudy* in January increased to 0.82 *pudy* in March and remained above the norm until the end of June (*ibid.*, p. 79).

14. *Ibid.*, pp. 2–3.

15. *Ibid.*

16. See chapter 2.

17. The MVD considered this to be one of its major accomplishments in the area of relief.

18. Korolenko testifies to both the power of the land captains and to their inexperience: "The *zemskii nachal'nik* is investigator, master, guardian [and] philanthropist. He draws up the lists, he verifies them, he organizes the grain stores, he gives them out. Now imagine in that position a man who knows the village and its ways as much as a person may know it who first studied in a *gymnasium* or a *korpus*, then in a military school, an academy, or university. The countryside, that's a vacation or a *dacha* for the summer months. And with such a preparation, a man finds himself grappling with the most vital and complex questions of rural life. . . ." *V golodnyi god*, p. 120.

19. *Pravitel'stvennyi vestnik*, May 19, 1892, p. 1.

20. TsGIA, f. Dep. Obshchikh del, op. 223, 1891, d. 194, "Vsepoddanneishii otchet Tambovskogo gubernatora za 1891 god," pp. 8–9. The liberal element of "society" was distrustful of the *zemskie nachal'niki*, and often argued that they would not do as good a job as the zemstvos in the work of relief. "Vnutrennee obozrenie," *Vestnik Evropy* (November, 1891), p. 357. No doubt some of the praise lavished on the new institution was designed to please its creators in the central bureaucracy. But the high regard for the work of the land captains was so general that it would be impossible to deny the value of the services they rendered.

21. In his memoirs of the famine of 1891, L. L. Tolstoi recalled an incident where some of the *stolovye* he had opened in a particular village were closed down by order of a *zemskii nachal'nik*. The land captain resented Tolstoi because the latter had set up his soup kitchens independently of the local charitable committee. Tolstoi appealed to the Governor, and the interference of the *zemskii nachal'nik* was terminated at once. "Zapiski iz epokhi goloda v 1891–92 godakh," *Vestnik Evropy* (July, 1899), pp. 59–64.

22. Candidates for the office of *zemskii nachal'nik* were chosen by the governors from lists prepared by the *uezd* marshals of the nobility, and then submitted to the MVD for confirmation. The governor could recommend the removal of a land captain but could not act until he received the approval of the MVD. A. Ianovskii, "Zemskie uchastkovye nachal'niki," *Entsiklopedicheskii slovar'*, 1894, XIIa, 506–7.

23. *Otchet Nizhegorodskoi . . . upravy po prodovol'stvennoi operatsii*, pp. 24–25. These estimates were those presented at the December session of the provincial zemstvo assembly; but in July, the Lukoianovskii *uezd* zemstvo had requested 1,675,000 *pudy* of grain—more than any other *uezd*. *XXVII ocherednoe Nizhegorodnoe gubernskoe zemskoe sobranie 10–18 dekabria 1891 goda* (N. Novgorod, 1892), pt. I, pp. 229–30. At the time these original estimates were made, the Marshal of the Nobility of Lukoianovskii *uezd*, M. A. Folosofov, wrote that starvation threatened the area unless large scale help was given. Korolenko, *V golodnyi* god, pp. 104–5.

24. Korolenko, *V golodnyi god*, pp. 201–3, 216–17. A letter from Boboedov to Governor Baranov complaining about the restrictions the *uezd* food supply commission was imposing on relief work is preserved in Korolenko's personal archive. The letter is dated January 5, 1892. GBL, f. Korolenko, raz. I, k. 2, d. 1496, "Materialy iz perepiski Lukoianovskogo zemskogo nachal'nika s Nizhegorodskim gubernatorom," pp. 2–4.

25. ZhNPK, November 17, 1891, pp. 10–11.

26. ZhNPK, January 9, 1892, pp. 8–9; ZhNPK, January 15, 1892, pp. 8–10, 21–30.

27. ZhNPK, February 2, 1892, appendix, pp. 1–6. The report is primarily concerned with the situation in Arzamasskii *uezd*.

28. *Zhurnal Nizhegorodskogo gubernskogo blagotvoritel' nogo komiteta* [hereafter ZhNBK], February 19, 1892, appendix, pp. 16–17. The journals of the charitable committee are often included among the numbers of ZhNPK. Many times the journal of the charitable committee has its own pagination.

29. ZhNBK, February 15, 1892, p. 6. Zybin noted the lack of unity among the *zemskie nachal'niki* as to how to conduct such operations. He stressed the need for strong central direction from the charitable committee.

30. Baranov to the *uezd* marshals of the nobility, January 5, 1892, GBL, f. Korolenko, raz. I, k. 26, d. 1498, "Materialy po sluzhebnoi perepiske lukoianovskikh dvorian," pp. 3–5.

31. ZhNPK, February 2, 1892, p. 1.

32. Baranov to M. A. Filosofov, February 17, 1892, No. 812, GBL, f. Korolenko, raz. I, k. 26, d. 1498, "Materialy po sluzhebnoi perepiske lukoianovskikh dvorian," pp. 5–6.

33. Filosofov to Baranov, February 21, 1892, No. 85, *ibid.*, pp. 9–10.

34. *Ibid.*, p. 12.

35. *Ibid.*

36. *Ibid.*, pp. 12–13.

37. ZhNPK, February 26, 1892, pp. 1–2. Rutnitskii was the representative of the Tsesarevich's Special Committee. Guchkov had come to Nizhni-Novgorod strictly on his own. He had been studying in Germany when he learned of the famine. He returned to Russia at once, and proceeded to Nizhni to volunteer his services to Governor Baranov.

38. Baranov to Filosofov, March 11, 1892, No. 153, GBL, f. Korolenko, raz. I, k. 26, d. 1497, "Materialy po delovoi perepiske lukoianovskikh dvorian," p. 7. The original pagination of the documents given by the archivists is incorrect. I pointed out the error to the archival staff. Citations given in the footnotes is in accordance with my own, corrected, pagination.

39. *Ibid.*, pp. 7–8.

40. *Ibid.*, p. 8.

41. *Ibid.*, pp. 10–11. The tone of the letter would seem to imply that at this time Baranov felt the officials in Lukoianovskii *uezd* were attempting to reduce the peasants of the area to a state of permanent poverty and dependence. In a later document, submitted to the MVD, Baranov stated that he did not believe that Filosofov and his colleagues had any such plan in mind. He ascribed their resistance to increased relief to ignorance and stubbornness. Zapiska o Lukoianove, December 9, 1892, TsGIA, f. Dep. obshchikh del, op. 223, 1891, d. 124, "Vsepoddanneishii otchet Nizhegorodskogo gubernatora za 1891 god," p. 44.

42. ZhNPK, March 8, 1892, p. 3.

43. ZhNPK, March 15, 1892, p. 2. By this move Baranov was not infringing on the legal rights of either the marshal of the nobility or the *zemskie nachal'niki*. The Governor was simply altering the arrangements concerning the management of food supply which he himself had created.

44. *Statisticheskie dannye*, pp. 49, 69.

45. Baranov to Durnovo, April 11, 1892, No. 1611, GBL, f. Korolenko, raz. I, k. 26, d. 1498, "Materialy po sluzhebnoi perepiske lukoianovskikh dvorian," pp. 25–26.

46. Durnovo to Baranov, April 24, 1892, No. 2114, TsGAOR, f. Dep. politsii 3-oe deloproizvodstvo, 1892, d. 369, "Svedeniia po Nizhegorodskoi gubernii," pp. 4–5.

47. Baranov to Durnovo, May 1, 1892, No. 249, *ibid.*, pp. 6–10.

48. Baranov to Durnovo, May 1, 1892, supplement to letter No. 249, *ibid.*, p. 5v.

49. Durnovo to Baranov, May 6, 1892, *ibid.*, p. 5g.

50. A. I. Guchkov to Baranov, May 6, 1892, GBL, f. Korolenko, raz. I, k. 26, d. 1498, "Materialy po sluzhebnoi perepiske lukoianovskikh dvorian," pp. 40–41. Typical of the kind of abuse that prevailed in the district was an incident recounted by Obtiazhnov. He told of a certain peasant, Grigorii Iakushkin, who, along with a group of other peasants, complained when their village *starosta* stole some of the grain intended for the needy. The peasants who lodged the complaint were first intimidated by the local police and the *starosta*. Then the *zemskii nachal'nik* arrived. He listened to the testimony of the peasants, some of whom were eyewitnesses to the theft, and then found for the accused, basing his decision on statements gathered from the *starosta*'s relatives. Iakushkin was placed under arrest. Obtiazhnov to Baranov, May 8, 1892, *ibid.*, pp. 43–49.

51. ZhNPK, May 10, 1892, p. 3.

52. A. Boldyrev to Baranov, May 17, 1892, GBL, f. Korolenko, raz. I, k. 26, d. 1498, "Materialy po sluzhebnoi perepiske lukoianovskikh dvorian," pp. 51–53.

53. Guchkov to Baranov, May 18, 1892, *ibid.*, pp. 55–57.

54. This account of the struggle between the nobles of Lukoianovskii *uezd* and the local

zemstvo is drawn from Korolenko's *V golodnyi god*, pp. 140–42. With regard to the Valov case, an investigation held after the famine found him to be innocent of all charges (*ibid.*, pp. 141–42).

55. A. S. Norman, letter to the Special Committee, January 15, 1892, TsGIA, f. Osobogo Komiteta, d. 100, "Perespiska po Tambovskoi gubernii," p. 176.

56. *Ibid.*

57. *Ibid.*

58. *Ibid.*

59. Journal of the Iambirnskaia *volost'* committee, October 13, 1891, *ibid.*, p. 181.

60. Journal of the Iambirnskaia *volost'* committee, November 6, 1891, *ibid.*, p. 187. The information contained in the journal seems to relate mostly to charitable relief and not to zemstvo loans. At this point, however, due to a lack of funds the committee was giving out charitable aid on a loan basis (of the thirty-seven *pudy* given out, twenty-four *pudy* were considered as loans). When more funds became available, this practice was stopped. Journal of the Iambirnskaia *volost'* committee, November 16, 1891, *ibid.*, pp. 188–89.

61. Journal of the Iambirnskaia *volost'* committee, November 22, 1891, *ibid.*, p. 190.

62. The committee generally met every two weeks, but sometimes more frequent sessions were held. The documents in the Leningrad archive contain the journals of the following sessions: October 13, October 28, October 31, November 6, November 16, November 22, November 27, December 13, December 31, January 13, 1892, January 27, February 24.

63. Journal of the Iambirnskaia *volost'* committee, November 27, 1891, *ibid.*, p. 191.

64. *Ibid.*

65. In the committee's journal for January 13, 1892, it was reported that: "In checking over the lists [of certain villages] the committee found several mistakes with regard to the requests of some peasants. . . . [The committee] decided to prevent some [of the peasants] from receiving loans for a period of from two weeks to two months; to remove some others from the rolls completely; and [in the case of] some obviously well-to-do peasants, . . . to try to recover the bread given to them. . . ." (*ibid.*, p. 195.)

66. Norman to the Special Committee, January 15, 1892, *ibid.*, p. 176.

67. *Ibid.*

68. *Ibid.*, pp. 176 and 199.

69. Pleve to Bobrinskii, January 23, 1892, *ibid.*, p. 175.

70. Bobrinskii's note is without date, *ibid.*, p. 175.

11. CONCLUSIONS

1. Vypiska iz zhurnala Komiteta Ministrov, February 25, 1892, *Prodovol'stvennoe delo*, II, 134.

2. See Table 2.

3. An extremely valuable survey of earlier famine relief efforts in Russia can be found in *Prodovol'stvennoe delo*, III, 143–350.

4. British relief efforts in Ireland are discussed at length in Woodham-Smith, *The Great Hunger* and R. D. Edwards and T. D. Williams, eds., *The Great Famine: Studies in Irish History*, 1845–52 (Dublin, 1956). Bhatia, *Famines in India* is the most thorough study of food supply operations on the subcontinent.

5. Mikhailovskii's proclamation, entitled "Svobodnoe slovo," was dated January 1892. The text is produced in M. S. Aleksandrov, "Gruppa narodovol'tsev (1891–1894)," *Byloe*, No. 11 (November, 1906), pp. 16–17.

6. If the size of strictly private relief operations can be taken as an index of the public's ability to manage the food supply campaign, Mikhailovskii's optimism does not seem very well founded. We have no total figures of the sums disbursed by private hands, but they may not have exceeded 5 or 6 million rubles. My reasoning is based on the fact that L. N. Tolstoi, the most important figure in private relief operations, raised about 141,000 rubles during 1891–92. Ernest J. Simmons, *Leo Tolstoi* 2 vols.; New York, 1960, II, 179. It seems unlikely that many others engaged in private charity would have been able to obtain anything like this sum.

7. In his study of the problem of famine, Alonzo E. Taylor writes, "In view of the frequency of occurrence of famine, more or less available for investigation, the recorded studies of famine are so few as to embarrass the student and the critic. One has to choose between a large number of cases poorly studied, or a small sample well studied." "Famine" (unpublished typescript, Food Research Institute, Stanford, 1947), p. 33.

8. Taylor states, "We possess no specific criteria to separate famine as morbidity or mortality from many inter-current diseases. Nor are we in position, by analysis of death and health records to separate the effect of famine, contrasted with infectious diseases, upon the death rate. Thus we can yet set up no demography of famine" (*ibid.*, p. 81).

9. The great Irish famine is a case in point. The literature about the subject is considerable; yet historians are chary about estimating the demographic impact of the crisis. A major scholarly study of the event begins with the statement, "It is difficult to know how many men and women died in Ireland in the famine years. . . . Perhaps all that matters is the certainty that many, very many died." Edwards and Williams, eds., *The Great Famine*, p. vii. This volume has no special section on famine demography, and only the crudest estimate of the disaster's impact upon the death rate.

10. The question whether or not people starved during the famine of 1891–92 cannot be answered with any certainty. No deaths from starvation were listed in the *Otchet* of the MVD's Medical Department, but this is not final proof that starvation did not take place. Rural officials and governors would be unlikely to report such instances if they did occur, and some other cause of death might be given in government records. I. K. Sukhopliuev, who made a considerable study of this problem, claimed that during famines in Russia, starvation frequently happened but that it went unmentioned in official reports. "Posledstviia neurozhaev v Rossii," *Russkaia mysl'* (June, 1906), 150. But available evidence for 1891–92 seems to indicate that if starvation occurred, it was rather rare. I found few documented cases of starvation among the memoirs and government records I examined. In a real sense, however, the question of starvation is irrelevant. Most mortality in a famine situation is due to diseases which attack the human organism, rather than genuine starvation.

11. There can be little doubt that famine always results in an increase in the rate of morbidity. The question which disturbs students is whether the increase in disease is due to weakness

caused by malnutrition or to the various social consequences of famine. For a good discussion of the problem see, William H. Foege, "Famine, Infections and Epidemics," in *Famine: A Symposium Dealing with Nutrition and Relief Operations in Times of Disaster*, G. Blix, Y Hofvander, and B. Vahlquist, eds. (Uppsala, 1971), pp. 64–72.

12. For a study of the impact of cholera in an earlier period, see Roderick E. McGrew, *Russia and the Cholera 1823–1832* (Madison and Milwaukee, 1965). High death rates from cholera often coincided with famines, however. Thus 1848, which saw a serious crop failure, also witnessed high cholera mortality (690,000 deaths). See M. S. Onitskanskii, *O rasprostranenii kholery v Rossii* (SPb., 1911), pp. 1–2, and Kahan, "Natural Calamities and Their Effect upon Food Supply in Russia," p. 373.

13. An excellent discussion of typhus, its causes and its relation to famine, can be found in Cecil Woodham-Smith, *The Great Hunger*, pp. 182–91.

14. On the role of beggars as carriers of disease during the Irish famine see *ibid.*, pp. 186–87. See also, Foege, "Famine, Infections and Epidemics," pp. 66–67.

15. This figure is often cited in Soviet historical works. See A. M. Anfimov, "Prodovol'stvennye dolgi kak pokazatel' ekonomicheskogo polozheniia krest'ianstva dorovoliutsionnoi Rossii (konets XIX—nachalo XX veka)," *Materialy po istorii sel'skogo khoziaistva i krest'ianstva SSSR*, IV (1960), 294. Also P. N. Pershin, *Agrarnaia revoliutsiia v Rossii* (2 vols.; Moscow, 1966), I, 58.

16. Onitskanskii, *O rasprostranenii*, pp. 1–2.

17. V. I. Pokrovskii, "Vliianie kolebanii urozhaia i khlebnykh tsen na estestvennoe dvizhenie naseleniia," in *Vliianie urozhaev i khlebnykh tsen na nekotorye storony russkogo narodnogo khoziaistva*, A. I. Chuprov and A. S. Posnikov, eds. (SPb., 1897), II, 171–370. Pokrovskii's data are not without flaw, but they are extremely useful and accessable.

18. This norm is derived by averaging the number of deaths in the famine provinces for the three years preceding the disaster and the two years following. In those provinces where bad harvest recurred in 1892 and where the local death rates for 1893 seemed excessively high, the data for 1893 are ignored and mortality is figured on the basis of the four years 1888–90 and 1894. See Table 4.

19. *Otchet meditsinskogo departamenta Ministerstva vnutrennikh del za 1892 god* (St. Petersburg, 1896), pp. 42–99.

20. In a number of areas, of course, the rise in the death rate was considerably higher. See Table 3.

21. Bhatia, *Famines in India*, p. 189.

22. The official account of the famine of 1896–97 indicated that mortality rose by about 20 percent in Bengal and Madras. In Bombay and Central Provinces the death rate jumped by 50 percent and more. *Report of the Indian Famine Commission, 1898* (London, 1898), pp. 155, 173–77, 182–86.

23. According to official statistics the *lowest* percentage rise in the death rate occurred in Central Provinces, an increase of 64 percent. *Report of the Indian Famine Commission, 1901* (London, 1901), p. 70.

24. *Ibid.*, pp. 4–7.

25. For a recent study of Soviet attempts at relieving the distress, see Charles M. Edmondson,

"Soviet Famine Relief Measures, 1921–1923" (unpublished Ph.D. dissertation, Florida State University, 1970).

26. H. H. Fisher, *The Famine in Soviet Russia, 1919–1923: The Operations of the American Relief Administration* (New York, 1927), p. 557.

27. Frank A. Golder and Lincoln Hutchinson, *On the Trail of the Russian Famine* (Stanford, California, 1927), p. 18. Edmondson notes, however, that other estimates by knowledgeable persons placed the death rate much higher. "Soviet Famine Relief Measures," pp. 325–26.

28. The most thorough calculation of mortality in 1932–33 is Dana Dalrymple, "The Soviet Famine of 1932–34," *Soviet Studies*, XV (January, 1964), 259.

29. Golder and Hutchinson provide numerous vignettes of life during the 1921 famine. See also Edmondson, pp. 33–41 and *passim*. Dalrymple gives the best survey of the available descriptions of the post-collectivization disaster.

30. Sukhopliuev, "Posledstviia neurozhaev," pp. 158–65. In Tula province, where, if the death rate is any indication, the impact of the famine was less severe than in other areas, the number of landless peasant households rose by 11 percent. The number of households which possessed horses declined from 137,000 to 133,200. Households possessing more than two horses decreased from 31,420 to 28,730. The Governor stated that in the wake of the disaster a quarter of the inhabitants of the province were without work animals. TsGIA, f. Dep. obshchikh del, op. 223, 1892, d. 199, "Vsepoddanneishii otchet Tul'skogo gubernatora za 1892 god," p. 6).

31. In a letter to Vyshnegradskii, Durnovo noted that the poverty resulting from the famine "was so great that the economic situation of the population has been severely shaken, and there is no basis for supposing that it will be possible to recover in full the food supply loans without the danger of further impoverishing the peasant economy." Durnovo to Vyshnegradskii, June 27, 1892, No. 6259, TsGIA, f. Departamenta okladnykh sborov Ministerstva Finansov (No. 573), op. 1, d. 1207, "O l'gotakh sel'skomu naseleniiu postradavshikh ot neurozhaia mestnostei po vozvratu vydannykh emu prodovol'stvennykh sud," p. 1. The Minister of Finance and the Emperor supported Durnovo's view. The peasants were allowed to return the loans in the form of grain on a *pud*-for-*pud* basis, instead of repaying in cash. Later most of the arrears on the loans were cancelled. In all, the government received only a small portion of its relief monies back.

32. G. B. Masefield, *Food and Nutrition Procedures in Times of Disaster* (Rome, 1967), p. 13. See also *Famine: A Symposium*, p. 192.

33. The discussion of the fate of Imperial Russia is spread over many years and works. Naturally enough, much of the debate concentrates on the period from 1905 to 1917, but remarks concerning that era have strong implications for the late nineteenth century as well. In the most recent version of the dispute, the main catalyst is Leopold Haimson's article "The Problem of Social Stability in Urban Russia, 1905–1917," *Slavic Review*, XXIII (December, 1964), 619–42, and *ibid.*, XXIV (March, 1965), 1–22. Haimson's remarks provoked stimulating replies by Arthur Mendel ("Peasant and Worker on the Eve of the First World War") and T. H. Von Laue ("The Chances for Liberal Constitutionalism"), which appeared in the March, 1965 issue of the *Slavic Review*. The views of Haimson, Mendel, and Von Laue were then subjected to penetrating criticism by George Yaney, "Social Stability in Prerevolutionary Russia: A Critical Note," *Slavic Review*, XXIV (September, 1965), 521–27. Since 1965, the argument has continued and others have joined in.

Useful summaries and extensions of the debate can be found in the articles by Mendel and Von Laue which appeared in *Russia under the Last Tsar*, T. G. Stavrou, ed. (Minneapolis, 1969). While this is not the place to make a further contribution to this discussion, one comment seems in order. In the main, too much attention has been focused on the question of the chances for the success of Russian liberalism. Too little time has been spent pursuing the line suggested by Yaney regarding the ability of the established bureaucracy to adapt to new conditions and to meet new challenges.

34. The government never published an official account of its struggle against the famine of 1891–92, although it would do so after later crisis. Much raw material was presented in the various ministerial histories and in sources like *Statisticheskie dannye*. This kind of information was little used by Russian journalists and historians, however.

35. Cited by G. V. Plekhanov, *Vserossiiskoe razorenie* (SPb., 1906), p. 60.

36. In January, 1892, the MVD addressed eighteen provinces currently experiencing food supply difficulties. In February, 1893, twenty-seven other provinces were asked to consider the reform of the famine relief system. For a convenient list of the questions posed by the Ministry, see Veselovskii, *Istoria zemstva*, II, 323–24.

37. Of the eighteen provinces originally polled, a majority in six local conferences favored zemstvo domination of relief. Ministerstvo vnutrennikh del. Khoziaistvennyi departament, *Svod mnenii mestnykh prodovol'stvennykh soveshchanii ob izmenenii destvuiushchikh pravil o obespechenii narodnogo prodovol'stviia* (2 vols., SPb., 1893), I, 91. Only the conference in Ufa and scattered members of other conferences wanted a takeover by the administration (*ibid.*, pp. 93–94). The other conferences supported some kind of joint zemstvo-administrative control, but the specifics of the arrangement desired varied considerably. For details, see *ibid.*, pp. 97–129. Of the twenty-seven *gubernii* questioned later, a larger percentage of the conferences favored administrative control, and fewer supported the zemstvos. The bulk of these conferences pressed for some kind of formalized cooperation between state and zemstvo agencies. *Svod mnenii*, II, 36–51.

38. For the information on the reaction of Russian doctors to the crisis, I am indebted to the work of Nancy Frieden.

39. The words are those of the Tver petition as cited in George Fischer, *Russian Liberalism* (Cambridge, Mass., 1958), p. 74.

40. There was, of course, a strong antibureaucratic flavor about the zemstvo petitions, a clear protest against administrative arbitrariness. The fact that Nicholas' accession stimulated zemstvo aspirations is significant, however. As the head of the Special Committee, he symbolized the link between the government and "society" which the famine engendered. The Soviet historian P. I. Shlemin also stresses the limited character of zemstvo demands in the wake of the famine. Shlemin does not make a connection between Nicholas' work during 1891–92 and the hopes that his accession generated, but he does note that the change of rulers raised many unfounded expectations. See Shlemin's articles "Zemskoe dvizhenie i liberal'naia intelligentsiia na rubezhe 80–90 godov XIX veka," *Voprosy istorii SSSR* (Moscow, 1972), pp. 191–202, "Zemsko-liberal'noe dvizhenie i adresa 1894/95 g," *Vestnik Moskovskogo universiteta*, seriia IX, No. 1 (1973), pp. 60–73, and the *avtoreferat* of his dissertation *Zemsko-liberal'noe dvizhenie na rubezhe XIX–XX vekov* (Moscow, 1973).

41. See, for example, Polovtsov's extended conversation with the Emperor, *Dnevnik*, II, 402–3.

42. Strong public outcry prevented the government from implementing this measure.

43. Pleve's program provided for a more regular system of administering relief during a famine crisis. The draft law proposed that a central good supply council be set up under the MVD to provide overall direction for relief operations. Provincial and *uezd* councils would also be established. Another innovation proposed by the project was the formation of smaller food supply districts corresponding to the *volost'* (Ermolov, *Nashi neurozhai*, I, 206–8). This draft did not become law at once, however. Not until 1900 did the main features of the project receive legal sanction.

44. The "Witte system" and the justifications for it are presented in detail in Von Laue's *Sergei Witte*, especially pp. 71–119.

45. An example of this kind of thinking was the opinion of the majority of the State Council concerning the food supply law of 1900. See *Otchet po deloproizvodstvu Gosudarstvenogo Soveta za sessiiu 1899–1900 gg.* (SPb., 1900), I, 424–25.

46. An MVD circular dated August 17, 1901 stated that "beginning with the crop failure of 1891–92 and during all subsequent misfortunes of the same character, it was frequently revealed that some philanthropists while giving material aid to the inhabitants of the afflicted regions [also] tried to arouse . . . discontent with the existing order. . . ." Quoted by D. N. Zhbankov, "O pomoshchi golodaiushchim," *Vrach*, No. 50, 1901, p. 1538.

BIBLIOGRAPHY

A NOTE ON SOURCES

Material on the famine of 1891–92 abounds, but surprisingly little has been used by historians. The best sources for the study of government relief policy are to be found in the Central State Historical Archive in Leningrad (TsGIA). The *fond* of the Economic Department of Ministry of Internal Affairs (No. 1287) has the single most valuable collection of documents on the famine. The files of the Economic Department contain a large portion of the day-to-day correspondence between the provincial governors and the MVD. In addition, this *fond* holds many of the reports of special agents sent into the famine region, extracts from hard-to-get zemstvo records, and communications from private citizens. Another rich vein of material is the *fond* of the Special Committee on Famine Relief (No. 1204). These papers have much information on the activities of charitable groups during the crisis and reveal a good deal about the work of state institutions as well.

The Central State Archive of the October Revolution in Moscow (TsGAOR) has considerable data on the famine. Particularly germane to this study were documents in the *fond* of the Department of Police, 3rd *Deloproizvodstvo* (No. 102). These papers have information on the conditions in the famine stricken *gubernii*, and shed light on the reaction of the central government to the crisis. Of great value, too, were the personal *fondy* of V. K. Pleve (No. 586) and Nicholas II (No. 601). The materials in Pleve's archive are of a varied character, but give insight into numerous aspects of relief work. The papers of Nicholas II deal mostly with the operation of the Special Committee on Famine Relief and supplement material held in the Leningrad Archive. The *fond* of the Emperor Alexander III was of little relevance to this study. This file is an artificial collection, composed of random documents.

Another major repository of material relating to the famine is the Manuscript Division of the Lenin Library (GBL). Here the most important papers are those of V. G. Korolenko. Korolenko's files contain a mass of information on his own activities during the hungry year, but also hold many documents which must have come from state archives. These records provide a valuable supplement to the *dela* in TsGIA. The Central State Historical Archive's holdings on Nizhni-Novgorod are incomplete, and the Korolenko papers fill in many gaps. Particularly significant are the materials relating to the so-called "*lukoianovskaia istoriia.*"

Of the published sources dealing with the famine, by far the most useful is the collection entitled *Prodovol'stvennoe delo*. This body of documents is virtually the complete record of the work of the Committee of Ministers during the crisis. It contains the reports submitted to the Committee by the various Ministries as well as extracts from the journals of the

Committee itself. Appended to the official memoranda are papers relating to the history of famine relief in Russia.

Zemstvo records comprise another major source of information for the historian of the famine. The discussions in the zemstvo assemblies tell much about the reaction of provincial "society" to the crisis and reveal many of the problems of relief work at the local level. Of particular relevance are the special reports prepared by the provincial *upravy* and statistical bureaus. These works contain a wealth of data which help make clear the causes of the famine and enable the student to gauge the effectiveness of relief operations. Beyond this, zemstvo documents provide a perspective on the famine which is often quite different from that of government officials in St. Petersburg.

Contemporary journalism provides a vast mine of material for the history of the famine. But the quality of Russian newspapers and magazines of this period is so varied as to make general comments almost impossible. Speaking broadly, however, both the capital and provincial press are great storehouses of information, but they should be used with caution. This is especially true of the major newspapers and the "fat" journals whose views are often clouded by ideological preconceptions. The provincial press overwhelms the student with the enormous detail it presents. The writings of emigre polemicists is of little use to someone trying to reconstruct the events of the famine year. These works are of interest mainly to the historian of revolutionary ideas.

The quality of available memoir literature is also varied. The accounts of those who worked in the famine regions provide valuable color and give much insight into the problems of local relief. But, on the whole, they tend to be anecdotal. A striking exception is V. G. Korolenko's justly famous *V golodnyi god*. This work, half journalism, half memoir, is a major source of information on events in Nizhni-Novgorod during the crisis and gives valuable insight into provincial politics. Unfortunately, there is nothing which provides a comparable view of decision-making at the highest levels. The key figures of the famine year, Durnovo, Pleve, Vyshnegradskii, Giubbenet, did not write their memoirs. As a result, the historian is often at a loss to explain the actions of government leaders. The diary of A. A. Polovtsov helps to fill the gap somewhat, but Polovtsov was abroad during the crucial period from July to October when the basic pattern of government relief was established. Witte's memoirs give some background on the railroad crisis, but they should be used with great care.

There is almost no secondary literature on the famine of 1891–92. The official histories of the Committee of Ministers and the Ministry of Internal Affairs provide much useful information but little analysis. The most important discussions of the problem of famine in Russia are the two works by A. S. Ermolov: *Neurozhai i narodnoe bedstvie*, and *Nashi neurozhai i prodovol'stvennyi vopros*. In the first book Ermolov makes a detailed investigation of the causes of the crisis of 1891; in the second he presents a broad survey of Russian famine relief measures. Both works display Ermolov's erudition with regard to agriculture and his intimate knowledge of food supply operations.

ARCHIVAL COLLECTIONS

Archive of Russian and East European History and Culture, Columbia University

Liubimov, D. N. "Russkaia smuta nachala deviatisotykh godov 1902–1906: Po vospominaniiam lichnym zapiskam i dokumentam."

Mel'nikov, N. "19 let na zemskoi sluzhbe (avtobiograficheskie nabroski i vospominaniia)."

Troitskii, K. K. "Iz vospominanii chinovnika osobykh poruchenii V klassa pri Ministre vnutrennikh del."

Otdel rukopisei Gosudarstvennoi Biblioteki SSSR imeni V. I. Lenina (GBL)

Fond Kireevikh-Novikovikh (No. 126).
Fond V. G. Korolenko (No. 135).
Fond S. M. Petrovskogo (No. 224).

Tsentral'nyi Gosudarstvennyi Arkhiv Oktiabrskoi Revoliutsii (TsGAOR)

Fond Aleksandra III-go (No. 677).
Fond Departamenta Politsii, 3-oe deloproizvodstvo (No. 102).
Fond T. I. Filippova (No. 1099).
Fond Nikolaia II-go (No. 601).
Fond V. K. Pleve (No. 586).

Tsentral'nyi Gosudarstvennyi Istoricheskii Arkhiv SSSR (TsGIA)

Fond Departamenta Obshchikh Del MVD (No. 1284).
Fond Departamenta Okladnykh Sborov Ministerstva Finansov (No. 573).
Fond Departamenta Zheleznodorozhnykh Del Ministerstva Finansov (No. 268).
Fond Filippovykh (No. 728).
Fond Kantseliariia Ministra Vnutrennikh Del (No. 1281).
Fond Khoziaistvennogo Departamenta MVD (No. 1287).
Fond Iu. S. Nechaeva-Mal'tseva (No. 1005).
Fond Obshchoi Kantseliairii Ministra Finansov (No. 560).
Fond Osobogo Soveshchaniia ob Obshchestvennykh Rabotakh (No. 1225).
Fond Osobogo Komiteta dlia pomoshchi nuzhdaiushchemusia naseleniiu v mestnostiakh, postignutykh neurozhaem (No. 1204).
Fond Vol'nogo Ekonomicheskogo Obshchestva (No. 91).

GENERAL SOURCES

Afanas'ev, N. I. *Sovremenniki: Albom biografii.* 2 vols. St. Petersburg, 1909–1910.
Aleksandrov, M. S. "Gruppa narodovol'tsev (1891–1894)," *Byloe*, No. 11 (November, 1906), pp. 1–27.
Ames, Edward. "A Century of Russian Railroad Construction 1837–1936," *American Slavic and East European Review*, VI (December, 1947), 57–74.
Anfimov, A. M. "Prodovol'stvennye dolgi kak pokazatel' ekonomicheskogo polozheniia krest'ianstva dorevoliutsionnoi Rossii (konets XIX-nachalo XX veka)," *Materialy po istorii sel'skogo khoziaistva i krest'ianstva SSSR*, IV (1960), 293–312.
Annenskii, N. F. "Eshche neskol'ko slov o prodovol'stvennoi nuzhde," *Russkoe bogatstvo* (March, 1898), pp. 161–83.
—— "Khronika vnutrennei zhizni," *Russkoe bogatstvo* (July, 1896), pp. 153–65.
—— "K voprosu o neurozhaiakh poslednikh let," *Russkoe bogatstvo* (September, 1898), (December, 1898), pp. 114–37.
—— "Organizatsiia prodovol'stvennogo dela (v period 1891–92 godov)." (In *Nizhegorodskaia guberniia po issledovaniiam gubernskogo zemstva*, Vol. III.) St. Petersburg, 1906.
Arsen'ev, K. K. "Iz nedavnei poezdki v Tambovskuiu guberniiu: Vpechatleniia i zametki," *Vestnik Evropy* (February, 1892), pp. 835–50.
—— "V neurozhainykh mestnostiakh," *Vestnik Evropy* (February, 1893), pp. 829–44.
B., V. [V. V. Biriukovich]. "Zemsko-prodovol'stvennoe delo," *Vestnik Evropy* (May, 1889), pp. 365–75.
"Baranov." *Novyi Entsiklopedicheskii slovar'*. Vol. V.

Baron, Samuel H. *Plekhanov, the Father of Russian Marxism*. Stanford, California, 1963.
Belokonskii, I. P. *V gody bespraviia: Vospominaniia*. Moscow, 1930.
—— "Zemstvo i narodnoe khoziaistvo. I. Statistika," *Severnyi vestnik* (May, 1892), pp. 16–33.
—— "Zemstvo i narodnoe prodovol'stvie," *Severnyi vestnik* (March, 1892), pp. 7–25.
Bennett, M. K. "Famine." *International Encyclopedia of the Social Sciences*. Vol. V.
Berenshtam, M. "Iz nedalekogo proshlogo (Vospominaniia o poezdke 'na golod')," *Russkoe bogatstvo* (April, 1898), pp. 153–71.
Berg, I. "Strakhovanie poseva," *Russkii vestnik* (August, 1893), pp. 164–206.
"Besedy v I. Otdelenii Obshchestva po voprosam o prichinakh neurozhaia 1891 goda i merakh protiv povtoreniia podobnykh neurozhaev v budushchem." *Trudy Imperatorskogo Vol'nogo Ekonomicheskogo Obshchestva* (1892), I, 67–106, 107–44, 163–206, 289–336, 337–80.
Bhatia, B. M. *Famines in India: A Study in Some Aspects of the Economic History of India (1860–1945)*. Bombay, 1963.
Billington, James H. *Mikhailovskii and Russian Populism*. Oxford, 1958.
Birzhevye vedomosti (St. Petersburg).
Blank, P. B. "Chem ustranit' vozmozhnost' goloda v Rossii," *Russkii vestnik*, No. 8 (1874), pp. 638–57.
Bleklov, S. M. *Za faktami i tsiframi. Zapiski zemskogo statistika*. Moscow, 1894.
Blinov, Nikolai. *Zemskaia sluzhba: obshchedostupnye besedy glasno-krest'ianina*. Moscow, 1887.
Blix, G., Y. Hofvander, and B. Vahlquist, eds. *Famine: A Symposium Dealing with Nutrition and Relief Operations in Times of Disaster*. Uppsala, 1971.
Bobrinskii, A. "Amerikanskaia pomoshch' v 1892 i 1893 godakh," *Russkii vestnik* (February, 1894), pp. 252–64.
Bogdanovich, A. V. *Tri poslednikh samoderzhtsa: Dnevnik A. V. Bogdanovich*. Moscow and Leningrad, 1924.
Bohr, Paul Richard. *Famine in China and the Missionary: Timothy Richard as Relief Administrator and Advocate of National Reform, 1876–1884*. Cambridge, Mass., 1972.
Carlyle, R. W. "Famine Administration in a Bengal District in 1896–97," *Economic Journal*, X (1900), 421–30.
Chernyshev, I. V. *Agrarno-krest'ianskaia politika Rossii za 150 let*. Petrograd, 1918.
Cheshikhin, V. E. *Piat'desiat' let zhizni Nizhegorodskikh zemstv: Ocherk razvitiia zemskogo khoziaistva*. N. Novgorod, 1914.
Chuprov, A. I. and A. S. Posnikov, eds. *Vliianie urozhaev i khlebnykh tsen na nekotorye storony russkogo narodnogo khoziaistva*. 2 vols. St. Petersburg, 1897.
Curti, Merle. *American Philanthropy Abroad: A History*. New Brunswick N.J., 1963.
Czap, Peter. "Peasant Class Courts and Peasant Customary Justice in Russia 1861–1912," *Journal of Social History*, I (Winter, 1967), 149–78.
Dalrymple, Dana G. "The Soviet Famine of 1932–1934," *Soviet Studies*, XV (January, 1964), 250–84.
Dashkevich, L. V. *Nashe ministerstvo vnutrennikh del*. Berlin, 1895.
Dashkov, D. "K prodovol'stvennomu voprosu (Pis'mo iz derevni)," *Russkoe obozrenie* (December, 1893), pp. 738–53.
Davydova, S. A. *Zapiski o zhenskikh rabotakh v Voronezhskoi i Nizhegorodskoi guberniiakh*. St. Petersburg, 1894.
Dmitriev, M. *Neurozhainyi god 1891–92 v Nizhegorodskoi gubernii*. N. Novgorod, 1893.

Durtskoe-Sokol'ninskii, D. "Nashe sel'skoe khoziaistvo i ego budushchnost', *Vestnik Evropy* (October, 1891), pp. 698–734.

Edgar, W. C. "Russia's Conflict with Hunger," *The Review of Reviews*, V (1892), 691–700.

Edmondson, Charles M. "Soviet Famine Relief Measures, 1921–1923." Unpublished Ph.D. dissertation, Florida State University, 1970.

Edwards, R. D., and T. D. Williams, eds. *The Great Famine: Studies in Irish History, 1845–52*. Dublin, 1956.

Egiazarova, N. A. *Agrarnyi krizis kontsa XIX veka v Rossii*. Moscow, 1959.

Elenev, F. P. "1868 god v Smolenskoi gubernii," *Russkii vestnik* (June, 1892), pp. 237–60.

Emel'ianov, A. P. *Golod v otrazhenii russkoi literatury i publitsistiki*. Kazan, 1921.

Erisman, F. "Pitanie golodaiushchikh," *Russkaia mysl'* (April, 1892), pp. 128–55.

Ermolov, A. S. *Nashi neurozhai i prodovol'stvennyi vopros*. 2 vols. St. Petersburg, 1909.

[Ermolov, A. S.] *Neurozhai i narodnoe bedstvie*. St. Petersburg, 1892.

Ertel', A. "Makar'evskoe popechitel'stvo (Iz istorii nedavnogo goloda)." *Russkaia mysl'* (January, 1893), pp. 228–50.

F., F. "Po povodu goloda," *Vestnik Evropy* (September, 1891), pp. 390–95.

Famine Inquiry Commission. *Report on Bengal*. New Delhi, 1945.

Feoktistov, E. M. *Vospominaniia za kulisami politiki i literatury 1848–1896*. Leningrad, 1929.

Fischer, George. *Russian Liberalism*. Cambridge, Mass., 1958.

Fisher, H. H. *The Famine in Soviet Russia, 1919–1923: The Operations of the American Relief Administration*. New York, 1927.

Flerovskii, N. [V. V. Bervi]. *Tri politicheskie sistemy: Nikolai I, Aleksandr II i Aleksandr III*. [London], 1897.

G., N. "Pis'ma iz derevni," *Russkoe bogatstvo* (February, 1892), pp. 149–55.

Gershenkron, A. *Continuity in History and other Essays*. Cambridge, Mass., 1968.

Gessen, V. "Gubernator, kak organ nadzora," *Severnyi vestnik* (January, 1898), pp. 183–211.

Gofshtetter, I. "Bor'ba s golodom," *Russkoe bogatstvo* (November, 1891), pp. 222–29.

—— "Vodka ili khleb," *Russkoe bogatstvo* (October, 1892), pp. 180–84.

Golder, Frank A. N. and Lincoln Hutchinson. *On the Trail of the Russian Famine*. Stanford, California, 1927.

Golovachev, D. "Pereselentsy v 1892 godu," *Vestnik Evropy* (August, 1893), pp. 803–12.

Golubev, P. A. "Narodnoe prodovol'stvie i podat'," *Russkaia mysl'* (June, 1895), pp. 85–107.

—— "Podat' i narodnoe khoziaistvo," *Russkaia mysl'* (May, 1893), pp. 137–150; (June, 1893), pp. 47–67; (July, 1893), pp. 1–29.

Gosudarstvennyi Sovet, *Otchet po deloproizvodstvu Gosudarstvennogo Soveta za sessiiu 1899–1900 gg*. St. Petersburg, 1900.

Gradovskii, A. D. *Sobranie sochinenii*. 9 vols. St. Petersburg, 1899–1904.

Grazhdanin (St. Petersburg).

Haimson, Leopold H. "The Problem of Social Stability in Urban Russia, 1905–1917," *Slavic Review*, XXIII (December, 1964), 619–42; XXIV (March, 1965), 1–22.

—— *The Russian Marxists and the Origins of Bolshevism*. Cambridge, Mass., 1955.

Hodgetts, E. E. Brayley. *In the Track of the Russian Famine: The Personal Narrative of a Journey through the Famine Districts of Russia*. London, 1892.

Hourowich, Isaac. *The Economics of the Russian Village*. New York, 1892.

Hsiao, Kung-Chuan. *Rural China, Imperial Control in the Nineteenth Century*. Seattle, 1960.

Iakovlev, A. F. *Ekonomicheskie krizisy v Rossii*. Moscow, 1953.

Ianovskii, A. "Zemskie uchastkovye nachal'niki," *Entsiklopedicheskii slovar'*. 1894. Vol. XII A.

Imperatorskoe Vol'noe Ekonomicheskoe Obshchestvo. *Sbornik otvetov na predlozhennye Imperatorskim Vol'nym Ekonomicheskim Obshchestvom voprosy po izucheniiu neurozhaia 1891 god*. St. Petersburg, 1893.

Izmailov, A. *Zheleznye dorogi v neurozhai 1891 goda*. St. Petersburg, 1895.

"Iz obshchestvennoi khroniki," *Vestnik Evropy* (August, 1891), pp. 866–81; (September, 1891), pp. 426–40; (November, 1891), pp. 417–32; (December, 1891), pp. 867–81; (March, 1892), pp. 440–54; (May, 1892), pp. 428–40; (June, 1892), pp. 867–82; (July, 1892), pp. 462–74; (January, 1893), pp. 454–71; (February, 1893), pp. 926–36; (April, 1893), pp. 863–74.

"Iz provintsial'noi pechati," *Severnyi vestnik* (August, 1891), pp. 43–55; (October, 1891), pp. 63–76; (November, 1891), pp. 53–60; (December, 1891), pp. 70–89; (January, 1892), pp. 45–57; (February, 1892), pp. 110–17; (March, 1892), pp. 26–38; (April, 1892), pp. 53–61; (May, 1892), pp. 43–54; (June, 1892), pp. 59–74; (August, 1892), pp. 45–57.

"Iz zhizni i pechati," *Russkii vestnik* (July, 1891), pp. 362–75; (September, 1891), pp. 288–303; (October, 1891), pp. 368–81; (November, 1891), pp. 341–54; (December, 1891), pp. 340–58; (March, 1892), pp. 400–13; (April, 1892), pp. 357–70; (June, 1892), pp. 323–38; (June, 1893), pp. 357–73.

K., P. [M. P. Petrov.] "Letnie vpechatleniia (Iz poezdki v Samarskuiu guberniiu)," *Severnyi vestnik* (January, 1893), pp. 20–29.

K., S. [S. N. Krivenko.] "Khronika vnutrennei zhizni," *Russkoe bogatstvo* (February, 1892), pp. 108–29; (April–May, 1892), pp. 94–120.

Kahan, Arcadius. "Natural Calamities and Their Effect upon the Food Supply in Russia (An Introduction to a Catalogue)," *Jahrbücher für Geschichte Osteuropas*, XVI (N. F.) (September, 1968), 353–77.

Kartavtsev, E. E. "Nashe zakonodatel'stvo o narodnom prodovol'stvii: Istoricheskii ocherk," *Vestnik Evropy* (January, 1892), pp. 628–78.

Karyshev, N. *Zemskaia khodataistva 1865–1884 gg*. Moscow, 1900.

Kazanskaia guberniia v sel'sko-khoziaistvennom otnoshenii po svedeniiam poluchennym ot korrespondentov, za 1891 g. Kazan, 1892.

Kazanskaia guberniia v sel'sko-khoziaistvennom otnoshenii po svedeniiam poluchennym ot korrespondentov, za 1892 g. Kazan, 1893.

Kazanskaia gubernskaia zemskaia uprava. *Otchet o deistviiakh Kazanskoi gubernskoi zemskoi upravy s 1-go sentiabria 1890 po 1-e sentiabria 1891 goda*. Kazan, 1891.

—— *Otchet o deistviiakh Kazanskoi gubernskoi upravy s 1-go sentiabria 1891 po 1-e sentiabria 1892 goda*. Kazan, 1892.

Kazanskoe gubernskoe zemskoe sobranie. *Postanovleniia XXXIV ekstrennogo Kazanskogo gubernskogo zemskogo sobraniia 4–5 iiulia 1891 goda*. Kazan, 1891.

—— *Postanovleniia XXXV ekstrennogo Kazanskogo gubernskogo zemskogo sobraniia 19–21 sentiabria 1891 goda*. Kazan, 1891.

—— *Postanovleniia XXXVII ekstrennogo Kazanskogo gubernskogo zemskogo sobraniia 18–22 fevralia 1892 goda*. Kazan, 1892.

—— *Postanovleniia XXVII ocherednogo Kazanskogo gubernskogo zemskogo sobraniia 7–23 dekabria 1891 goda*. Kazan, 1892.

—— *Postanovleniia XXVIII ocherednogo Kazanskogo gubernskogo sobraniia 4–22 dekabria 1892 goda*. Kazan, 1893.

Keep, J. L. H. *The Rise of Social Democracy in Russia*. Oxford, 1963.

Kindersley, Richard. *The First Russian Revisionists: A Study of Legal Marxism in Russia.* Oxford, 1962.

Kizevetter, A. A. *Mestnoe samoupravlenie v Rossii, IX–XIX st. Istoricheskii ocherk.* Moscow, 1910.

—— *Na rubezhe dvukh stoletii.* Prague, 1929.

[Komitet Ministrov]. *Prodovol'stvennoe delo. Pechatnye predstavleniia Ministerstv Vnutrennikh Del, Putei Soobshcheniia i Finansov, kopii s vypisok iz zhurnalov Komiteta Ministrov po prodovol'stvennym delam, i sostavlennye kantseliarieiu Komiteta Ministrov spravki k sim delam, raspolozhennym po zasedaniiam Komiteta.* 3 vols. n.p. [St. Petersburg], n.d. [1891–92].

Korf, P. L. "Poezdka v neurozhainye mestnosti Kurskoi gubernii," *Trudy Imperatorskogo Vol'nogo Ekonomicheskogo Obshchestva* (1892), II, 109–120.

—— "Po povodu neurozhaia nyneshnego goda," *Trudy Imperatorskogo Vol'nogo Ekonomicheskogo Obshchestva* (1891), II, 203–21.

Kornilov, A. A. *Sem' mesiatsev sredi golodaiushchikh krest'ian.* Moscow, 1893.

Korolenko, V. G. "Nekotorye osobennosti organizatsii prodovol'stvennogo dela v Nizhegorodskom krae," *Russkaia mysl'* (July, 1893), pp. 59–73.

—— "Tretii element (Pamiati N. F. Annenskogo)." In *Sobranie sochinenii.* 10 vols. Moscow, 1955, Vol. III.

—— *V golodnyi god.* In *Sobranie sochinenii.* 10 vols. Moscow, 1955, Vol. IX.

Lamzdorf, V. N. *Dnevnik 1891–1892.* F. A. Rotshtein, ed.; Iu. Ia. Solov'ev, trans. Moscow and Leningrad, 1934.

Lavrov, S. M. *Ocherk zemskoi meditsiny Nizhegorodskogo uezda (1866–1899 gg).* N. Novgorod, 1899.

Lazarovich, S. "Krest'ianskaia tesnota i zasukhi poslednikh let v Novorossiskom krae," *Severnyi vestnik* (May, 1893), pp. 13–25.

"Lebeda," *Novyi entsiklopedicheskii slovar'.* Vol. XXXIV.

Leontovich, F. I. "Golodovki v Rossii do kontsa proshlogo veka," *Severnyi vestnik* (March, 1892), pp. 47–76; (April, 1892), pp. 33–63; (May, 1892), pp. 41–60.

Lugovoi, A. "Derevenskie nuzhdy i obshchestvennye raboty," *Russkoe bogatstvo* (July, 1892), pp. 96–116.

McGrew, Roderick E. *Russia and the Cholera 1823–1832.* Madison and Milwaukee, 1965.

Mak-Gakhan, V. "Pis'ma iz Ameriki: Kak amerikantsy pomogaiut Rossii," *Severnyi vestnik* (April, 1892), pp. 94–102.

Maklakov, V. A. *Vlast' i obshchestvennost' na zakate staroi Rossii.* (*Vospominaniia*) [Paris, 1936].

Maksimov, V. E. *Ocherki po istorii obshchestvennykh rabot v Rossii.* St. Petersburg, 1905.

Maress, L. N. "Pishcha narodnykh mass v Rossii," *Russkaia mysl'* (October, 1893), pp. 43–67.

Margulies, O. *Yidishe Folksmasn in Kamf kegn zeire Unterdriker (Etiudn).* Moscow, 1940.

Martov, L., P. Maslov, and A. Potresov. *Obshchestvennoe dvizhenie v Rossii v nachale XX-go veka.* 4 vols. St. Petersburg, 1909–12.

Masefield, G. B. *Famine: Its Prevention and Relief.* London, 1963.

—— *Food and Nutrition Procedures in Times of Disaster.* Rome, 1967.

Mendel, Arthur P. *Dilemmas of Progress in Tsarist Russia: Legal Marxism and Legal Populism.* Cambridge, Mass., 1961.

—— "Peasant and Worker on the Eve of the First World War," *Slavic Review*, XXXIV (March, 1965), pp. 23–46.

Meshcherskii, V. P. *Moi vospominaniia.* Part III, 1881–94. St. Petersburg, 1912.

Ministerstvo gosudarstvennykh imushchestv. Departament zemledeliia i sel'skoi promyshlennosti. *1888 god v sel'skokhoziaistvennom otnoshenii po otvetam, poluchennym ot khoziaev*. St. Petersburg, 1888–90.

—— *1889 god v sel'skokhoziaistvennom otnoshenii po otvetam, poluchennym ot khoziaev*. St. Petersburg, 1889–90.

—— *1890 god v sel'skokhoziaistvennom otnoshenii po otvetam, poluchennym ot khoziaev*. St. Petersburg, 1890–92.

—— *1891 god v sel'skokhoziaistvennom otnoshenii po otvetam, poluchennym ot khoziaev*. St. Petersburg, 1891–92.

—— *1892 god v sel'skokhoziaistvennom otnoshenii po otvetam, poluchennym ot khoziaev*. St. Petersburg, 1893–94.

Ministerstvo vnutrennikh del. *Ministerstvo vnutrennikh del: Istoricheskii ocherk*. 2 vols. St. Petersburg 1901.

—— *Obshchii obzor deiatel'nosti Ministerstva vnutrennikh del za vremia tsarstvovaniia Imperatora Aleksandra III*. St. Petersburg, 1901.

—— *Obshchii otchet po obshchestvennym rabotam proizvedennym soglasno vysochaishemu poveleniiu ot 28 noiabria 1891 g., v guberniiakh postradavshikh ot neurozhaia*. St. Petersburg, 1895.

Ministerstvo vnutrennikh del. Khoziaistvennyi departament. *Istoricheskii obzor pravitel'stvennykh meropriiatii po narodnomu prodovol'stviiu v Rossii*. 2 vols. St. Petersburg, 1893.

—— *Svod nmenii mestnykh prodovol'stvennykh soveshchanii ob izmenenii destvuiushchikh pravil o obespechenii narodnogo prodovol'stviia*. 2 vols. St. Petersburg, 1893.

—— Meditsinskii departament. *Otchet meditsinskogo departamenta Ministerstva vnutrennikh del za 1892 god*. St. Petersburg, 1896.

—— Tsentral'nyi statisticheskii komitet. *Sbornik svedneii po Rossii 1896 g. Statistika Rossiiskoi Imperii*. St. Petersburg, 1897, Vol. XL.

—— *Statisticheskie dannye po vydache ssud na obsemenie i prodovol'stvie naseleniiu postradavshemu ot neurozhaia v 1891–1892 gg. Vremennik tsentral'nogo statisticheskogo komiteta*, No. 28. St. Petersburg, 1894.

—— *Urozhai 1891 goda v 60 guberniiakh Evropeiskoi Rossii. Statistika Rossiiskoi Imperii*. St. Petersburg, 1892, Vol. XIX.

—— *Urozhai 1892 goda v 60 guberniiakh Evropeiskoi Rossii. Statistika Rossiiskoi Imperii*. St. Petersburg, 1893, Vol. XXVI.

Miropol'skii, A. L. "O narodnom prodovol'stvii (Pis'mo v redaktsiiu)," *Russkaia mysl'* (October, 1891), pp. 120–24.

M-skii, N. [Miklashevskii, N. N.] "Na pervykh obshchestvennykh rabotakh," *Vestnik Evropy* (December, 1902), pp. 833–45.

Naumov, A. N. *Iz utselevshikh vospominanii, 1868–1917*. 2 vols. New York, 1954.

Nelidova, L. "Iz poezdki na Volgu v proshlom godu," *Vestnik Evropy* (March, 1893), pp. 204–54; (April, 1893), pp. 453–533.

Nifontov, A. S. "Statistika urozhaev v Rossii XIX v. (po materialam gubernatorskikh otchetov)," *Istoricheskie zapiski*, No. 81 (1968), pp. 216–58.

Nizhegorodskaia gubernskaia prodovol'stvennaia komissia. *Zhurnaly sobraniia Nizhegorodskoi gubernskoi prodovol'stvennoi komissii* [N. Novgorod, 1891–92].

Nizhegorodskaia gubernskaia zemskaia uprava. *Otchet Nizhegorodskoi gubernskoi zemskoi upravy po prodovol'stvennoi operatsii 1891–92 gg*. N. Novgorod, 1893.

—— Statisticheskoe otdelenie. *Urozhai 1891 goda v Nizhegorodskoi gubernii*. N. Novgorod, 1891.

Nizhegorodskie gubernskie vedomosti.

Nizhegorodskoe gubernskoe zemskoe sobranie. *XXVI ocherednoe Nizhegorodskoe zemskoe sobranie 3–7 dekabria 1890 goda i chrezvychainye . . . sobraniia sozvyvavshiesia v 1891 godu.* N. Novgorod, 1891.

—— *XXVII ocherednoe Nizhegorodskoe gubernskoe zemskoe sobranie 10–18 dekabria 1891 goda.* N. Novgorod, 1892.

Obolenskii, V. A. *Ocherki minuvshego.* Belgrade, 1931.

Onitskanskii, M. S. *O rasprostranenii kholery v Rossii.* St. Petersburg, 1911.

-ov. [I. I. Ivaniukov.] "Ocherki provintsial'noi zhizni:" *Russkaia mysl'* (June, 1893) pp. 192–213.

Pavlovsky, George. *Agricultural Russia on the Eve of the Revolution.* London, 1930.

Pershin, P. N. *Agrarnaia revoliutsiia v Rossii.* 2 vols. Moscow, 1966.

Petlin, N. S. *Opyt opisaniia gubernii i oblastei Rossii v statisticheskom i ekonomicheskom otnosheniiakh.* 2 vols. St. Petersburg, 1893.

Petrov, M. "Dolgi postradavshikh gubernii," *Severnyi vestnik* (April, 1893), pp. 17–30.

Petrunkevich, I. I. "Chto govoriat tsifry," *Russkaia mysl'* (December, 1891), pp. 297–306.

P. K. [M. P. Petrov], see K., P.

Plekhanov, G. V. *Vserossiiskoe razorenie.* St. Petersburg, 1906.

Pogozhev, A. V. "Apatiia golodaniia i gigiena," *Russkoe bogatstvo* (April–May, 1892), pp. 18–41.

Pogozheva, A. V. "Otchet A. V. Pogozhevoi," *Russkaia mysl'* (January, 1893), pp. 250–51.

Pogrebinskii, A. P. *Ocherki istorii finansov dorevoliutsionnoi Rossii.* Moscow, 1954.

Pokrovskii, F. "V. G. Korolenko pod nadzorom politsii (1876–1903). K sorokaletiiu literaturnoi deiatel'nosti," *Byloe*, No. 13 (July, 1918), pp. 3–37.

Pokrovskii, S. A. *Vneshniaia torgovlia i vneshniaia torgovaia politika Rossii.* Moscow, 1947.

Polnoe sobranie zakonov Rossiiskoi imperii. St. Petersburg, 1830–1917.

Polovtsov, A. A. *Dnevnik gosudarstvennogo sekretaria A. A. Polovtsova*, P. A. Zaionchkovskii, ed. 2 vols. Moscow, 1966.

Pravitel'stvennyi vestnik (St. Petersburg).

Propper, Stanislav M. *Was nicht in die Zeitung kam: Erinnerrungen der Chefredakteurs der "Birschevyja Wedomosti."* Frankfurt a.M., 1929.

Provintsial'nyi nabliudatel'. [N. F. Annenskii and V. G. Korolenko.] "Tekushchaia zhizn' (Razmyshleniia, nabliudeniia i zametki)," *Russkaia mysl'* (January, 1893), pp. 122–44.

Queen, G. S. "American Relief in the Russian Famine of 1891–1892," *Russian Review*, XIV, No. 2 (1955), 140–50.

Reeves, Francis B. *Russia Then and Now.* New York, 1917.

Report of the Indian Famine Commission, 1898. London, 1898.

Report of the Indian Famine Commission, 1901. London, 1901.

Report of the Russian Famine Relief Committee of the United States. Washington, D.C., 1893.

Robbins, Richard G. "Russia's System of Food Supply Relief on the Eve of the Famine of 1891–92," *Agricultural History*, XLV (October, 1971), 259–69.

Robinson, Geroid T. *Rural Russia under the Old Regime.* New York, 1932.

Romanovich-Slavatinskii, A. V. "Goloda v Rossii i mery pravitel'stva protiv nikh," *Izvestiia Kievskogo universiteta*, XXXII (1892), 27–68.

Rossiiskoe obshchestvo krasnogo kresta. *Obzor deiatel'nosti Rossiiskogo obschestvo krasnogo kresta v 1891 i 1892 godakh po okazaniiu pomoshchi naseleniiu postradavshemu ot neurozhaia, i po bor'be s kholernoi epidemiei.* St. Petersburg, 1893.

Russkie vedomosti (Moscow).

Russkie vedomosti, 1863–1913: Sbornik Statei. Moscow, 1913.

Sazanov, G. P. *Obzor deiatel'nosti zemstv po narodnomu prodovol'stviiu (1865–1892)*. 2 vols. St. Petersburg, 1893.

Scarfe, Wendy and Allan. *Tiger on a Rein: Report on the Bihar Famine*. London, 1969.

Scott, Richenda. *Quakers in Russia*. London, 1964.

Semenkovich, V. N. "Zemstvo i narodnoe prodovol'stvie," *Russkoe obozrenie* (September, 1892), pp. 339–45.

Seredonin, S. M. et al. *Istoricheskii obzor deiatel'nosti Komiteta Ministrov*. 5 vols. St. Petersburg, 1902–1905.

Sergeevskii, Ivan. [N. S. Rusanov.] *Golod v Rossii*. Geneva. 1892.

Shafranov, P. A. "Neurozhai khlebov v Rossii i prodovol'stvie naseleniia v 20-kh godakh nastoiashchogo stoletiia." *Russkoe bogatstvo* (May, 1898), pp. 82–115; (June, 1898), pp. 114–34; (July, 1898), pp. 119–54.

Shchepkin, V. "Golod v Rossii: Istoricheskii ocherk," *Istoricheskii vestnik*, XXIV (1886), 489–521.

Shingarev, A. I. *Vymiraiushchaia derevnia. Opyt sanitarnoekonomicheskogo issledovaniia dvukh selenii Voronezhskogo uezda*. St. Petersburg, 1907.

Shlemin, P. I. "Zemskoe dvizhenie i liberal'naia intelligentsiia na rubezhe 80–90 godov XIX veka." In *Voprosy istorii SSSR*. Moscow, 1972.

—— "Zemsko-liberal'noe dvizhenie i adresa 1894/95 g.," *Vestnik Moskovskogo universiteta*, seriia IX, istoriia, No. 1 (1973), pp. 60–73.

—— *Zemsko-liberal'noe dvizhenie na rubezhe XIX–XX vekov*. Avtoreferat disertatsii. Moscow, 1973.

Shmurlo, E. "Nuzhda v Cheliabinskom uezde," *Severnyi Vestnik* (June, 1892), pp. 20–42.

Shvanebakh, P. Kh. *Denezhnoe preobrazovanie i narodnoe khoziaistvo*. St. Petersburg, 1901.

—— *Nashe podatnoe delo*. St. Petersburg, 1903.

Simmons, Ernest J. *Leo Tolstoy*. 2 vols. New York, 1960.

Singh, Musafir. *People Can Avert Famine*. New Delhi, 1970.

S. K. [S. N. Krivenko], see K., S.

Skliarov, L. F. *Pereselenie i zemleustroistvo v Sibiri v gody stolypinskoi agrarnoi reformy*. Leningrad, 1962.

Skvortsov, A. I. *Ekonomicheskie etiudy*. Vol. I: *Ekonomicheskie prichiny golodovok v Rossii i mery k ikh ustraneniiu*. St. Petersburg, 1894.

Skvortsov, I. "Pishcha i zdorov'e: Golodanie i ego posledstviia," *Russkoe obozrenie* (April, 1892), pp. 644–75.

Slonimskii, L. Z. "Ekonomicheskaia programa—'Neurozhai i narodnoe bedstvie,'" *Vestnik Evropy* (May, 1892), pp. 345–64.

Smith, Charles Emory. "Famine in Russia," *North American Review*, CLIV (May, 1892), pp. 541–51.

Sobranie uzakonenii i rasporiazhenii pravitel'stva. St. Petersburg, 1862–1917.

"Sobytiia i novosti," *Severnyi vestnik* (October, 1891), pp. 77–85; (January, 1892), pp. 115–28; (February, 1892), pp. 118–24; (March, 1892), pp. 100–14; (April, 1892), pp. 119–32; (August, 1892), pp. 103–15.

Sofinov, P. "Vnutrenniaia politika Aleksandra III," *Istoricheskii zhurnal*, No. 5 (1937), pp. 60–78.

Solov'ev, V. S. "Narodnaia beda i obshchestvennaia pomoshch'," *Vestnik Evropy*, (October, 1891), pp. 780–93.

Southard, Frank A. "Famine," *Encyclopaedia of the Social Sciences*. Vol. VI.

"Sovremennaia letopis'," *Russkoe obozrenie* (July, 1891), pp. 405–26; (October, 1891), pp. 842–61; (November, 1891), pp. 420–45; (December, 1891), pp. 850–82.

Stadling, Jonas, and Will Reason. *In the Land of Tolstoi: Experiences of Famine and Misrule in Russia.* London, 1897.
Starr, S. Frederick. *Decentralization and Self-Government in Russia, 1830–1870.* Princeton, 1972.
Stavrou, Theofanis G., ed. *Russia under the Last Tsar.* Minneapolis, 1969.
Stefanovskii, F. K. *Materialy dlia izucheniia svoistv "golodnogo" khleba.* Kazan, 1893.
Stepniak, S. [S. M. Kravchinskii.] *Chego nam nuzhno i nachalo kontsa.* London, 1892.
Steveni, William B. *Through Famine-stricken Russia*, London, 1892.
Sukhopliuev, I. K. *Bibliograficheskii obzor izdanii po voprosu o obezpechenii narodnogo prodovol'stviia.* Vol. I: *Obzor pravitel'stvennykh izdanii.* Moscow, 1907.
—— "Neurozhai i massovye zabolevaniia golodaiushchego naseleniia," *Russkaia mysl'* (March, 1906), pp. 42–54.
—— "Neurozhai i obshchestvennye raboty," *Russkaia mysl'* (October, 1906), pp. 52–70.
—— "Posledstviia neurozhaev v Rossii," *Russkaia mysl'* (June, 1906), pp. 147–83.
Tambovskaia gubernskaia zemskaia uprava. *Otchet Tambovskoi gubernskoi zemskoi upravy po prodovol'stvennoi operatsii.* 5 vols. Tambov, 1891–92.
Tambovskie gubernskie vedomosti.
Tambovskoe gubernskoe zemskoe sobranie. *Zhurnal chrezvychainogo Tambovskogo gubernskogo sobraniia 3-4-go iiulia 1891 goda.* Tambov, 1891.
—— *Zhurnal chrezvychainogo Tambovskogo gubernskogo zemskogo sobraniia 8, 9 i 10 fevralia 1892 goda.* Tambov, 1892.
—— *Zhurnal chrezvychainogo Tambovskogo gubernskogo sobraniia 17 iiunia 1892 goda.* Tambov, 1892.
—— *Zhurnal ocherednogo Tambovskogo gubernskogo zemskogo sobraniia v dekabre 1891 goda.* Tambov, 1892.
Tarasov, I. "Strakhovanie posevov. O knige L. I. Grassa," *Severnyi vestnik* (July, 1893), pp. 58–63.
Taylor, Alanzo E. "Famine." Unpublished manuscript, Food Research Institute. Stanford, California, 1947.
Tolstoi, L. L. *V golodnye goda (Zapiski i stat'i).* Moscow, 1900.
—— "Zapiski iz epokhi goloda v 1891–92 godakh," *Vestnik Evropy* (June, 1899), pp. 682–716; (July, 1899), pp. 5–73.
Treadgold, Donald W. *The Great Siberian Migration: Government and Peasant in Resettlement from Emancipation to the First World War.* Princeton, 1957.
Troinitskii, V. A. "Neurozhai v Tobol'skoi gubernii 1891 g," *Istoricheskii vestnik*, CXXXIII (1913), 536–52.
Uspenskii, G. "Bezkhleb'e (Soobshcheniia povolzhskoi pechati)," *Russkaia mysl'* (November, 1891), pp. 92–106.
Ustav o obespechenii narodnogo prodovol'stviia. Svod zakonov Rossiiskoi imperii, Vol. XIII (1892).
Vendrikh, A. A. fon. *Otchet po upravleniiu perevozkami po zheleznym dorogam v mestnosti postradavshie ot neurozhaia (Dekabr' 1891 g-mart' 1892 g.)* St. Petersburg, 1896.
Vereshchagin, N. V. "Po povodu neurozhaia tekushchego goda." *Trudy Imperatorskogo Vol'nogo Ekonomicheskogo Obshchestva* (1891), II, 178–96.
Vernadsky, G. V. "Bratstvo 'Priiutino,'" *Novyi Zhurnal*, No. 93 (1968), pp. 147–71; No. 95 (1969), pp. 202–15; No. 96 (1969), pp. 153–71; No. 97 (1969), pp. 218–37.
Veselovskii, B. B. *Istoriia zemstva za 40 let.* 4 vols. St. Petersburg, 1909–11.
—— "Neurozhai v Rossii i ikh sotsial'no-ekonomicheskie prichiny," *Obrazovanie* (April, 1907), pp. 1–29.

Veselovskii, B. B. and Z. G. Frenkel', eds. *Iubileinyi zemskii sbornik*. St. Petersburg, 1914.

Vesin, L. "Neurozhai v Rossii i ikh glavnye prichiny," *Severnyi vestnik* (January, 1892), pp. 85–123; (February, 1892), pp. 41–75.

—— "Nishchenstvo na Rusi," *Severnyi vestnik* (March, 1893), pp. 19–33; (April, 1893), pp. 1–17.

Vestnik finansov promyshlennosti i torgovli (St. Petersburg).

Vlasov, K. "Golod v Sibiri i kniaz Golitsyn," *Istoricheskii vestnik*, CXXXII (1913), 129–54.

"Vnutrennee obozrenie," *Russkaia mysl'* (July, 1891), pp. 142–67; (August, 1891), pp. 175–200; (November, 1891), pp. 148–79; (December, 1891), pp. 199–224; (January, 1892), pp. 193–218; (February, 1892), pp. 168–98; (March, 1892), pp. 167–91; (May, 1892), pp. 178–202; (June, 1892), pp. 138–64; (October, 1893), pp. 159–80.

"Vnutrennee obozrenie," *Vestnik Evropy* (October, 1891), pp. 794–817; (November, 1891), pp. 353–78; (February, 1892), pp. 851–70; (March, 1892), pp. 380–401; (April, 1892), pp. 839–58; (May, 1892), pp. 372–95; (July, 1892), pp. 401–19; (September, 1892), pp. 349–73; (February, 1893), pp. 845–57.

Vokach, N. A. "Pereselencheskoe delo," *Russkaia mysl'* (August, 1892), pp. 65–82.

Volgar' (Nizhni-Novgorod).

Volin, Lazar. *A Century of Russian Agriculture: From Alexander II to Khrushchev*. Cambridge, Mass., 1970.

Volzhskii vestnik (Kazan).

Von Laue, T. H. "The Chances for Liberal Constitutionalism," *Slavic Review*, XXIV (March, 1965), 34–46.

—— *Sergei Witte and the Industrialization of Russia*. New York, 1963.

Voronov, L. N. "Ekonomicheskoe obozrenie," *Russkoe obozrenie* (June, 1891), pp. 877–89; (July, 1891), pp. 427–49; (August, 1891), pp. 852–75; (September, 1891), pp. 378–97; (October, 1891), pp. 862–75; (November, 1891), pp. 446–66; (April, 1892), pp. 876–87; (May, 1892), pp. 377–98.

—— Review of *Neurozhai i narodnoe bedstvie*. *Russkoe obozrenie* (May, 1892), pp. 440–52.

Vucinich, Wayne S., ed. *The Peasant in Nineteenth-Century Russia*. Stanford, Calif. 1968.

V-v, D. "Pis'ma iz gubernii. Po povodu rabot dlia nuzhdaiushchikhsia," *Russkii vestnik* (January, 1892), pp. 367–81.

—— "Pis'ma iz gubernii. Sevooborot i oroshenie," *Russkii vestnik* (July, 1891), pp. 343–61.

Walkin, Jacob. *The Rise of Democracy in Pre-Revolutionary Russia*. New York, 1962.

Watters, Francis M. "Land Tenure and Financial Burdens of the Russian Peasant, 1861–1905." Unpublished Ph.D. dissertation, University of California, Berkeley, 1966.

Weissman, Benjamin M. "The American Relief Administration in Russia, 1921–23: A Case Study in Interaction between Opposing Political Systems." Unpublished Ph.D. dissertation, Columbia University, 1968.

Westwood, J. N. *A History of Russian Railways*. London, 1964.

—— "The Vladikavkaz Railway: A Case of Enterprising Private Enterprise," *Slavic Review*, XXV (December, 1966), 669–75.

Wildman, Allan K. *The Making of a Workers' Revolution: Russian Social Democracy, 1891–1903*. Chicago, 1967.

Witte, S. Iu. *Vospominaniia*. A. L. Sidorov, ed. 3 vols. Moscow, 1960.

Woodham-Smith, Cecil. *The Great Hunger: Ireland 1845–1849*. New York, 1962.

Yaney, George L. "Social Stability in Prerevolutionary Russia: A Critical Note," *Slavic Review*, XXIV (September, 1965), 521–27.

Zaionchkovskii, P. A. *Krizis samoderzhaviia na rubezhe 1870–1880-kh godov*. Moscow, 1964.

—— *Otmena krepostnogo prava*. 3rd ed. rev. Moscow, 1968.

—— *Rossiiskoe samoderzhavie v kontse XIX stoletiia*. Moscow, 1970.

—— "Zakon o zemskikh nachal'nikakh 12 iiulia 1889 goda," *Nauchnye doklady vysshei shkoly*, No. 2 (1961), pp. 42–72.

Zakharova, L. G. *Zemskaia konterreforma 1890 g*. Moscow, 1968.

Zasodimskii, P. V. "Iz vospominanii (1891–1892 gg.)," *Istoricheskii vestnik* (1904), No. 3, pp. 763–77; No. 4, pp. 55–56, 498–514.

"Zemskie itogi," *Vestnik Evropy* (July, 1870), pp. 326–40.

Zemskii, V. G. [V. I Charnoluskii and G. A. Fal'bork.] "Vnutrenniaia khronika," *Russkoe bogatstvo* (October, 1891), pp. 197–210; (November, 1891), pp. 168–207.

Zolotov, V. A. *Khlebnyi eksport Rossii cherez porty chernogo i azovskogo morei v 60–90e gody XIX veka*. Rostov-na-Donu, 1966.

INDEX

STUDIES OF THE RUSSIAN INSTITUTE

PUBLISHED BY COLUMBIA UNIVERSITY PRESS

THAD PAUL ALTON, *Polish Postwar Economy*
JOHN A. ARMSTRONG, *Ukrainian Nationalism*
ABRAM BERGSON, *Soviet National Income and Product in 1937*
HARVEY L. DYCK, *Weimar Germany and Soviet Russia, 1926–1933: A Study in Diplomatic Instability*
RALPH TALCOTT FISHER, JR., *Pattern for Soviet Youth: A Study of the Congresses of the Komsomol, 1918–1954*
MAURICE FRIEDBERG, *Russian Classics in Soviet Jackets*
ELLIOT R. GOODMAN, *The Soviet Design for a World State*
DAVID GRANICK, *Management of the Industrial Firm in the USSR: A Study in Soviet Economic Planning*
THOMAS TAYLOR HAMMOND, *Lenin on Trade Unions and Revolution, 1893–1917*
JOHN N. HAZARD, *Settling Disputes in Soviet Society: The Formative Years of Legal Institutions*
DAVID JORAVSKY, *Soviet Marxism and Natural Science, 1917–1932*
HENRY KRISCH, *German Politics under Soviet Occupation*
DAVID MARSHALL LANG, *The Last Years of the Georgian Monarchy, 1658–1832*
GEORGE S. N. LUCKYJ, *Literary Politics in the Soviet Ukraine, 1917–1934*
HERBERT MARCUSE, *Soviet Marxism: A Critical Analysis*
KERMIT E. MC KENZIE, *Comintern and World Revolution, 1928–1943: The Shaping of Doctrine*
CHARLES B. MC LANE, *Soviet Policy and the Chinese Communists, 1931–1946*
JAMES WILLIAM MORLEY, *The Japanese Thrust into Siberia, 1918*
ALEXANDER G. PARK, *Bolshevism in Turkestan, 1917–1927*
MICHAEL BORO PETROVICH, *The Emergence of Russian Panslavism, 1856–1870*
OLIVER H. RADKEY, *The Agrarian Foes of Bolshevism: Promise and Default of the Russian Socialist Revolutionaries, February to October, 1917*
OLIVER H. RADKEY, *The Sickle Under the Hammer: The Russian Socialist Revolutionaries in the Early Months of Soviet Rule*
ALFRED J. RIEBER, *Stalin and the French Communist Party, 1941–1947*
RICHARD G. ROBBINS, JR, *Famine in Russia, 1891–1892: The Imperial Government Responds to a Crisis*

ALFRED ERICH SENN, *The Emergence of Modern Lithuania*
ERNEST J. SIMMONS, editor, *Through the Glass of Soviet Literature: Views of Russian Society*
THEODORE K. VON LAUE, *Sergei Witte and the Industrialization of Russia*
ALLEN S. WHITING, *Soviet Policies in China, 1917–1924*

PUBLISHED BY TEACHERS COLLEGE PRESS

HAROLD J. NOAH, *Financing Soviet Schools*

PUBLISHED BY PRINCETON UNIVERSITY PRESS

PAUL AVRICH, *The Russian Anarchists*
PAUL AVRICH, *Kronstadt 1921*
EDWARD J. BROWN, *Mayakovsky: A Poet in the Revolution*
MILTON EHRE, *Oblomov and His Creator: The Life and Art of Ivan Goncharov*
LOREN R. GRAHAM, *The Soviet Academy of Sciences and the Communist Party, 1927–1932*
PATRICIA K. GRIMSTED, *Archives and Manuscript Repositories in the USSR: Moscow and Leningrad*
ROBERT A. MAGUIRE, *Red Virgin Soil: Soviet Literature in the 1920's*
T. H. RIGBY, *Communist Party Membership in the U.S.S.R., 1917–1967*
RONALD G. SUNY, *The Baku Commune, 1917–1918*
JOHN M. THOMPSON, *Russia, Bolshevism, and the Versailles Peace*
WILLIAM ZIMMERMAN, *Soviet Perspectives on International Relations, 1956–1967*

PUBLISHED BY CAMBRIDGE UNIVERSITY PRESS

JONATHAN FRANKEL, *Vladimir Akimov on the Dilemmas of Russian Marxism, 1895–1903*
EZRA MENDELSOHN, *Class Struggle in the Pale: The Formative Years of the Jewish Workers' Movement in Tsarist Russia*

PUBLISHED BY THE UNIVERSITY OF MICHIGAN PRESS

RICHARD T. DE GEORGE, *Soviet Ethics and Morality*

PUBLISHED BY THE FREE PRESS

HENRY W. MORTON and RUDOLF L. TÖKÉS, editors, *Soviet Politics and Society in the 1970's*